D1563671

BOSTON BALLERINA

Boston Ballerina

A DANCER, A COMPANY, AN ERA

Laura Young

WITH JANINE PARKER

UNIVERSITY PRESS OF NEW ENGLAND

HANOVER AND LONDON

University Press of New England
www.upne.com
© 2018 Laura Young

Manufactured in the United States of America
Designed by April Leidig
Typeset in Garamond by Copperline Book Services, Inc.

For permission to reproduce any of the material in this book,
contact Permissions, University Press of New England, One Court Street,
Suite 250, Lebanon NH 03766; or visit www.upne.com

Library of Congress Cataloging-in-Publication Data
Names: Young, Laura, 1947– author. | Parker, Janine, author.
Title: Boston ballerina: a dancer, a company, an era / Laura Young, with Janine Parker.
Description: Hanover; London: University Press of New England, [2017] |
Includes bibliographical references and index. |
Identifiers: LCCN 2017026922 (print) | LCCN 2017028609 (ebook) |
ISBN 9781512601336 (epub, mobi, & pdf) | ISBN 9781512600797 (cloth: alk. paper)
Subjects: LCSH: Young, Laura, 1947– | Ballet dancers — United States — Biography. |
Ballerinas — United States — Biography. | Boston Ballet — History.
Classification: LCC GV1785.Y59 (ebook) | LCC GV1785.Y59 A3 2017 (print) |
DDC 792.8092 [B] — dc23
LC record available at https://lccn.loc.gov/2017026922

5 4 3 2 1

To my parents,
who gently supported me in my journey,
every step of the way.

_____

CONTENTS

Illustrations follow pages 84 and 180

ACKNOWLEDGMENTS

OVER THE YEARS, I have been asked to recount tales of my dancing days with Boston Ballet—stories not only about my career and the company's beginnings but also about the "dance boom" that exploded all around America in the 1960s and 1970s. Knowing what an enormous task that would be to put on paper, I procrastinated until Laura Chapman—one of my adult students, ballet aficionada, and now close friend—came into my life. Her support and penchant for extreme organization propelled this memoir forward and kept me on track. So first and foremost, my heartfelt thank you, Laura, for being the instigator and seeing it through to fruition.

A special thank you to Janine Parker, coauthor and longtime friend and colleague, who conducted and transcribed hours of interviews with me and wove them, along with the myriad of files that Laura Chapman, my niece Bridget Young, and I compiled for this narrative. Her writing reflects the deep knowledge of dance she possesses from years of working in the field in so many different capacities, and the close relationship we've had for over twenty years. She knows me well and has kept my voice intact throughout her writing.

To all of the photographers and their kith and kin, who so readily searched their archives and gave permission to use their photographs, my deepest thanks. It's heartwarming to communicate with these talented people once again, and gratifying that this lovely reconnection was made through our medium, the ballet. In addition, the folks at Harvard Theatre Collection kindly helped us locate and obtain images for this book.

Our sincerest thanks go to Karen Corsano, Dan Williman, and Jeffrey Gantz for their advice, insights, and overall generosity. Karen and Dan, longtime Boston Ballet subscribers, supporters, and volunteers, offered indexing expertise; Jeffrey, a superb writer and editor, provided us with a much-appreciated read through.

To Con Chapman, Gary Rzab, and Chris Mehl, our husbands, for putting up with us and giving us the room to do what needed to be done, thank you and much respect for hanging in there. Chris, the magic you wrought on so many of the photographs was invaluable! I am in awe of your photographic expertise; thank you for being readily available, no matter the hour.

Thanks to my brother, Jim, for his wise counsel and for always being ready to run follow spots, stage-manage, or be prop man for so many of our early productions. Like a child growing up, it took the village of all of our collective families to raise the company to adulthood.

To the donors, sponsors, volunteers, and board members, you have my eternal gratitude for believing in us all these years. While there were many who stepped up to the plate to keep us afloat when the need was great, several stand out for serving tirelessly on the board and opening their homes for fundraisers and galas. We danced in their living rooms, backyards, and once under a tent during a torrential thunder and lightning storm. Imagine dancing the *Black Swan* pas de deux with that as your backdrop! Bravi to our "pillars of society": John and Pamela Humphrey; Bill and Susan Poduska; Jill Levitt; Mark Goldweitz; Lew and Linda Lloyd; and Kay and Peter Lyons.

To *all* of the dancers, artistic and administrative staff, conductors, musicians, designers, dressers and crewmembers, your contribution to the success of this company is no small feat and a vital part of the whole. To the dancers of my generation, my thanks for your support and camaraderie through some pretty trying, yet exhilarating, times.

I am deeply grateful to my editor, Richard Pult, for his belief in this memoir and his understanding of our foibles and for guiding us in the right direction, and to the University Press of New England team for their diligence in production.

Finally, and formally, I give my thanks to my mentor, E. Virginia Williams, and to Sydney Leonard for having the drive and determination to make ballet thrive in Boston. I am most grateful to them both. None of this would have happened without them.

BOSTON BALLERINA

Romeo and Juliet, Life, Death, and Dancing

WHILE LYING "DEAD" on the bier in my debut as Shakespeare's famously doomed, star-crossed Juliet, tears started to well up as my thoughts turned to the one who had been my guiding mentor, E. Virginia Williams, Boston Ballet's founder. Just days earlier, she had died unexpectedly, right before the premiere of the production of *Romeo and Juliet* she had commissioned for the company. The date was May 8, 1984, more than twenty years after Virginia had formed her fledgling company, the New England Civic Ballet, which eventually became the now well-known Boston Ballet, one of the country's leading ballet companies.

It was uncanny that my real life's sorrows had merged for a moment with R&J's classic but fictitious tragedy. Telling stories through dance requires a delicate balance that is hard to get just right. Without words, it's up to the body to move within the choreography and the music, to convey the character, plot, thoughts, and feelings. Too little depth, and the story is unclear, or worse, trite; too much physical emoting, and the story is overwrought. The dancer must therefore find subtle ways to embrace and embody the character so that the audience can easily understand the story. The aim of a professional dancer is to express oneself as sincerely and authentically as possible so that the viewer can enter into this make-believe world up on the stage, even if only for an hour or two.

While it may sound counterintuitive, dancers try not to actually cry in a dramatic scene. Unlike an actor in a movie, real tears in dance can tip the drama into melodrama. So although it's not a rule, crying for real while dancing on stage is not encouraged. For one thing, it can ruin your makeup! For another, one must *immerse* oneself in the story but cannot afford to *lose* oneself in the story. It is, as I say, a delicate balance.

Although I had been yearning for the chance to take on the role of Juliet for a long time, I was by now a seasoned professional and could hardly be considered an ingénue overcome with some kind of opening-night hysteria. *Romeo and Juliet* was a ballet that Virginia had promised to Donn Edwards and me for years, and it was finally happening. Donn and I were one of three couples chosen to alternate the lead roles in what was Boston Ballet's first full-length version of the ballet. This was made even more exciting because it was a new production created for our company by the young and up-and-coming choreographer Choo San Goh, who up until now had not choreographed a full-length ballet. So, it was new territory and a very thrilling time for all of us.

In rehearsals, before Virginia died, we had joked about being careful not to breathe too noticeably in the crypt scene. After all, if the audience saw the lilies that were lying over the shroud on our chests rising and falling we would not be believable. On that day in May though, with the tears rolling down my cheeks, it took everything in my power not to make the shroud flutter, because I knew in my heart that Virginia's death would forever change the company dramatically.

––––––––––

MY STORY IS ONE filled with history and recollections of my coming of age as a ballet dancer during a particularly exciting and unique era. Borne along the first waves of professional ballet and modern dance in America in the 1930s, '40s, and '50s, my peers and I would help to usher in and ride the crest of the "dance boom" of the '60s and '70s. My long tenure with Boston Ballet gives me the ability to recount a chronology of events that should not be forgotten regarding the "balletization" of regional America.

I continue to marvel at our efforts. From our humble roots as a feisty little ballet company in Boston with our Yankee-driven leader to our triumphant performances across North America, Europe and Asia, it has been an exhilarating and noble journey, sometimes even a wild ride. We were indeed pioneers, and I was incredibly fortunate to have been in the right place at the right time.

I

If the Shoe Fits

MY FIRST PAIR of pointe shoes didn't fit properly. That was not a big surprise, as technically speaking, they weren't mine to begin with. They had been my mother's, and they were so big I had to stuff socks into the toes. After all, I was only seven years old when I found them while playing in my grandmother's attic.

As any ballet student knows, pointe shoes are highly individualized and must fit very snugly; they are never to be "grown into," and they are never to be shared. Though I hadn't quite learned this yet, I must have known that my newfound activity of playing records on my grandmother's 78 rpm record player while dancing around in my mother's old pointe shoes was something better kept to myself. So, by the time anyone discovered what I'd been doing, I was eight years old and had worn out the two pairs of shoes in that box in the attic: my mother's very first pair and her last before she "retired" from dancing. Although I imagine she sighed over their demise, my mother astutely brought the damning evidence to my ballet teacher, Miss Baker, who agreed to add pointe work to my regular ballet regimen. I guess they figured that this horse was already long out of the barn, and at least under Miss Baker's tutelage, they could make sure I didn't hurt myself.

I had begun going to Cecile Baker's School of Dance in North Quincy, Massachusetts, a couple of years earlier, at age six, somewhat as a "cure" for my sizable energy. Always an active child, I could be a handful on rainy days, and on one such day, my mother asked me if I'd like her to give me a ballet lesson. My eagerness was somewhat dampened when along with the dancing came corrections. "Oh, what do you know about ballet?" I demanded sassily. Very soon after, I was put into the care of Miss Baker.

As it turned out, my maternal grandmother, whose house I stayed at regularly while my parents were at work, already knew Cecile Baker. Not only was Miss Baker's studio conveniently located about a ten-minute walk from my grandmother's house, but also Cecile provided me with an excellent base, which later became a strong springboard. At my first recital, she choreographed a little dance to part of the *Les Sylphides* score, with that wonderful music by Frédéric Chopin, and I remember how she would sing the names of the steps to match the music. "Glide up the back wall, balancé, up the back wall, balancé, sauté arabesque . . ." And so, from her, at a young age, I learned to appreciate and explore musicality, and the beauty of the coordination of music with dance, without which a dancer is merely a technician.

Of course, the fact that music was already deeply ingrained in my family's household certainly added to my burgeoning comprehension. Classical music was always playing in our house. Family lore has it that my dad, James Vincent Young, had studied violin seriously under the concertmaster of the Boston Symphony Orchestra circa 1934. His chances at a professional career, however, were brought to a halt when he cut off the tip of one of his fingers in a woodworking accident. Although the concert hall was then not to be his arena, he did appear on the vaudeville circuit and in minstrel shows, and also competed in and won many local singing contests. A singer and dancer in those productions, he was what was called an "end man." Dad's favorite dancing partner, however, was his mother, who was lovingly referred to as "Mrs. 5 × 5"; she was very short and quite stout, but he could really whirl her around the dance floor. Later on at receptions, I came to appreciate how well he could whirl me around the floor! His mother was an accomplished accompanist for silent films at local theaters, and it was a perk for Dad to be able to see movies and vaudeville routines over and over again. No wonder he would later become an end man. Nana Young was a self-taught pianist and could transpose on the spot for any individual in singing auditions. Since the age of fourteen, Dad's sister Helen sang with the Johnny Long Orchestra, one of the most successful local big bands of the 1940s. This led to her touring with the USO twice during World War II. She was also a classically trained dancer, but her voice was what drew her to the stage.

My mother, who had a love of opera and musical theater, taught me arias from *Faust* and songs from *My Fair Lady* that we would sing together. Like my dad, my mom, born Adelaide Janet Coupal and known as Addie to her friends and Ma to her kids, had her own interrupted artistic career dreams. She had shown enough aptitude and potential that the great ballet master and choreographer George Balanchine took an interest in her when she studied with him, as did another revered teacher, Pierre Vladimiroff, at the recently opened School of American Ballet in New York City the summer after she graduated high school. So music and dancing was coming at me from both sides of the family. Mr. B, as Balanchine was eventually, and affectionately, called, had recently arrived in America and was constantly looking for future talent to cultivate: ballet was still a young art form in this country at the time, and well-trained classical dancers were a rarity. If the beginnings and height of my career were smack in the middle of the "dance boom" of the sixties, seventies, and eighties, that glorious era was surely pushed forward by the heady days of early "serious" ballet in America, when my mom and others like her were meeting the likes of Balanchine. It was also the very early days of modern dance.

Well, at the end of that summer, Mr. B, who would go on to cofound what is now one of the world's top ballet troupes, New York City Ballet, told my mother that if she stayed and continued studying with him and Vladimiroff he'd put her in his company. My grandmother, however, said no. She would not leave her husband behind to move to New York City with Addie, and New York City was no place for an eighteen-year-old young lady on her own. In addition, dancing was not considered a "proper" profession. Once back in Massachusetts, my mother burned all of her dance clothes, except for those two wonderful pairs of pointe shoes for me to find years later. Save the first and the last. I did it myself.

What a curious and unpredictable thing fate is. While it's fascinating for me to wonder "what if?" in terms of my mother and her own possible dancing career, I also realize that if she had indeed stayed in New York City, she might not have married my dad . . . and I might not have come along. But marry they did. Although they had gone to the same high school, they hadn't known each other well back then. But years later, when my dad was working at the deli located on the ground floor of the building where my mom worked as an x-ray technician, they began to connect. My dad made her sandwiches extra special, I think; he liked to say it was love at first bite. On May 30, 1941, they married, and a year later my older brother, James V. Jr., was born. In addition to my mother's ballet career detour, there was another potential near miss in my presence on earth, one that is both Young family legend and a sober reminder of a Boston tragedy. It so happens that on the evening of November 28, 1942, my parents were planning to go to the Cocoanut Grove, the popular Boston nightclub, with friends. However, my brother James, who was six months old, was sick, so my parents stayed home. But their friends went and, along with 490 other poor souls, perished in the deadliest nightclub fire on record. Five years later, on August 5, 1947, I, Lorraine Denise Young, was born at the Boston "Lying-In," which is now part of Brigham & Women's Hospital.

―――――

THE ATMOSPHERE at Miss Baker's school was very supportive. I don't know how easily a serious student, one who hopes to become a professional dancer, would fare in such a small studio now, given the competitiveness that seems rampant in the art form today. In 1960, Cecile put on a production of *The Sleeping Beauty* and I was given the lead role of Princess Aurora while four of my female classmates acted as my "cavaliers" in the Rose Adagio. They weren't jealous about the casting, realizing that it was just part of being in a small studio back then and very few young men were available to cast. Or perhaps it was the prevailing ethos in the American dance community in those pioneering days where, compared to ballet meccas such as Italy, France, and Russia, the genre was still in its youth.

My Prince in that *Sleeping Beauty* was none other than my mother! Turns out that her dancing days weren't quite over. Ma returned to dancing for a while in her early forties, and even got herself into good enough shape to dance on pointe again. I can't imagine being able to pull that off, after not dancing for so many years. I'm sure her body rebelled to a certain extent. One day, when my brother was rather sweetly massaging her sore calves, he must have "chopped" at them a bit too energetically because Ma said if she was ever able to get up off the couch she was going to kill him!

She also helped out behind the scenes, as secretary for the school, and my brother Jim worked as a stage assistant in the 1957 end-of-year recital and again as stage manager in 1959. For such a relatively small school, Miss Baker put on fairly impressive shows. We called them recitals back then. Now, the word "recital" isn't used with dance as regularly. Over time, it's become unpopular with most professional dance studios. Miss Baker, though, worked hard to give her students not only solid training but also respectable performance opportunities. Her devotion was supported by the like-minded, dedicated family members who volunteered their time and efforts.

From time to time she also brought in artistic support, and it was at Miss Baker's that I met her cousin, Sydney Leonard. Miss Leonard was a guest teacher at the school now and again and, as she was still dancing when I first met her, would appear with us in lead roles in the big performances. When they were younger, my mother and Sydney and Cecile had been classmates at Madame Maria Paporello's school, which was located on Huntington Avenue, across from the New England Conservatory. Like my mother, Sydney had dreams of pursuing dance as a career, but that was unrealistic, at least financially. In those days, in Boston at any rate, one couldn't make much of a living dancing full time, so Sydney secured a dependable job at the *Atlantic Monthly*, where she stayed for many decades. She worked there days and taught or took classes and attended rehearsals at night and on the weekends.

For her 1957 show, Miss Baker concocted a version of *The Nutcracker*. In "The Snowstorm" section, Miss Baker, my mother, my classmate Bunny (Gaylen Grohe), and I were "Ice and Snow" while Miss Leonard appeared as "Frost." She was beautiful! I remember her not only as a brilliant turner but mostly for the joy she exuded in her dancing; I wanted so much to emulate her. As I would learn in the years following, and as the legions of students she taught over the course of fifty-plus years can attest to, she was also a demanding teacher. Over time, some students felt that her strictness could be severe, but when I studied with her, I found her meticulousness to be anchored with encouragement. In any event, it was from her that I first learned many of the famous classical variations such as Aurora, Princess Florine (Bluebird's partner), Lilac Fairy from *The Sleeping Beauty*, and Odette from *Swan Lake*; and those are the ones I remember to this day.

Fortunately, Miss Baker was both wise enough and selfless enough to know when I outgrew her studio. And so, when I was twelve years old, she told me it was time for me to continue my training at another school where Miss Leonard taught, the Boston School of Ballet.

BY THE TIME I arrived at her school in the autumn of 1959, E. Virginia Williams and her fledgling company, the New England Civic Ballet, were housed on Massachusetts Avenue, having moved from Madame Paporello's former Huntington Avenue studio four years earlier. In her own memoirs, Sydney wrote that Virginia, born in Melrose in 1914, had been a shy but doted-upon child who was taken to dance classes as a way to bring her out of her shell. Although Virginia supposedly confessed to people that she was too "lazy" to really want to pursue a performing career, she must have overcome her shyness somewhat because she told Sydney that by the time she was an adolescent, she loved to tell other people what to do! During summer vacations, Virginia would come up with a "project" for the day, often a ballet or a play, and assign the other neighborhood children their roles and tasks. When she was only fourteen years old, she began teaching dance to some of those neighborhood children out of her family's Melrose house.

Her first "official" school she called the E. Virginia Williams School of Dance before changing it to the New England School of Ballet. By 1950, when she established the Boston School of Ballet on Huntington Avenue, she had studios in four suburban towns. The stability of those schools afforded Virginia some latitude as she worked on the building of her enterprise. If Virginia's own professional ballet background was spotty since she hadn't trained in a rigorous setting and was not particularly drawn to performing, she was steadfast in her dream of creating a company. As it happens, there were other, similar pioneers scattered about the country. Like Virginia, they too, along with dedicated faculties, dancers, students, staffs, and volunteers, were working tirelessly, with creativity and savviness, in pursuit of the at-the-time exotic goal of forming a ballet company.

"But first, a school," Balanchine famously said when talking about his own hopes of creating a ballet troupe in America. After all, if one is going to present "professional" concerts, one must have well-trained dancers. So Virginia and her ilk, whether or not they were aware of Mr. B's quip, set about establishing their own schools. Though Virginia wore many hats over the years, and toiled as hard as anyone else, she was admirably aware of her shortcomings. As soon as she could convince her to come aboard, she hired Sydney to join the faculty. Virginia did continue to teach though, always working to learn and improve upon her knowledge. She often went to New York City during the summers, where she'd sit in on various teachers' classes, absorb new ideas, pick up tricks of the trade, and find different ways in which to tackle various components of ballet technique. Balanchine himself, his School of American Ballet, and its company, New York City Ballet, were often part of her itinerary, a connection that grew and eventually proved extremely valuable.

While they couldn't have known it at the time, Virginia and her peers were to be the vanguards of regional ballet in America. And we, the young dancers who found our way into their studios, were to begin our careers in this brave, fertile, and exciting new world. But the first time I stepped foot into this professional realm, I was quite intimidated. This former big fish in the small pond shrank down, just as Alice did in that other wonderland.

2

Grand Jeté

Grand jeté. Origin: French. A commonly performed big leap; at the height of it, the dancer's legs are wide apart in a "split" position, one leg stretched front, the other stretched back.

MY BIG LEAP into the big pond of the Boston School of Ballet metaphorically wavered between excitedly testing the waters and treading water. I did manage, for awhile, to stay afloat: it probably helped that during that first year, I still had the comfort zone of Miss Baker's school to return to, for Miss Williams, having faced the suspicions of other local dance teachers who feared that she would "steal" their students, initially insisted that new Boston School of Ballet students must also continue to study a few times a week at their home studios.

Miss Williams was formidable. Always in high heels, she rarely got out of her chair while teaching, simply calling out steps for us to do. It was up to us to know the terminology and execute the exercises correctly. None of us wanted to be known as a slow learner. She could also be, in her own way, encouraging. If not overtly warm with her students, she was honest, both in her criticisms and in her plaudits. I felt she wanted us to be the best we could be, and she was going to help us achieve that any way she could. I believe she recognized that her teaching was limited since she had not actually performed, so she did everything from bringing in guest teachers to taking her dancers to renowned teachers, via summer trips to New York City as well as to the Northeast Regional Ballet Festival. This convention was formed in 1959 with the aim of bringing serious students from the surrounding states together for master classes and performances.

There was no guarantee for easy success, and it was brought home in various ways, including the feared and detested weekly weigh-ins, which were carried out in front of one's classmates. This would never be tolerated today. While most adolescents are hyperconscious of their growing, changing bodies, there is a tendency among dance students, ballet dancers in particular, toward harsh self-judgment in terms of body image. It's not that surprising, given the form-hugging and revealing tights and leotards, and the fact that we practice in front of mirrors, our twinned selves a constant reflection for hours and hours each day. Those mirrors, on the positive side, are meant to be "tools" for dancers, a way to check how details large and small look, so we can then compare the image with how it "feels," thus developing a kind of inner sight. The goal is to ultimately achieve correct form and line without the mirror, to be able to present these images to an audience with the assurance of the physical knowledge that the *sensation* is correct. We develop "an eye" and a visual understanding of what this correctness looks like, on others as well as ourselves. A sophisticated and necessary kind of sixth sense is born. On the negative side, that reflection can often be like an enemy to be fought and, unfortunately, one that is sometimes despised, even abused. It may sound like a stretch to say we can see every extra pound, but when one studies one's image with such obsessive focus, there is little that escapes a dancer's notice.

While this intense attention to detail and physical form is necessary for anyone hoping to achieve a high level of proficiency in dance, or for that matter, any other "elite" athletic pursuit, it's a slippery slope between maintaining one's body as a finely tuned instrument and becoming unable to know when enough is enough. In the early 1960s, the pursuit of ultra-thinness was becoming more popular among women in general, perhaps spurred by the fashion world; the name of the most prominent model of that era, known as "Twiggy," says it all. The ballet world certainly is now known for its many extremely slender artists, and while professional dancers have always been quite fit, it seems it was during these years that the look of today's "typical" ballet dancer was born. Some people in the field have attributed—or credited—George Balanchine for the hyperslim look that is especially connected with female ballet dancers. Many of the dancers Mr. B favored at that time were long, leggy, and indeed, quite thin, so there are those who feel that other dancers took note and sought ways in which to make their bodies fit that mold.

To me, it seems a bit farfetched to attribute the thirst for thinness to one man, even one as important as Mr. B. Regardless of how it all began, scales became studio fixtures, and crazy diets became the norm. I had at least one classmate who literally turned orange from carotene poisoning, the result of subsisting on a diet of carrots! I also knew several girls whose metabolisms became so out of whack from various wildly unhealthy diets that they never quite recovered. Anorexia nervosa and bulimia became major problems in the ballet world, particularly among female students.

As it happened, throughout my adolescence and even until I was in my early twenties, I was what I considered to be on the plumper side—for a dancer anyway. In my early teenage years, I put my own metabolism through the wringer with my own experiments in dieting, which included not eating until nighttime. When in class one evening I almost passed out during the barre, it occurred to me that maybe I needed to eat before class. At least my brain was still somewhat functional. Needless to say, I, for one, did not look forward to our public weigh-ins.

———————

THE STUDIOS AT 186 Massachusetts Avenue consisted of the main studio and "the pink room"—a smaller, pink-painted studio toward the back of the building, where we'd often be sent to work on details with the eagle-eyed Miss Leonard. We students regarded her with both fear and awe; she was encouraging, but quite strict. I still remember her corrections —"Sharp! Sharp!" she'd say, accentuated with a clap of her hands, pushing us to perform our movements with energy and clarity. "Do it again," which was often followed by, "Not yet, that's almost right, now do it again." When we still hadn't met her expectations, she would sigh in dismay, "Oh, oh . . . no."

Miss Williams, whose own early training was somewhat limited, resourced what she did know and came up with her own rather interesting ideas about how to achieve various aspects of technique. "You have to control the muscle, the muscles on top of your elbow," she'd vaguely say, when trying to help us with pirouettes. We didn't quite get it. In my own teaching, I've learned that the back muscles control and support the arms, thus keeping that little "elbow muscle" up!

Usually we would work with Miss Williams in the main studio, which was a much bigger, trapezoidal-shaped room where we had more freedom to fly in our grand jetés, as long as we watched out for the two poles smack in the middle. Indeed, those two poles often remained in the choreography in the form of gaping holes in the patterning when we transitioned to the stage. Everything had to be reblocked!

At the outset, I was definitely not one of Virginia's "favorites," or at least that's how it seemed at the time. "Laurie," she'd say in her distinctive voice, with a heavy Boston accent that was part mumble and part growl, "I don't know when you're going to get strong." I may have been strong enough in both will and body to put myself up on pointe at the age of seven, but Miss Williams had determined that, by the time I got to her, I was not strong. Her perception lasted for years and meant that she almost always cast me in more lyrical roles, many of which were wonderful, but of course I itched to prove that I could be powerful and quick too. For that, though, I had to bide my time.

Still, for a starry-eyed young dancer such as myself, trepidation was often tempered by the fact that the atmosphere in Boston was frequently electrified by the glamorous presence of various professional dancers whom Virginia brought in to appear with her newly formed performance group that she founded in 1958. The New England Civic Ballet was primarily composed of students and adults such as Sydney Leonard who were capable dancers but for one reason or another hadn't become professionals. The group performed all over the region, packing dancers, costumes, and music and the bulky equipment to play it on into whatever cars were available. Sydney remembers at one point traveling in an old hearse they'd acquired.

As at Miss Baker's, everyone—students, teachers, family members, and friends—helped out in various ways, whether it was transporting dancers, sewing costumes, building scenery, or running the sound for performances; the behind-the-scenes list goes on and on.

And although this early company was mostly made up of amateurs, with much of the support work performed by volunteers, Virginia ran it from the beginning, to the extent that she could, as a professional organization. We students had to audition to get in. An early acceptance letter, however, reflected that I was, in fact, very much still a student: "For continued membership," the brief document read, "it will be necessary for you to attend a minimum of four classes a week." And, of course, our nonprofessional status was also reflected in the fact that we weren't paid for our work and were required to pay a twenty-five-dollar costume fee. But this doesn't mean we were being exploited—far from it; we were thrilled to be allowed to join. It was a privilege, not something we took for granted.

Because Virginia managed to get some of the biggest stars of the ballet world to come and perform with our little ragtag group, we learned from the best. Her trips to New York City to watch master teachers at work had helped her develop connections within the larger community, networks that she and other pioneers of the American regional ballet movement cultivated and relied upon greatly, as they strove to establish their own footholds in the ballet world. Sometimes the networking went both ways: at that first Northeast Regional Ballet Festival, held in 1959 in Pennsylvania, Virginia and two of her company members, Sara Leland and Earle Sieveling, met Alexandra Danilova, Balanchine's former common-law wife who was dancing and teaching at New York City Ballet. Before long, Leland and Sieveling migrated to City Ballet, but Virginia and her New England Civic Ballet (NECB) were now in Mr. B's range of vision, and he took the company under his wing. Now, when Sara and Earle performed with NECB they returned as guest artists, and we were blessed with other City Ballet stars including Jacques d'Amboise, Melissa Hayden, Maria Tallchief, Edward Villella, and Patricia McBride.

In 1961, Virginia was invited by Balanchine to attend his rehearsals and classes once a month, a generosity sweetened by his invitation to talk with her about choreography, music, or whatever she wanted to know about while she was there. My head spins at the thought! Good thing Virginia knew what a once-in-a-lifetime kind of opportunity this was; she took him up on the offer, visiting Mr. B for two years.

The only negative to these visits is something that is humorous in retrospect but was somewhat agonizing at the time. Balanchine is known to have experimented with ballet technique in his classes, sometimes rather controversially. Of the various things he tried out on his dancers, some he kept and some he threw out. To this day, some things remain controversial among Balanchine-inspired teachers: did he say the heels should *never* touch the floor when landing from jumps or did he just say that the best way to execute some very fast jumping sections was to keep the heels up? Because Virginia was visiting only once a month, she might watch a class in which Balanchine was trying something out before perhaps deciding it wasn't any good a day later, and discarding it. Not knowing this, Virginia would come back to Boston and try these concepts on us, her unwitting lab mice.

During one such month our barre—the beginning of ballet class that is the all-important and usually logical progression that warms up the body —began with grand plié and was followed directly by grand battement. The former, a deep bend of the knees, is often one of the first exercises, and the latter, a high kick of the leg, is usually one of the last, as the muscles of the legs must be sufficiently stretched and warmed in order to avoid injury. Well, it was a good lesson learned that if I wanted to survive as a dancer, I should arrive a half hour early to class and warm myself up!

———

IN ANY EVENT, as a student member of New England Civic Ballet, I was able to not only watch but also sometimes be up on stage (albeit in the background) with great dancers. Virginia was adamant that we needed to see how it should be done, what real dancing looked like. While a few of these artists did the "drive-by"—that is, they performed as contracted but didn't interact much with the rest of us, most of them really invested themselves into mentoring those of us just starting out. How they approached their work informed even the youngest corps de ballet members. At all times we were observing and trying to absorb as much as we could from them.

The overarching lesson for me was one in humility. As with so many other young dancers who start out in a small studio where they may have been the "star," here there were constant reminders of one's place in the pecking order, of how far one had to go. Very occasionally, and comically, the lessons were primers in how *not* to behave: one of the couples who guested with the company several times would carp at each other onstage, both swearing like sailors! But we had plenty of reasons to stay humble and an abundance of inspirational examples to push us to keep working hard.

Eventually, as I did move up in the ranks of the company, I, like others in my position, benefitted most directly from the guests who would often take the time to work with the midlevel dancers. Indeed, although it would be a while before I attained that status, Sara Leland would prove to be an invaluable resource for me when it came to the Balanchine repertory we began performing. For, along with the borrowed stars Balanchine also let NECB, and other similar fledgling companies, borrow some of his ballets. Although companies other than New York City Ballet can perform Balanchine works today, they have to get permission, pay sizable licensing fees, and follow various strict guidelines that were put in place after Mr. B's death in 1983. Of course, he didn't just let any company perform his works, but in those days he was relatively free with these precious loans, and they were timely. The presence on NECB's programs of world-class ballets performed by world-class dancers no doubt helped quicken the pace of the company's growth.

Virginia was also always bringing in guest teachers, such as the revered Vera Volkova and Simon Semenoff, and when possible, eminent choreographers to teach and coach us in their ballets. I still marvel at the names of the greats with whom we had the honor and pleasure to work: Hans Brenaa, Anton Dolin, Fernand Nault, Birgit Culberg, Agnes de Mille, Pearl Lang, John Butler, Talley Beatty, Merce Cunningham, Norman Walker, and Geoffrey Holder.

In the presence of those stars, while mostly serving as the greatest kind of inspiration, they also presented a sobering aspect: on any given day one could dream of aspiring to their heights and even think it possible, or else feel that it was out of one's reach, an impossible dream after all.

A year after joining the Boston School of Ballet, I had a crisis of doubt, my early dreams of becoming a professional dancer crushed. We had been given permission to perform Balanchine's *Scotch Symphony*, and I wasn't put into the first cast—or even the second. I—along with only one other dancer—was put in the third cast, which effectively meant I wasn't going to be performing the ballet. To me this meant that I wasn't really cut out for this business. Thus, my future place in this world seemingly unrealistic, I quit dancing.

3

Return to Forever

June 7, 1961

Dear Laurie,

I think it is time for you to seriously consider working toward a ballet career.

You have a talent given by God to only a few people—certainly—you need much work to train and develop this talent to meet professional standards. <u>Everyone</u> has to work to become good dancers.

<u>NO ONE</u> is born a great dancer.

That letter, signed "With affection, Miss Williams," went on to state that even some of her most prized students—such as Sara Leland and Fern MacLarnon, who had gone on to successful careers with New York City Ballet and American Ballet Theatre respectively—hadn't in her opinion been as advanced as I was when they were my age. She wrote that of the thousands of students she had seen come and go, only a few had "the gifts of brains, natural grace, stage and personality and the bodies capable of becoming fine dancers." She concluded with a push and a promise: "So think about this—I will help you—and I think you'll love being a ballet dancer. Think about it." Not long after my self-imposed "fall from grace," I had indeed returned, but this letter was a big sign that I'd done the right thing.

I hadn't told anyone why I quit ballet, and certainly not Miss Williams. I just quit, stoically suffering in the way that only teenagers can, my sincere misery spiked with a hint of melodrama. My parents gave me the ability to find my own way through this. They were supportive in whatever it was

I wanted. And they probably knew me well enough to realize I'd soon be bored. Although it seemed great at first, I didn't really do anything with the extra time I had on my hands. I hung out with classmates, but after a while that couldn't fill the hole I was feeling inside.

And, oh, what a world I returned to! In that first year with New England Civic Ballet, before my little "intermission," I performed on a program in which Sara and Fern were the guests, along with Eleanor D'Antuono, Jacques d'Amboise (Jack), Melissa Hayden (Milly), and Paul Sutherland. Jack and Milly were notable not only for their physical abilities but also for their "colorful" onstage asides to one another. Eleanor was another of Virginia's former students who went on to become a well-known and respected figure in the ballet community, dancing with the touring group Ballet Russe de Monte Carlo and the Joffrey Ballet (back then called the Robert Joffrey Theater Ballet), and eventually became a principal dancer with American Ballet Theatre. Paul also danced for Joffrey, a company that, though not nearly as big as City Ballet or Ballet Theatre, became a beloved fixture in the New York City dance scene, particularly throughout the 1960s, '70s, and '80s. The group's eclectic and often daring repertoire provided audiences with an exciting, refreshing take on ballet. Joffrey and his co-director, Gerald Arpino, tapped into some of the most striking social and political issues of that era; psychedelic "rock ballets" such as Joffrey's 1967 *Astarte* were performed alongside older ballets that were decidedly *not* about fairies and swans, such as Kurt Jooss's 1932 brilliant but grim antiwar masterpiece *The Green Table*.

Virginia too, as the years went on, would seek out adventurous and new choreography for the company, but the classics always remained the bedrock of the repertory. The program on December 30, 1960, provides an interesting window into how far the company had come in a few years and how far it had to go. It was held in Boston's John Hancock Hall; those guest artists, along with some up-and-coming homegrown dancers such as Earle Sieveling and Virginia Zango, performed lead roles in the evening's double-bill presentation of *The Nutcracker* and *Les Sylphides*. Performing *The Nutcracker* only once is nearly impossible to imagine today. Now of course *The Nutcracker*, set to Peter Tchaikovsky's well-known score, has become a huge holiday tradition in America, and Boston Ballet performs it more than forty times between Thanksgiving and the New Year. For many dancers, the ballet is both a continual rite of passage and a gauge for how well one is, or perhaps isn't, progressing. Originally choreographed by Lev Ivanov and Marius Petipa in 1892 in St. Petersburg, Russia, most productions include ample performance opportunities for children and adults alike. To a young dancer, the array of roles is like a daunting yet irresistible stairway to be ascended, each step seeming even more wondrous than the last. From baby mouse to polichinelle, party child, soldier, and angel, the pathway after those children's roles becomes steeper, and one that many students are unable to keep climbing.

It's in these middle years, especially for female students, where attrition may set in. Their changing bodies often can't handle the increasingly difficult classwork. While there is no such thing as the mythological "perfect ballet body," tight, inflexible musculature and hips that have a limited range of turnout are examples of physical issues that make the lines and bravura steps in classical ballet particularly difficult to achieve. And those pointe shoes! Though at first they beckon glamorously, they can become instruments of torture when young dancers discover that the slippers' satiny sheen is in great contrast to the hard work and physical strength needed to get up onto one's toes. Adolescence can wreak havoc on the progress of a ballet student, who may exhibit many positive physical attributes including flexibility when younger but whose unpredictable growth during puberty may suddenly introduce limits where there were none before. For those who are able to make the leap to that next level, a new range of roles opens up again: corps de ballet parts such as snowflakes or flowers; demi-soloist or soloist parts in the ballet's various "sweets" dances such as Chocolate, Coffee, Tea, or Marzipan. Finally, on the top landing are the coveted principal roles of the Snow Queen, Dew Drop, and ultimately, the Sugar Plum Fairy.

In that 1960 performance, I appeared as one of the children in the first-act party scene of *The Nutcracker*, near the bottom but, like my peers, looking way, way up with glittering eyes. Indeed, the next year, when we performed *The Nutcracker* at the Springfield Trade School, while I was still in the party scene (and now I was playing a boy; a not-uncommon situation in the often male-bereft ballet world) I had earned a spot in the snow corps de ballet, whirling and waltzing to Tchaikovsky's beautiful melody with eleven other young snowflakes.

In 1961 I performed as a "card" in the croquet game scene in Miss Leonard's *Alice in Wonderland* and then, in later performances of the ballet that year, as a "gardener" alongside my friend Susan Magno. I was becoming a dancer! My life was happily consumed with classes and rehearsals. Although I was always aware of how hard everything was, I relished the challenges. There were times when I'd panic and feel I wasn't progressing fast enough, and that maybe it was all a waste of time, but it never felt like a sacrifice. I loved going to class, although I hated that I was always fifteen minutes late for our 3:00 class, because I got out of school at 2:30 and it took forty-five minutes to get from Cohasset to Boston.

From the time I was fourteen we had class every day, sometimes three or even four classes; if there was rehearsal then we had fewer classes, but occasionally rehearsal went until 1:00 in the morning. Of course later, when the company was unionized, that sort of thing would never happen, but back then, we'd be told, "Nope. It's not right yet. Do it again." And do it we did.

As I got older, I occasionally found time for some outside fun with my high-school friends. If rehearsals in Boston ended early enough, for instance, I'd be able to get to a Friday-night party in Cohasset well after it started but still enabling me to have a somewhat normal teenage existence. Indeed, I managed to do many "normal" teenage things, both romantic—with my boyfriend Stewart throughout high school, whom I continued to date for a couple of years after graduation—and rebellious. Like many young people, I took up smoking. Between bumming cigarettes from other people and swiping some from Dad's pack, I didn't actually buy my own until I was sixteen. Of course, my parents eventually found out. One evening, Ma and Dad picked up my girlfriend, Cindy, and me after an evening of bowling at the community center. She and I had snuck a cigarette in the anteroom of the nearby post office, back in the days when—hard to imagine now—people smoked everywhere. We unwittingly ratted ourselves out when we got in the car, with that unmistakable and lingering smell everywhere, on our clothes and in our hair.

While ballet absorbed most of our time, my dancer friends and I also had fun outside of all the serious work we did in the studio. In the summer, we'd briefly escape the stifling heat inside and sit out on the fire escape, eating watermelon and spitting the seeds out into the alley below. In addition to Susan Magno, my pals in those early days included Linda DiBona, Virginia Dunton (later Stuart), and Carol Ravich, wonderful dancers who contributed greatly to the company's early success. Actually, Susie left pretty early on when she got a contract to dance with the Joffrey Ballet, but like the others who'd started out with Virginia, she returned to guest with us. As with the other guest artists, there was something to learn when she visited. In particular, her pirouettes had improved dramatically. It seemed to me this was due to the way she was holding her leg in the passé position, very high and turned out. I immediately began applying that to my own turns, and to this day, when I teach pirouettes to students, I encourage them to get their knees up and well turned out, and to focus the eyes and spot like crazy.

The fact that I recognized and applied this technique to my own pirouettes doesn't mean that I became one of those phenomenal turners. Remember that there's no such thing as a perfect ballet body. Well, it's rare for even a professional dancer to be excellent at *every* skill set; one, of course, must be pretty darn good at most things in order to make it in this field, but the best at everything? Nah. And, indeed, pirouettes were not my strongest suit—but I never stopped working on them.

What I loved about those early years is something that continued throughout my career with Boston Ballet: the dancers were all in it for each other and for the good of the company. Of course there is going to be occasional jealousy or bad feelings in a situation in which dancers have to compete for roles, but over-the-top movies such as *Black Swan* notwithstanding, there is often a lot of camaraderie amidst dance companies.

For her part, I think Virginia rather enjoyed the fact that we were like a little family; she was the hen, and we dancers were her chicks.

DURING THESE YEARS while I was inching my way along the ballet student's journey from caterpillar to butterfly, the New England Civic Ballet was making relatively huge strides itself: its repertoire and quality of dancers were increasing, and the company's exposure was expanding. In 1962,

NECB performed for the first time at Jacob's Pillow Dance Festival as part of its thirtieth-anniversary season. The program listed us as "Boston Ballet, formerly New England Civic Ballet," and although it was at the time technically incorrect, it was a bit of foreshadowing that would soon prove to be true. Jacob's Pillow, situated on eighty bucolic acres in the Berkshires of western Massachusetts, is an important and revered institution in the dance world, particularly here in the United States; its main stage, the Ted Shawn Theatre, was the first built specifically for dance in this country. Shawn, one of the early modern dance pioneers, had purchased the property, a former farm, in the 1930s and set about, with his performing group known as his "Men Dancers," refurbishing the old barns into studios. All these decades later, the Pillow has continued its tradition of presenting dancers and companies of all genres from around the world.

Today, the usual schedule is for two different companies to come each week and perform either in the Shawn or in the newer theater, the Doris Duke, but back then, each week was usually composed of a variety of performers. NECB performed Virginia's ballet *The Green Season*, as well as Michel Fokine's 1911 *Spectre de la Rose* and the company premiere of Balanchine's *Scotch Symphony* (yes, that *Scotch Symphony*!). *The Green Season* eventually became a signature piece for the company, since it was clearly liked by audiences, so much so that Robert Joffrey asked Virginia to stage it for his company.

In 1963, the company garnered more local attention when it performed for the first time at the Boston Arts Festival, which back then was presented in the city's famous Public Garden. This time around the guest artists were City Ballet stars Patricia McBride and Edward Villella, who performed the leads in *Scotch Symphony*. As you may have guessed by now, this Balanchine ballet was becoming a regular in our repertoire, as well as another Balanchine work, the exuberant crowd-pleaser *Stars and Stripes*. In addition to her *The Green Season*, Virginia's *Chausson Symphony* was performed, as was *Jazz 63*, a new piece choreographed by company member Joseph Cassini and performed by him and Nina Pillar, a young dancer with an uncannily prodigious technique. As it happens, Balanchine was in attendance for this company milestone. One paragraph of an otherwise glowing *Boston Herald* review of the performance, written by Elinor Hughes, is a telling indicator of the company's status at this time, which seemed to be somewhere between an awkward duckling and a graceful swan: "Everything was delightful, in fact, except that the music, in addition to being canned, was also poorly reproduced and for the most part distressingly harsh and unpleasing."

Live music was, in fact, something that was considered by Virginia to be an important aspect in terms of quality, of professionalism, but, like everything else, live music was expensive and therefore something that was, at the time, intermittent. Virginia took it upon herself to make the edited music tapes and proceeded to make the edits with Scotch tape instead of editing tape. Eventually, her Yankee frugality resulted in a significant moment in history at a Jacob's Pillow performance of *Giselle*. Violette Verdy, who was guesting with us and was about to start the act 2 adagio, stood in her augmented fifth position for what seemed to be forever. One of Virginia's "Scotch tape edits" had come apart, and all the tape was on the floor! Future Boston Ballet (BB) member, Leslie Woodies, who was interning backstage as a Jacob's Pillow student, was the poor soul running the tape machine. Ever the professional, Violette remained in character, still in her perfect fifth position, while Leslie scooped it back up and rewound to the start point. What a horrible start to that intense adagio, but she carried on flawlessly. From then on, two recorders were run in sync, so that if one failed, the other was ready to kick in. And Virginia was no longer allowed to do any editing.

Even as we scored important performance opportunities such as the ones at the Pillow and the Boston Arts Festival, we continued participating in the Northeast Regional Ballet Festival, including the one in May 1963, when it was held in Detroit, Michigan. Both Balanchine and Joffrey were in attendance as guests of honor. I don't know whether or not she had much contact with either of them during that festival, but Virginia and her company had apparently remained on Balanchine's radar, because by the end of that year, news came of a major break. Virginia was to be one of seven recipients of a new Ford Foundation grant designed to help New England Civic Ballet become Boston's first professional dance company. The Ford Foundation, in addition to being one of this country's biggest privately funded supporters of the arts, was also America's first foundation to fund dance. Balanchine served as a national talent scout for the foundation, and it was he who recommended that Boston's growing troupe be a recipient of the grant.

The grant—which initially Virginia, believe it or not, turned down, fearful that she could not raise the required "challenge" amount that was originally a stipulation—in the end amounted to $144,000, spread out over the course of three years. Naturally, in those days it was monumental to such an organization that relied heavily on volunteering family members to help out the few "official" employees who themselves were each doing the work of several people. Sydney Leonard was still working full time at the *Atlantic Monthly*, so she must not have been making much for her duties as assistant to Virginia, which included teaching, coaching, and countless tasks. As she said in her memoirs, "We did every scrap of work ourselves, everything."

For years, another mainstay on the staff was the company's executive director, Ruth Harrington—always "Mrs. Harrington" to us—Sara Leland's mother. Though people that hold that title today usually have their own staff to do all the "small stuff," Mrs. Harrington was down in the trenches with everyone else. I can still picture her at performances, collecting money and distributing tickets from an old Capezio pointe shoebox!

Along with Balanchine's New York City Ballet and its affiliate School of American Ballet, ballet companies in Houston; Pennsylvania; San Francisco; Utah; Dayton, Ohio; and Washington, D.C., were the other awardees. While this seminal grant turned out to be a huge boost for ballet in the United States, it created some backlash within the dance community. Some decried the fact that only ballet companies, no modern troupes, were given grants, and others complained that only those who'd had some association with Balanchine were favored.

We dancers were blissfully unaware of any bitterness. All we knew was that the company was on the rise. And, as always, there were classes to take and rehearsals to do today, tomorrow, and beyond.

4

Relevé

Relevé. Origin: French. Literally "raised up"; in ballet it is a movement in which the dancer rises onto the balls of the feet or even the tips of the toes.

ON JANUARY 25, 1965, Virginia and we, her steadfast band of hardworking dancers, teachers, staff members, and volunteers, began the first official season as a professional entity, The Boston Ballet Company. While this "inaugural" program, at John Hancock Hall, still included guest artists, more and more of the homegrown dancers were able to take on prominent roles. So, while New York City Ballet members Sara Leland, Carol Sumner, Suki Schorer, and Robert Rodham, for example, performed the leads in Balanchine's 1929 masterpiece *Apollo*, our own Susan Magno, Linda DiBona, Carol Ravich, and Nina Pillar comprised the cast of Anton Dolin's crowd-pleasing restaging of the 1845 *Pas de Quatre*. The importance of the event was underscored by the fact that we were accompanied by our own "Boston Ballet Company Orchestra," which was led that evening by the eminent conductor Hugo Fiorato, also on loan from NYCB. In those tentative, formative, sink-or-swim years that every young organization must navigate, we were surely buoyed up by the fact that Balanchine continued to share his ballets, his dancers, and other resources, including Maestro Fiorato. In programs, Balanchine was listed as "artistic advisor" to the company, a very public stamp of approval.

Indeed, it was an important moment for Boston, a city that is known to be both metropolitan and provincial. It's a "big" city with international status, and yet small-town charms can be found within many of its neighborhoods. The cover of the brochure for that first season —"The Premiere Season of The Boston Ballet Company"— invited potential audience members to subscribe to "A History-Making Event." And, in fact, each of the three performances, which comprised that first modest Boston season (January 25, February 15, and April 5), sold out completely. While we continued to perform in cities and towns around the region (during the previous year, 1964, the company appeared throughout Massachusetts in places such as Attleboro, Cape Ann, and Framingham, as well as at Dartmouth College in New Hampshire), we were now gaining traction in our own hometown.

The announcement of the Ford Foundation grant, and with it the fact that Boston was about to have its first professional ballet company, was newsworthy enough for five company members to appear on the cover of the *Boston Globe*'s March 1964 "Magazine" section. Titled "Boston—City of Culture," this special edition featured stories and lavish photographs of various local cultural institutions. In that cover picture, the dancers were costumed in the Romantic-era-inspired costumes from Michel Fokine's 1909 *Les Sylphides*, a ballet we performed frequently in the early days, and posed in the beautiful indoor garden of Boston's beloved Isabella Stewart Gardner Museum. It was here that Virginia had her favorite photo taken on one of the balconies overlooking the garden. In an accompanying piece about our company—the new kid on the block—Margo Miller wrote, "In Boston, dance has been a stepchild compared to the other arts, but now a local troupe is clamoring for attention."

While these moments of celebrity, if you will, were thrilling, they were also fleeting. The hard work continued, as did the necessary trekking about. In 1965, along with our Boston engagements, we performed in venues in Brockton, Cape Cod, Cohasset, Falmouth, and Worcester, and, of course, in Virginia's "Williams Dance Review" held at Malden High School. Rising stars or not, we were still expected to appear on this annual program with students from Virginia's flagship Malden school, which was still moving along, producing future hopefuls *and* helping to pay the bills of the company.

And the local critics, for their part, weren't going to go easy on us just because we were making history. The prominent Elliot Norton, mostly revered (and sometimes feared) for his vast knowledge of and critical writings on the theater, reviewed the January 25 performance. At the time, it was not uncommon for a theater or music critic to review dance performances; in fact, it's another indication of how "young" dance still was in this country relative to other performing arts. This changed over the ensuing decades as dance critics and criticism became more widespread. In any event, Norton was one of our frequent reviewers in those early days, and whether or not he would have had more enthusiasm for us if dance criticism had been his "specialty" is impossible to know. "Of The Boston Ballet Company," his piece opened, "which began its season Monday evening at John Hancock Hall, it can be said that its first program was unhackneyed, its dancing generally commendable though hardly inspired, its orchestra first-rate, its decor dismal, its lighting somewhat erratic." As this paragraph illustrates, Norton was often dry, even acerbic, when writing about the company. "Unhackneyed!" With such faint praise, we weren't likely to rest on our laurels. Thankfully, others were more generous. Elinor Hughes began her review of that evening thus: "The opening night of the Boston Ballet Company's first season . . . was, even when soberly regarded, an auspicious occasion."

———

IT SEEMS PARTICULARLY fitting to me that my own appearance on that season debut program in January 1965 was as a member of the *Scotch Symphony* corps de ballet. Choreographed in 1952, Balanchine's dance, which takes its title from the score by Felix Mendelssohn, is an abstract meditation that evokes both the woodland "sylphs" of Scottish legend as well as the legendary feisty earthiness of that land's people. Thus, of the lead females, one is costumed in a diaphanous bell-type skirt, reminiscent of the Romantic tutu, while another one is outfitted in a cheeky kilt. It is by turns wistful and playful, and as with so many of Mr. B's dances, intensely musical. As if a curse of some kind had been lifted, this ballet, which had previously given me so much grief, would become something I danced many times over the years, and usually as one of the leads. Not bad for this former member of the "third cast!" In fact, earlier on the day of the premiere season's first concert, I performed one of the main *Scotch* roles at Harvard University's Loeb Drama Center, across the Charles River in Cambridge. I guess I wasn't quite ready for "prime time," but Virginia and others were surely pushing me along, apparently seeing potential in me.

How quickly we all were propelled forward. It's rather dizzying to think of it now, but within a few months, I had also taken over one of the four spots in *Pas de Quatre*. First choreographed in 1845 by Jules Perrot (one of the original choreographers of the Romantic era's most well-known ballet, *Giselle*), *Pas de Quatre* was originally a showcase for four of the leading ballerinas of their time, Fanny Cerrito, Lucile Grahn, Carlotta Grisi, and Marie Taglioni. While these names are mostly known only to ballet dancers and balletomanes today, in their own time they were wildly acclaimed. It is said that a group of Taglioni's fans cut up a pair of her pointe shoes and cooked them in a stew—which they then reportedly ate.

In addition to their "star" status, there were reports of bitter rivalries amongst the four legends. While they are probably *somewhat* apocryphal, those gossipy stories continue to be told, mostly with tongue-in-cheek affection. The English choreographer and dancer Anton Dolin's 1941 restaging of *Pas de Quatre* is, accordingly, both a loving tribute and a sly parody of that bygone era. How incredible it still is to me that Dolin himself came to stage the ballet on the company. It was, to be honest, scary to be in the studio with such an icon, but he was very methodical in rehearsals with us. He completely understood that we were not all full-fledged professionals yet and worked with us in such a way that we were brought up to another level.

Another challenge we were given for that first season's opening program, and another way for us to grow artistically, was to learn and perform *Reflections*, the most modern work the company had yet done. Although choreographer Norman Walker's movement was quite contemporary compared to what most of us were used to, it was also balletic enough that it was a great way for the company to begin to tackle different kinds of material. I was only an understudy for that first performance, but we all loved it. It didn't matter what the style was, what mattered, and what always matters to a dancer, is how does it feel to do it? And *Reflections* had that most glorious feeling of all: it completely reflected the music and made the dancing euphoric. Though there would be some new pieces that came along that were, shall we say, less than wonderful, this was a lovely way to jump into the continually morphing genre sometimes called "modern ballet." It's notable that Virginia put such a new work on that all-important January program. Today, it's business as usual for companies to present out-of-the-box ballets alongside more traditional-looking works, but it seems that there was a bit of riskiness for her to do so at that precise moment, when we had so many eyes on us and so much to prove to potential audience members. By doing so just then, however, she showed Boston what it could expect from its first professional ballet company. To her dancers, she indicated what she would expect from *us* going forward.

And we were ready to do whatever it took, to try it all, to work, to learn, to improve, and to be better artists. While we knew that the presence of all of those great guest dancers was deeply beneficial to us—believe me, we were in awe of them, and a lot of our growth came from observing and emulating them—we were naturally hungry for our own recognition, for bigger roles. Virginia wanted that too, and she and we achieved it gradually but not slowly. On February 15, the second performance of that debut Boston season, only four guests appeared with us, compared to the seven on January 25. And we apparently managed to hold our own with them; dancing in act 2 of *Swan Lake*, with Sonia Arova and James Capp in the lead roles of Odette and Prince Siegfried, I and three others were noted by several of the local critics. "'Swan Lake' tests the quality of the corps de ballet and the young Boston dancers passed the test triumphantly," wrote Kathleen Cannell, "and in the pas de quatre of the little cygnets, four dainty soloists, Linda di Bona [*sic*], Nina Pillar, Carol Ravich and Laurie Young stopped the show." Elinor Hughes wrote of we four little swans, that "the warmest reception of the evening was reserved for the four young members of the resident company . . . [who] were superb as they performed with flawless grace and precision."

Now that we were unionized, legally we had to be paid. Though we were now able to call ourselves "professional dancers," we were still part of a family. So, we cashed the first checks we received—to prove to the union that we'd been paid—and then turned the money right back over to the company. We knew the company couldn't really afford it, and we wanted the company, our family, to survive. We had ambitions to achieve, dreams to live.

RETURNING TO *Pas de Quatre*, in the company's first go-round with the ballet I was originally second-cast as the effervescent, flirtatious Fanny Cerrito, but soon after the debut season's opening performance, my friend Susie (Magno) left to begin her tenure with the Joffrey Ballet. Susie had been dancing the role of Taglioni—the mature "stateswoman" of the four ballerinas based on the real-life Marie Taglioni—in the first cast, and when she left I was moved into her position. It was my first fully leading role with the now fully professional Boston Ballet Company, and the first time I performed it was for the grand opening of the Prudential Center, another institution that would become a Boston landmark.

IN JUNE OF that noteworthy year, I marked another personal milestone, though of quite a different nature, when I graduated from Cohasset High School. As I mentioned earlier, I managed to have some life outside the ballet, and my senior year of high school was filled with memories and experiences I cherish to this day. I continued to enjoy good times with school pals, including my boyfriend Stewart, and my best-friends group of Cindy, Sam, and Diane, who were all engaged in theater in some form or another. I had sung and acted a bit in some school plays, and in my senior year I choreographed the production of *Bye Bye Birdie* for Cohasset High School's first-ever presentation of a musical. And for the record, those performances sold out too.

Along with the pride, relief, and celebration that graduating from high school usually affords, many find that it's also a time of major uncertainty, and I was no exception. Although I was clearly making progress as a dancer, beginning to get lead roles and some recognition along with them, I was still in the corps de ballet, the lowest rank. Actually, at the time, we weren't even given that title; in programs, the leading dancers were listed in capital letters, and then the rest of us were just listed below, in alphabetical order by last name and with only a first initial. So, while I may have performed as the iconic Marie Taglioni on a particular evening, my name still languished at the bottom of the heap on the printed program—literally, as "Young" was rarely followed by any names beginning with a *Z*. I was thrilled when Virginia Zango joined the company, but for many more reasons than I wasn't last anymore. She was the one who taught me how the way one uses and works the feet can make a significant difference in the overall line. Not having the ultimate body structure, I took her advisements to heart to make the very best of what I possessed. We all taught each other. Any new tidbit of information was readily circulated throughout our ranks. By now there were four female principal dancers, but I wasn't one of them. It seemed to me that Virginia had her favorites, and I was not to be one of those either.

And so, I had my second lapse of faith in terms of my ability to cut it in this field. Once again, just as when I was thirteen and briefly quit dancing, I began to consider leaving the company, but I never told Virginia about it. It seemed it was time to make a backup plan: mine was applying to and being accepted into the University of Miami's marine biology program. My family, as always, was loving, supportive, and strong. Ma told me, "You know, if this isn't making you happy, don't worry about it. We'll send you to college, and you can go do something else. But if you want to dance, you've got to make a decision here." With uncanny timing, Virginia took a leap of faith and made me a principal as I was trying to figure it all out. Later on, injuries may have threatened my ability to continue dancing, but that second crisis of doubt was my last.

So, I stayed in Massachusetts, although I did make a big move of another kind when I left my family's home later that year and joined forces with my longtime school buddy Diane. She and I got a one-bedroom apartment on Beacon Street, in Brookline. My departure from the proverbial nest wasn't an act of defiance but rather a bid for survival: driving home one night after another late rehearsal, I woke up on the shoulder of the expressway. "Ma," I said the next day, "I gotta get an apartment. I'm gonna die."

GRADUATING FROM high school, becoming a principal dancer, and moving away from home . . . to these hallmarks of young adulthood was added a formal touch: Virginia changed my name, at least professionally. Although the practice of "exoticizing" one's name to something either Russian sounding or European sounding was by then not quite as frequently done as it had been in earlier decades, directors still often tweaked or changed dancers' names. I had been toying with the idea already, but even I knew that my romantic notions of being called something such as "Lara Ivanova Maladaya" were a bit over the top. Virginia, as usual, was decidedly unsentimental about the whole thing. "Laurie," she said, in that voice of hers, "when you're thirty, you're not going to want to be called Laurie. I think you should change your name to Laura." I never said yay or nay to the idea, but one day my name appeared on a program as "Laura Young," and it stayed like that. Lorraine turned Laurie was now Laura.

5

Allegro

Allegro. Origin: Italian, literally, "lively, gay"; in ballet it is used to describe sequences in which the dancer is airborne, executing either brisk, complicated footwork (petit allegro) or soaring, bounding leaps (grand allegro).

YES, I WAS GROWING UP. We all were: my fellow dancers and the company itself, all very quickly. Not only was Boston Ballet relying less and less on guest artists to perform the leading roles, but also we "homegrown" dancers were even beginning to perform elsewhere as the guest artists ourselves. Although one of my first such appearances was quite modest—a benefit performance for former company dancer Denise Plouffe's ballet school — it was nonetheless a particularly exciting opportunity for me. I danced the role of the Sugar Plum Fairy for the first time as a professional, with fellow Boston Ballet dancer Leo Guerard as my Cavalier. I had danced many of the variations Miss Leonard had taught us at local Grange Hall meetings as a sort of "half-time" event, and most often, it was the Sugar Plum variation so I was fairly comfortable with the solo parts. As for the pas de deux sections with Leo, he was ever gallant, was a steady partner, and possessed a dry wit that set me at ease in the partnering. While my debut wasn't in a big-city venue, it was certainly a big deal for me: I had arrived, at the top of that *Nutcracker* ladder.

Of course, big responsibilities aren't unusual among accomplished young dancers who, like musical prodigies, tend to grow up fast. Not only are such young artists working in intense atmospheres, but also they are required to present themselves on stage with a maturity and professionalism beyond their years, often portraying characters whose stories involve experiences way beyond anything a young adult has yet to encounter. While most dancers continue to develop and ripen their physical, emotional, and intellectual talents as they get older, the desirable traits of hyperflexibility, strength, stamina, and the ability to move fleetly, stealthily, or sinuously must be trained into the dancer at an early age when the body is at its most pliable. No wonder young students are often compared to lumps of clay.

It's also not unusual for ballet dancers to go directly into their professional dancing careers upon graduating from high school, putting college off until later, earning a degree through a correspondence school, or forgoing college altogether. The latter situation is more rare now but was still typical when I was beginning my career. Conversely, the majority of modern dancers have traditionally gone to college first and thus tend to start performing professionally at an older age than their ballet counterparts. And starting later often enables modern dancers to dance long into their later years. Martha Graham, whose father, like my own grandmother, didn't approve of dance for young women, didn't take a class until she was in her early twenties. There is that "improper" stigma attached to dancers again. In any event, Graham and many of her peers ended up being largely responsible for the presence of dance on many American college campuses today, particularly modern and contemporary forms. One such iconic college dance program offered at Vermont's Bennington College grew from the summer dance festivals that former Graham student Martha Hill started in 1932. Later, Hill founded another respected dance department at Connecticut College. Today, modern, ballet, jazz, tap, and other forms of dance are included in the curricula of the majority of college dance programs.

In contrast, in the early 1930s when Graham's choreographic career was beginning to take hold, three "baby ballerinas" were making headlines with their appearances with the Ballets Russes de Monte Carlo. Irina Baronova and Tamara Toumanova were twelve and Tatiana Riabouchinska was fourteen when they first caught the eye of none other than George Balanchine before he had made his way to America. While many people in the field would agree that the punishing performing schedule that these three "babies" would end up enduring is not a healthy life for a young person, those of us who experienced similarly exhausting schedules reveled in the progress we made in our chosen art form.

Ballet has deep roots in being a "youth-driven" art form. Is it because of that need for physical pliability? Or is it about a young person's willingness to take risks and try anything that is asked—or demanded—of them? Regardless of the answer, I was young when I began taking class and rehearsing for many hours at a stretch, often late into the night, but I didn't resent it one bit. Maybe it could be argued that we were all exploited, but that doesn't feel like the experience I had. Today of course, a professional ballet school wouldn't be legally allowed to keep students for such extended periods of time. Don't get me wrong: it's a good thing that these rules are in place. I guess I'm just grateful that my "total immersion" as a young dancer was such a positive one for me. Otherwise, to quote Bette Midler, "Why bother?"

At eighteen, I still had a good deal of maturing to do in spite of regularly portraying princesses and other roles depicting authority and responsibility on stage. I am struck now though by something we didn't seem to notice then: in reviews and articles we were frequently referred to as "girls," while the company males were usually called "men" in the exact same articles. It's true that the feminist movement, a few short years away, called attention to just that sort of disparity, but that nomenclature remained in our field for a long time, and you still hear it used in some professional companies today. Often, it's at least democratic, that is, all dancers are called either boys and girls, or ladies and gentlemen, but it's an interesting dichotomy. We young dancers were expected to behave with seriousness and maturity but were often referred to as children.

IN 1966 MY BROTHER JIM, five years my senior, took the very adult step of getting married. And wouldn't you know it, he married a dancer from the company, my friend Phyllis Heath. Jim and Phyllis ultimately had two children, Aaron and Bridget. When Phyllis was six months pregnant with Aaron, and I was sidelined by an injury, I was horrified to see her fall during a performance. Fortunately, all was well, but it seemed to be a sign that maybe it would be a good time to go on maternity leave. When Aaron was four years old, he inadvertently gave me a company nickname that has stuck with me to this day. He'd been brought to a performance of *The Nutcracker*, and when he saw me as the Sugar Plum Fairy take my place on stage, he called out from way back in the audience, "La-La!" Everyone heard him, and the nickname was perpetuated. Meanwhile, Bridget's own daughter Riley, my grandniece, is continuing the ballet tradition in the Young family and studies at Boston Ballet School where I am one of her teachers. She's on her own journey now, working hard, and doing quite well. *And* she has lovely long legs, just like her grandmother Phyllis.

———————

FOR THE COMPANY'S second Boston season in 1966, the repertoire was once again a bold mix. Virginia had made it clear with the first season that she wasn't interested in playing it safe by scheduling only tried-and-true or purely decorative ballets. The "subscription series"—one performance in January, one in February, and one in March—was exciting and, yet again, ambitious for such a young company. As in the 1965 series, we presented an entirely different program for each show. The ambition was noted, and not condescendingly, by local and New York critics alike. Clive Barnes wrote in the *New York Times* about the January show that "its program must have surely constituted the most varied and ambitious one ever offered by an American dance company based outside New York." Barnes's review ended by stating, "The real hope of the company was that here was a program in which the choreography was first-rate throughout. On such a basis, with good training and the help of a loyal and intelligent audience, anything can be achieved."

Our growing Balanchine repertoire was well represented with *Allegro Brillante*, the *Stars and Stripes* pas de deux, *Donizetti Variations*, *Prodigal Son*, and *Serenade*, while *Les Sylphides* and *Napoli, Act III* represented the more traditional side of ballet. Other classically based pieces included *Le Combat (The Duel)*, a choreodrama by Ballet Theatre star William Dollar that featured NYCB stars Melissa Hayden and Conrad Ludlow, and Virginia's new *Stephen Foster Suite*, a series of abstract vignettes reflecting the varying moods of Foster songs. Arthur Miller's *After the Fall* had recently opened in Boston, and then closed soon after, and we acquired the set at a very reduced cost to use in *Foster Suite*. Because it was so massive, it would only fit in nearby Horticultural Hall, and so that's where we ended up rehearsing. Doing the cakewalk and thrashing our skirts on a platform that was only six feet wide made for a fairly hairy situation—if anyone fell, it would be onto a concrete floor twenty feet below. As you can imagine, we were *very* careful.

Although we still depended upon guest artists for the leads in the Balanchine works, it was hardly a sore point for us, particularly because the only two who appeared in the season-opening performance, Sara Leland and Earle Sieveling, had begun their careers with Virginia in Boston. The presence of those well-known and highly accomplished dancers, and the Balanchine repertoire itself, was good for the company and good for us, and we knew it. We were the only American company other than NYCB that Balanchine allowed to perform *Prodigal Son* at that time, which was quite a coup. Choreographed in 1929 for the original Ballets Russes, Balanchine revived the highly theatrical *Prodigal Son* in 1960 for the young Edward Villella, updating some of the movements to capitalize on Villella's powerful physique and showcasing his particularly robust elevation. The revival and Villella were a hit, and by the time Mr. B allowed us to perform the ballet, Villella was something of a legend in the role. Boston Ballet was already garnering more and more press, but Villella's appearance attracted even more buzz in that 1966 season.

Over time, many of us would take over the lead roles in all of these Balanchine ballets, but even dancing in the corps of a ballet such as *Serenade* was a gift. Musicality is one of the most celebrated hallmarks of Balanchine's ballets, and *Serenade*, set to Tchaikovsky's Serenade for Strings, is sublimely musical. It has its devilishly difficult sections too, but as usual, Balanchine married the steps to the music as if they were jigsaw pieces, meant to be forever fitted together. It makes sense to the ear and to the body, and thus the steps flow organically. Choreographed in 1934, it was the first ballet he made for his initial ensemble of dancers in America. He was often quoted as saying that *Serenade* was in many ways an exercise for those young amateurs, to teach them various aspects of stagecraft. Had my mother stayed in New York, she no doubt would have experienced his early choreographic genius firsthand. The poetically simple opening is a beloved image to ballet lovers everywhere. Seventeen women costumed in pale blue, calf-length skirts of floating tulle stand, their faces inclined to their right hand extended on an upward diagonal, as if blocking out the light of the moon. In unison, each stretches through her fingers and then bends the arm, the hand briefly trailing across the brow, then the heart, and finally meeting the other hand so the two form the most basic of port de bras. Their legs, in parallel up to now, sweep suddenly into first position, the heels of the feet connecting and the toes reaching out to opposite sides. And then? Glorious dancing, which, I am still proud to remember, we in the corps apparently delivered. In his *New York Times* review, Barnes wrote, "*Serenade* stands or falls on its ensemble, and it was the dancing here that offered the clearest promise for the company's future. Any company that can dance *Serenade* like this obviously deserves to succeed. Indeed, it can hardly fail."

We continued to present modern works too, including Joyce Trisler's *Perilous Time* and Anna Sokolow's *Time + 6*. Both had been commissioned for the company and were, in their own very different ways, meant to be reflective of the turbulence of the times. *Perilous Time*, which we had first performed in 1965, was intense, the dancers in flesh-colored costumes accented here and there with ominous bloodlike splotches. Trisler, a lovely modern dancer with the Alvin Ailey American Dance Theater, choreographed and performed the lead for the premiere, and then Phyllis Heath, my sister-in-law, took over that role in 1966. That was also the year I first worked with Miss Trisler, when she staged the summer stock production of *Brigadoon* in which I played Bonnie Jean. I would work with her again a year later when she staged her concert solo piece *Journey* on me while I was guesting at New Jersey's Garden State Ballet. After several performances, she told me that the solo, set to Charles Ives's composition "The Unanswered Question," was mine to perform any time I wanted. Even though, as it turned out, I never had the chance to take her up on her generous offer, it was a tremendous vote of confidence, a big gift to a young dancer.

Whereas Trisler's piece was unabashedly violent—one of the characters is murdered—*Time + 6* depicted a group whose moods ranged from alienation to agitation. We wore jeans, had our hair down, and danced to Herb Pomeroy's jazz orchestra. One writer called it a "beatnik ballet," and many viewers saw the piece as a comment on the seemingly growing indifference seen among some young people at the time. I believe it was the first time Sokolow had worked with ballet dancers, and I for one was intimidated by this legendary figure in the modern dance world. While Sokolow may have had a clear idea that involved a certain portrayal of young people, it didn't mean we dancers portraying these young people "got" what she was looking for. I remember rehearsing one day, with my long, long hair everywhere; it was in my eyes, in my mouth, and covering my partner completely at times, and I obviously wasn't doing what I was supposed to be doing, because Sokolow came up to me with a very sour look. When she told me to "make a face with my fanny" I knew I'd never figure it out. Alas, I was turned off by Sokolow and hardly inspired to dig deeper at that point. It was rare for me, but ugh, I just hated working on that dance. On the bright side, most of the critics and, from what we could tell, most of the audience members liked *Time + 6* a lot more than I did.

It was a savvy idea for the company to sell the season as a whole. One couldn't buy a ticket to only one or two of the three Boston season shows. Thus, the subscription-only purchase discouraged any potentially wary viewers of opting out of any performances. On the one hand, it was a great way to introduce viewers to works they might not have seen, but it was also a great way to effectively guarantee full houses. And such a bargain we were! In 1966, those subscription series, meaning the entire three programs, ranged in price from nine to twelve dollars.

Of course, twelve dollars went a lot farther then than it does now, but one thing hasn't changed: then, as now, we needed every cent. Although the company was awarded a second Ford Foundation grant in 1966—this one for three hundred thousand to be spread out over three years, and yet another in 1970 and then again in 1972—everything was always tight. For this second season, though the sight lines weren't perfect, we were now performing at the Back Bay Theater, located directly across the street from our studios. It was something of a step up from the John Hancock Hall where the stage was very shallow and inordinately hard. We were on a never-ending cycle that required us to keep moving forward at a high level while not quite making enough money to pay for it all. We were hardly alone then, nor are we today. Like arts organizations everywhere across America, Boston Ballet has to continually find the balance between offering quality works—often with expensive, opulent costumes and scenery—that keep its audience happy through a diverse repertory and raising enough funds to be able to accomplish it all. In addition, the expense of keeping the women in pointe shoes is prohibitive. They are so expensive that we were only given one pair per season, specifically for performance. We were personally responsible for our rehearsal shoes. As the budget grew over the years, however, so did our supply of pointe shoes. And although dancers don't earn anything even remotely close to what other elite athletes earn—such as baseball, basketball, or football players—the dancers must be paid according to the union (American Guild of Musical Artists [AGMA]) rates. Meanwhile, the musicians, the directors, the regisseurs, the teachers, the production and design crews, and the administrative staff must all be paid too. It's an expensive endeavor, and almost always, ballet companies struggle to pay the bills.

At least we weren't alone on this uphill battle, and it wasn't a secret either. Elinor Hughes wrote a piece in the *Boston Herald* titled "The Theater Needs Help, But How?" and in it she discussed the financial difficulties that theatrical organizations faced. "True, though the government won't help or not very much, we have generous private foundations, but they can't do the whole job." In another article that year, one highlighting the situation for dance specifically, Joan B. Cass wrote, "Disregarding many reasons which prevented this art from taking roots in America, it is enough to focus on the uncontestably major factor: money, since it is impossible to mount elaborate dance productions without the expenditure of huge sums." Cass did see reasons for hope, citing not only private foundations such as Ford but also the recent development of the National Council on the Arts, which had been established in 1964 and advises the chairperson of the National Endowment for the Arts. "No one ever doubted that American dancers have talent and vitality," she summed up. "It is exciting to realize that they are being given the means to shape these qualities into a Golden Age of Dance."

Those Ford Foundation grants were crucial and deeply important to Boston Ballet's launch, as was the support that came from individual donors and volunteers. The first official iteration of organized volunteers, then called the Boston Ballet Society, was founded in 1965 with its principal responsibility being to raise funds for the company and raise awareness of the importance of ballet as a cultural enhancement to the city. They were our grassroots ambassadors. Among the early society members was the mother of fellow company member Ellen O'Reilly, Jacqueline, who spearheaded the creation of the Arts Lottery, forerunner to the Massachusetts Cultural Council. Others included Ruth and Roland Burlingame, lifelong friends from my hometown, and Russell Curry, ballroom dance instructor extraordinaire who later choreographed a fabulous dance for us.

———————

THE QUALITY THAT an audience experiences, of course, is the sum of much more than the beautiful costumes and elaborate set. One of the most important aspects of a ballet's success lies in how it is staged. Staging is the process of setting an already-existing ballet on a different cast or company than the original, and it's a beloved and important tradition in the ballet world, which rarely relies on scores or scripts, as do musicians and actors. In the case of our premiere of the third act of *Napoli*, August Bournonville's 1842 masterpiece, Virginia secured no less than Hans Brenaa, one of the leading experts of the Bournonville style, to come to Boston to work with us and stage the ballet. Born in Copenhagen, Brenaa was a direct "descendent" of Bournonville's and danced in the Royal Danish Ballet before embarking on his invaluable work as a teacher and curator of the technique. *Napoli* was full of the usual Bournonville characteristics: buoyant allegro; exacting, elegant port de bras; and simple but very difficult pirouettes that demanded crystal-clean finishes. Technical ability is paramount in any Bournonville ballet.

As if an antidote to my dismal experience with Anna Sokolow, working with Brenaa was easily one of the highlights of my career. So much so that when I later directed Boston Ballet School's Summer Dance Program (SDP), I hired Brenaa to come and teach and coach our students. Oh, what a master he was! "Nay!" he would heartily call out to correct us during rehearsals. He was very direct. And, oh, what a character! He'd sit at the front of the studio, watching us dance while he smoked his cigar and drank his Danish beer. He'd jump up to dance something out for us, and when he sat back down his little bald head was sleek with perspiration. He'd turn to the side, bend over, sweep his finger swiftly down his balding pate like a squeegee, and "shwooeet!" Off came the sweat! Of course we giggled—in many ways, I guess we were in fact still kids.

6

Onstage, Offstage

M Y BIG MOMENTS of doubt about whether I was suited to ballet as a career may have been behind me, but a lifetime of dealing with injuries was just beginning. Fortunately, I wasn't overly prone to injuries, but they are an unavoidable part of the profession, and I had my share. A dancer, like any other athlete, is going to have aches and pains by nature of the work. Some are just varying levels of daily muscle soreness, some are individual chronic "issues" that have to be monitored proactively, and some are debilitating problems that require immediate attention. Often, a dancer can still perform "through" an injury, sometimes with a cortisone shot or other short-term analgesic care, but sometimes a brief hiatus is required in order to rest the affected area. Occasionally, surgery and longer-term rehabilitation are necessary.

More often than you may think, a dancer can be unaware of the severity of an injury. Some people believe our pain threshold is higher because of a life dealing with daily aches. I've known many colleagues who were surprised to learn they'd been dancing with a broken bone in their foot or even a broken vertebra. Later in my career, I was dancing with a certain amount of "mysterious" pain in my left thigh. When I finally got it checked out, my doctor told me I had a stress fracture in my femur and was in danger of it snapping if I didn't rest it.

Injuries are always difficult—frustrating, hugely demoralizing, and occasionally terrifying. But over time, one learns how to cope by reworking one's technique to accommodate an injury and discover if an imbalance may be present. Of course, this kind of wise long view takes time to acquire. While it was disappointing to have to sit out our second "official" *Nutcracker* season in December 1966 due to an ankle injury, I could take some solace in that it gave me the perfect opportunity to observe and learn from our guest artist that season, Maria Tallchief. Balanchine's former wife, Tallchief was the first Native American dancer to attain principal status with a ballet company in the United States, and it was a title she held for many years at New York City Ballet. For this reason alone she was an important figure in the dance world, but she was also a stunning ballerina, both physically beautiful and dramatically powerful. Once again, we were given the priceless opportunity of being exposed to a top-notch artist.

———————

MY INJURY that December, a chipped bone in the ankle, was possibly the result of what was for us at the time a bustling fall season. In early September, we had performed on the South Shore of Massachusetts; in mid-October, the North Shore. And in late October we traveled to perform in a major dance festival at Chicago's Harper Theater. In total, the company presented eight ballets in those fall performances while rehearsing for *The Nutcracker* and preparing for our 1967 Boston season, which required that we get an additional eight ballets ready.

It was often dizzying, but in reality the exciting, sometimes frenetic pace was one we were getting used to as the company rapidly acclimated to its professional status. My body too was figuring out how to roll with the punches, and although I was out for *Nutcracker*, I was back in time for our third Boston season's opener in late January. My ankles, however, continued to be one of my weak points—my Achilles' heel, I guess you could say. I eventually needed surgery on my right ankle. But along the way, Virginia Zango (Ginny) helped me learn how to strengthen them, which also ultimately helped my feet look better overall. Ballet dancers obsess over the line and shape of their feet, especially for those like me who don't have naturally beautiful, super-curved arches. I remember admiring the beauty of Ginny's feet one day, to which she responded, "Oh, honey, I worked hard to get these.

You have to keep pushing. I'm telling you, these are 'worked' feet!" I took her words to heart and put her suggestions to practice, eventually "working" my own feet into making a rather decent arch.

While our bodies needed to get used to performing more often, our hearts and minds were champing at the bit. Emboldened by that second Ford Foundation grant, as well as the fact that the first two Boston seasons had been completely sold out, an additional performance was added to each of the Boston concerts in January, March, and April. The financial boost also allowed us to get paid weekly, rather than via a series of contracts, which were on a performance-by-performance basis. This was a symbolically significant difference to us: per-show contracts are for guests; regular salaries are for company members. Initially, we did not have parity in rehearsal versus performance weeks, but being paid for what we loved to do was a revelation. Maybe, just maybe, a career path was forming.

The doubling of the Boston performances enabled us to both continue to build our repertory and revive existing ballets. Was it also of symbolic significance that, in the third and final set of the Boston season, we offered a program without any Balanchine works? I don't mean that the company was in any way disassociating itself with Balanchine, who had been such an invaluable and generous mentor with Virginia and the company, and would indeed continue to be for a while, but it seems that, whether calculatedly or not, it was an important step for the company to take, to show that it could stand without always leaning on Balanchine. Perhaps the most obvious way to gauge how we fared in our independence was the fact that, in various reviews, though the writers as usual had a plethora of varying reactions, not one mentioned the absence of his works.

What they *all* noted, however, was the spectacular fall I took in the company's premiere of David Lichine's 1940 *Graduation Ball*. The ballet is a comic romp set in a girls' finishing school, with male military academy cadets invited to the title's main event. Anthony Williams and I were cast in the divertissement pas de deux, and, I didn't actually fall; I was dropped. But in Tony's defense, it was opening night and the tutu for my costume hadn't been finished before then, so we hadn't rehearsed with me in it. In one breathtaking moment the female is lifted while in a big grand jeté, legs split apart; at the top of the lift, the male gives her a kind of "pop" and she closes her legs quickly together while he turns her fully around (still midair, mind you) before catching her in a "fish dive."

In a classic "fish," one of the female's legs is bent and tucked up, and the other is stretched behind in arabesque; her partner has either moved her into this position from a standing pose or, more dramatically, as in *Grad Ball*, first tossed her and then caught her in this position. When it came time for the "pop" poor Tony couldn't see me for a moment, now that I was wearing the tutu, which flew up and all around me during the turn. He was a very good partner with whom I had danced many times, and he told me later that he never knew when I got around, because when he looked up, there was only a tutu! Well, "pop" *up* I went and "plop" *down* I went, straight through his arms. I landed on my back and lay there for a moment until he bent over, picked me up, and kindly propped me back onto my legs. Tony whispered, "Sauté to the corner" and after answering "okay" in a smallish, still dazed voice, I did and prepared to do it again because the choreography called for a repeat of the very same lift-throw-catch. It may have been somewhat abrupt, but you can bet Tony caught me the second time around. Personally, I blocked it out and have no recollection of that second lift. I do remember, however, that Tony carried me backstage and laid me upon a bed of roses in the dressing room, making me think I might have died. But no, Virginia appeared and proceeded to remove my eyelashes, which were hanging askew, along with my tiara, and sent me off for x-rays. My mother and grandmother were in the audience that night, aghast at what they had seen, and they carefully took me to the hospital and home with them. Fortunately, I had no serious injuries, so off I went to rehearsal the next day to do it all over again. As always, the show must go on! Dancers fall. Then we get up and resume whatever it was we were doing, which is usually dancing.

ALTHOUGH NO ONE mentioned the absence of Balanchine and everyone mentioned my unexpected plummet, at least Alta Maloney focused on another mark of the company's growth in her *Boston Traveler* review: "It was the first performance of the final program for the Boston Ballet Company's season last night at the Back Bay Theater, and it was almost incredible. Not that it was perfect. But it showed the increasing confidence of the Artistic

Director, E. Virginia Williams, in the ability of her company, and virtually no dependence on imported stars." And in an article in the January 22, 1967, *Boston Globe*'s Sunday magazine section, the recognition we were receiving, and not just the local kind, was noted. The headline of the big spread read "Boston Ballet's Third Season/a graceful leap into national esteem." The piece mentioned that among those paying attention to Boston Ballet were eminent choreographers. Before, Virginia had to actively scout around to attract, then hopefully contract, desired choreographers to set or restage works on us. Certainly she continued to seek out such talents, as do all artistic directors, but now many of the creators were already aware of this up-and-comer. For the '67 season, noted modern choreographers John Butler and Talley Beatty were on board. Butler, a former dancer with Martha Graham's company, made a new work on us, *Aphrodite*, bringing with him the great Carmen de Lavallade to dance the title role.

The Beatty piece we performed was the Boston premiere of his well-known and respected 1959 work *The Road of the Phoebe Snow*. It marked the first time the Duke Ellington/Billy Strayhorn accompaniment was performed live, by the Herb Pomeroy Jazz Orchestra. Like Butler, Beatty brought guests in to dance with us, Consuelo Atlas and Miguel Godreau, two stunning dancers on loan from the Alvin Ailey American Dance Theater. The choreography was a blend of jazz and modern, which for me, unfamiliar with triple contractions of the spine and the like, was a supreme challenge. Although I was not cast that first time around, I loved learning it and hoped I'd get the opportunity to perform it one day. It was an abstract ballet that depicted a group of poor people living along train tracks, and was a big, dramatic piece that unfolded through celebratory dancing, love duets, a rape, and finally, a tragic death. The "Phoebe Snow" was a passenger train that operated between Chicago and New Jersey but was discontinued in 1966. Though Beatty originally conceived it as a piece about the "Negro condition"—as many referred to it at the time—the '67 program notes stated, "This present performance marks the first time a group other than an all-Negro company has attempted this work, bearing out the fact that this is a universal story of conflict, not of color."

Our company may have looked as segregated as most of the country at that time, but as many of us were supporters of the civil rights movement we were thrilled to, even subtly, be able to embrace racial equality via our art form. Brava Virginia!

––––––––––

THE ROAD OF THE PHOEBE SNOW became a company mainstay for a while, and we grew to fit into its specific physical grooves so that guest artists were no longer needed to properly carry this dance. Many of us, myself included, simply hadn't had much, if any, training in anything other than classical ballet, so we had a learning curve to navigate. Finally in the midseventies, I got my chance to perform it. Today, even the most classically trained ballet dancers know it's wise to have some modern, jazz, and increasingly, hip-hop dance training under their belts, since companies that perform traditional ballets also have contemporary repertory that employs all kinds of movement genres. To develop and then maintain the chops required to perform in a *Swan Lake* or a *Giselle*, as well as have the ability to morph physically and perform in modern and postmodern works, is demanding but expected of dancers these days. We were some of the earliest "lab rats" of this now-routine crossover. In a *Boston Herald* interview, Butler told Joan B. Cass that "The line is disappearing between ballet and modern dance. . . . I think the war is over. All these dancers can handle both vocabularies. I certainly found this to be true with the Boston Ballet Company. I was very impressed at how quickly they caught on. They are receptive and surprisingly well-disciplined for their youth."

Of course, serious dancers are known for being "well-disciplined," but I think a lot of what Butler was getting at was a willingness to experiment, and it seems to me that our particular experience in those early days had a lot to do with this artistic flexibility. Often, we were just thrown into things, and there's nothing like simply having to do something to compel you do it. But that process gave us a rich education. Along with a varied repertoire that Virginia established from the very beginning, we always had wonderful teachers, from our own eagle-eyed Miss Leonard to the many guest teachers brought in over the years, including the aforementioned Russian masters, Vera Volkova, and Simon Semenoff from the Bolshoi. We also had important snippets of a musical education, whether from our longtime accompanist "Mr. Hobbs," Virginia's second husband, who would often offer astute advice from behind his piano, or by the inherent musicality within the dances themselves, especially the Balanchine ballets. When Mr. Hobbs was not available to play for class, the record player was warmed up and we all learned how to land softly, so we didn't make the record skip—yet another good habit, reinforced by necessity.

While we grew and benefitted from those visiting choreographers, we soon hired our own resident choreographer. Virginia had created some lovely ballets herself. Indeed, in that Boston season, we performed three of her works, the popular *The Green Season*, *Sea Alliance*, and a revival of her *Chausson Symphony* from the New England Civic Ballet days. But choreography wasn't her main strength or priority, and she knew it. Building Boston's first ballet company was her main focus. So, in the spring of 1967, the first "Vestris Competition" was held—named, curiously, after Auguste Vestris, the Romantic-era celebrity renowned much more for his dancing than his choreography. The event—sponsored by a charitable trust run by a local attorney and a ballet-loving couple from Ontario—ultimately accepted applications from thirty-one choreographers from across the United States. The applicants could create a work using any concert dance idiom, with the idea that each would set a short section on Boston Ballet dancers, which would then be videotaped. After viewing the excerpts, a jury selected a handful of finalists, three of whom were awarded top prizes.

One of the top three ballets, *Arietta*, entered our repertory, and its choreographer, Samuel Kurkjian, became our resident choreographer. Sam, whose organic, flowing, and beautiful choreography was a sheer delight to perform, worked very quickly. He always had an idea of what he wanted to do and would say to us, "Do this, do this, do this . . . yes, that's what I want." But if you showed him something that you liked instead, he'd usually take it and say, "Ooh, I like that, keep that." He was also an excellent teacher—warm, droll, and firm. When he initially joined the company, he was still dancing and we danced occasionally together, but soon he turned to choreography as his main focus. However, because he was such a gregarious and witty man, he appeared in "character" roles in many productions over the years. He lit up the stage in those moments, as he always lit up any room he walked into.

———————

IN THE FOURTH Boston season program, we offered the usual hearty dose of Balanchine fare, including works we'd previously performed—*Apollo*, *Concerto Barocco*, *Serenade*, and *Scotch Symphony*—and one that we hadn't, *Symphony in C*. The last time we'd performed *Apollo*, the four leading roles were filled by guest artists; this time, only two were. As with *Prodigal Son*, Boston Ballet was the first American company other than New York City Ballet that Balanchine allowed to perform *Symphony in C*, and we did so without any guests, a major feat. This abstract ballet, set to Georges Bizet's symphony, is glorious, regal, and really, really hard. One of Mr. B's more classically oriented ballets, the large cast of women are costumed in traditional, elegant tutus; the men, in handsome tunics and tights. Oh, how we worked on this daunting ballet—as did our mothers, who lovingly sewed our costumes. The night before we opened, we got changed after rehearsal—at 1:00 a.m., mind you—and went back into the studio. All twenty-four tutus were laid out on the floor and had yet to be attached to the bodices along with hand-sewn jewels. All the moms were there, sewing their brains out late into the night for the afternoon dress rehearsal and evening performance that were the next day.

Many of the fathers regularly contributed sweat equity too; my dad and Jerry DiBona (Linda's dad) made the staircase for our first production of *Apollo*. It was gorgeous but famously much heavier than necessary for a stage set. Jerry, a professional carpenter, designed a stairway that could have passed code for a house. How the stagehands cussed over that one!

———————

ALONG WITH THE new ballets were newer faces in the company, many of whom also became pals: Robin Adair (Bird); Jerilyn Dana (PeeWee); Geraldine Gagnon (Jodine); David Moran (later renamed David Drummond by Virginia), and young little Edra Toth (Edie), to name a few. Edie, who was only fourteen when she made her *Giselle* debut with us, was one of those "baby ballerinas" and made her mark on the company immediately. But one newbie in particular, Anne Marie Sarazin, would become one of my closest and most cherished friends, and someone who danced with the company for nearly as long as I did. Soon, via Virginia's habit of changing people's names, her first name was tweaked to Anamarie, although her eventual nickname was "Rose," courtesy of the parking lot attendant who always mistakenly called her Rosemarie.

Anne Marie, Anamarie, Rose—what a beauty! Dark-haired and dark-eyed, she danced with a mixture of intensity and feistiness, always crackling like a bonfire. A few years later, when Elaine Bauer joined the company —another beauty, both poetic and sleek like a panther—she also joined our little cozy coterie. We three—LaLa, Lefty, and Rose—became inseparable. Elaine's nickname referred to her preferred turning side, which is the opposite of most dancers' preference. We even had a group nickname conferred on us: the Gumm Sisters. For a while, Jerilyn Dana was a "fourth" honorary Gumm Sister, but she left to join Les Grandes Ballets Canadiens soon after Elaine arrived. She laughingly called herself a "Chiclet."

When, eventually, each in our trio got married, our husbands had no choice but to get along as well. They may have done so anyway, but it certainly helped that they were all in "the biz" too. Elaine and I married fellow company dancers, and Anamarie married the company's stage manager, Aloysius Petruccelli.

———

AS A CHARTER MEMBER of Boston Ballet, until my retirement from the stage more than a quarter century after I'd begun dancing for Virginia, I saw a lot of dancers come and go, and the majority of my experience with all of those artists within the company was positive. Of course, an aspect of the profession is competitive, and sure, in all of that time there were a few who got jealous about this or that, and then issues would arise, but such situations were rare. Because Lefty, Rose, and I, and others, such as Jerilyn, would often be in the position of sharing roles, we would coach each other— offering ideas on how to fix or improve a step, position, or transition—and "borrow" from one another too. We were always of the mind that the look would be different on someone else, because of personal dancing style. So, if we saw something that worked really well on another, we'd adjust it and try it ourselves. All were very friendly and supportive because ultimately it was the company's success that mattered the most. I like to think our camaraderie from the top influenced the rest of the company.

But this kind of support wasn't "cliquish," kept only within our circle. Years later, when Marie-Christine Mouis left the prestigious Paris Opera Ballet to become a principal dancer with us, she told critic Christine Temin that she was surprised by our professionalism. "Elaine Bauer taught her the first role she danced in Boston . . . and that in itself was refreshing to Mouis," Temin wrote in the *Boston Globe*, going on to quote Marie-Christine: "In Paris, this would never happen, someone coming from the outside and dancing your part." And, of course, Elaine not only taught her the part but also did so with her usual warmth. And as was our wont, Marie-Christine became "MC" and eventually "Merry Christmas."

7

Pas de Bourrée and Bourrée

Pas de bourrée. Origin: French. In ballet it is most often used as a transitional step that connects one step with another. In pas de bourrée, the dancer more or less stays in place; in the step just called "bourrée," the dancer travels lightly, briskly, as if skimming along the floor.

WITH MY ANKLE the culprit again, I was out for the first two sets of performances of Boston Ballet's fourth season in January and March 1968. As I told writer Joan B. Cass the following summer, I took a certain amount of the blame for my moody right ankle. "The first trouble came from overstressing the joint," I told her. "I was dancing so much and being foolish by not warming up properly before rehearsals. . . . It was my own fault—being dumb—young—not realizing what you can do to your own body."

Though I was temporarily sidelined, the company's continual propulsion was evident, not only in the progressive works by contemporary choreographers, but also in the classic ballets we slowly amassed in our repertoire. The right mix of traditional and contemporary works can be difficult territory for a ballet company to navigate. There are as many audience members who are mainly interested in the "tried-and-true" ballets as there are viewers who find the older ballets stuffy and dated. The former may be reluctant to take a chance on the more avant-garde dances, creating a challenge for artistic directors trying to plan repertory. For the latter, it may just be a matter of

personal taste, but it's also possible that they've seen too many tepidly performed productions of the so-called warhorses. One too many boring *Swan
Lakes* is almost like eating a mealy peach at the beginning of the season: it's
easy to be turned off from going back for more.

In March, the company presented its first production of *Giselle*. Originally choreographed in 1841 in Paris by Jules Perrot and Jean Coralli, amaz-
ingly, this famous ballet reportedly hadn't been seen in Boston since 1846.
To stage our version, we were blessed to have Dimitri Romanoff, regisseur
from American Ballet Theatre. One of the very few Romantic-era ballets
still performed today, *Giselle* is the story of a young, naïve peasant girl who
falls in love with Albrecht, a nobleman who disguises himself as a peasant
in order to be near her. While the story is based on timeless themes—love
and betrayal, life and death—the ballet is also rife with many of the ideas
and qualities prevalent among artists during that period. Though Albrecht's
elaborate deception can be seen as "caddish" behavior, many dancers portray
him instead as the "brooding" romantic poet, yearning for something more
than what is stipulated for him by society. In the second act of the ballet, the
era's fascination with Gothicism and the supernatural is seen in the setting
of the forest graveyard of the "wilis," mythological ghosts of women who die
before their wedding night. At the end of the first act, Giselle is so overcome
by the discovery of Albrecht's true identity and the news that he's already
engaged that she dies, poor innocent thing that she is. And thus Giselle
becomes one of the wilis under the command of their queen, Myrtha, who
directs them to avenge their heartbreaks by trapping and killing men who
wander into the forest.

Betrayal, madness, death, and murder . . . hardly a bland night at the ballet, when you think of it that way. The role requires that the dancer, in turn,
be youthfully exuberant yet shy, innocent, and then mortally destroyed by
shock—all in the first act. In the second act, the dancer's movements and
overall demeanor must somehow be muted so the audience can believe she
has become a spirit, weightless and drained of her former life force. Interestingly, Giselle, as a wili newbie, still has a shadow of her former humanity
intact and ultimately protects Albrecht from Myrtha, saving his life. The
ballet therefore is also a tale of forgiveness. Because of the great dramatic
range, and the formidable technical demands, the role of Giselle is a highly

desirable one, often described as the "Hamlet" for ballerinas. However, even if I hadn't missed the company premiere because of my injury, I wasn't ready for the supreme challenge of this particular role—yet.

Boston Ballet's debut of *Giselle* was recognized by critics as the major and important step that it was, and they applauded this first production for the most part. While Rose (Anamarie Sarazin) performed as Myrtha, Virginia relied on guest artists for the main roles of Giselle and Albrecht. As was often the case with visitors, she mined New York City Ballet's deep bench of talent: Edward Villella, who had made such a big impression when he guested with us in the title role of Balanchine's *Prodigal Son*, was Albrecht to Violette Verdy's Giselle. As the press reported, there were debuts galore: the company's production, Villella's first time in this role, and the first time the French ballerina, Verdy, performed the title role in America.

Verdy would play another very important role with Boston Ballet but of quite a different nature when, many years later, she succeeded Virginia as artistic director.

———

THOUGH WE HADN'T YET tackled *La Sylphide*, the other Romantic-era ballet still in repertories today, we had often performed *Les Sylphides*, choreographer Michel Fokine's early twentieth-century ode to the Romantic era. It was on the April 1968 program, with the beloved Italian ballerina Carla Fracci guesting in one of the female leads and American Ballet Theatre's Royes Fernandez partnering her. Boston Ballet's Carol Ravich and Edra Toth were cast in the other female principal parts.

Although I was back in the saddle by now, I was still trying to get my full strength back and thus only performed once on this program, in the beautifully haunting adagio section of Balanchine's *Symphony in C*. My partner in the pas de deux, Robert Steele, was one of the company's most elegant men and a tall, strong partner. Because of his height, lifts with him were huge, which we jokingly call "nosebleeds." He had excellent classical technique, which was even more refined after he returned from a year with the Royal Danish Ballet, the first American, by the way, to land a contract with that company. For a while we were offstage partners too. He'd cook me dinner at his Back Bay apartment that had an enviable view of the Charles River through a large picture window. We weren't romantically involved for a long time, but we had lovely times together: I once even knitted him an afghan.

Although it was disappointing to miss out on the chance to perform in *Les Sylphides* opposite the exquisite Fracci, getting the opportunity to watch her from the wings was surely a very fine consolation prize.

Perhaps dancing in my first recital at Cecile Baker's school to the Frédéric Chopin score makes me especially biased, but how can anyone resist the sweeping pull of those waltzes and mazurkas? Widely considered to be the first abstract or plotless ballet, it is the music and the movement in *Les Sylphides* that provide the only "drama" to Fokine's masterwork. It's hard to imagine now, when there are easily as many abstract ballets as there are "story ballets," but in 1909, Fokine's pure dance poem was considered revolutionary, even shocking to some, despite its gentle lyricism and formal, almost chaste manner. But then again, much of what was being created during the 1909–1929 history of the original Ballets Russes, founded by the Russian "impresario" Serge Diaghilev, was considered groundbreaking. Though not a dancer himself, Diaghilev had a vast knowledge and appreciation of the arts, particularly music and painting, and from the time he was a young man, surrounded himself with like-minded colleagues. Fokine was that group's first ballet master and choreographer; Balanchine was one of its last. In addition to *Les Sylphides*, Fokine created other famous works such as *Scheherazade*, *Carnaval*, *Le Spectre de la Rose*, and *Petrouchka*, several of them also renowned for the performances featuring the legendary Vaslav Nijinsky in the lead male roles.

After Diaghilev's sudden death in 1929, there would be offshoots of the Ballets Russes "brand," but the amount of innovation and adventurousness that occurred during the twenty-year span of Diaghilev's prototype, and the stunning list of great artists involved in these two decades, is mind-boggling. Along with Fokine, other choreographers included Balanchine, Léonide Massine, Vaslav Nijinsky, and his sister Bronislava Nijinska. Their ballets were set to music by such composers as Claude Debussy, Sergei Prokofiev, Maurice Ravel, Erik Satie, and Igor Stravinsky; costume and set designs were by artists such as Léon Bakst, Alexandre Benois, Natalia Goncharova, Pablo Picasso, and Nicholas Roerich. And then, of course, there were the dancers, among them many celebrated figures from Russian ballet history:

Not only Nijinsky but also Adolph Bolm, Tamara Karsavina, Serge Lifar, and Anna Pavlova.

It has often been noted that ironically this "Russian Ballet" company never performed in Russia. The group grew out of the frustrations that Diaghilev, Fokine, and others shared in terms of what they perceived as stagnation within the great Russian arts institutions, particularly with the venerated Mariinsky Theater, home to one of the world's greatest orchestras and one of the world's greatest ballet companies and academies. While the "hub" of ballet during the Romantic era was largely situated in France and Italy, it was in Russia, and particularly St. Petersburg, that the major accomplishments of the next period of ballet, the Classical era, occurred. Between the 1860s and the end of that century, the two major Classical-era choreographers working in St. Petersburg, Marius Petipa and Lev Ivanov, had created a host of major ballets that dramatically changed the landscape then and are regularly performed to this day, including *The Sleeping Beauty, Swan Lake, The Nutcracker, Don Quixote, La Bayadère, Paquita*, and *Raymonda*.

As important as those ballets were and continue to be, by the turn of the century there were some in Russia who, like Fokine, were ready to push the field even further, only to find themselves denied or even forbidden permission to do so. One of Fokine's pet peeves was what he saw as the superficiality of many of the characters in the story ballets, both in the manner in which dancers portrayed them and particularly in their choreography. He wanted to create ballets in which the movement was as true to the character as possible, rather than just impose a series of stock ballet choreography onto any scenario. In a way, *Les Sylphides'* lack of a story at all was Fokine's ultimate pushing of the boundaries. He wanted every aspect of a production to be "authentic." He had seen Isadora Duncan, the "mother of modern dance," perform, and perhaps it was her near nakedness that emboldened him to request that the females in one of his ballets dance barefoot. This apparently outrageous costume detail was prohibited, so Fokine got the last, rather sly word in by painting toenails on the dancers' tights.

––––––––––

SUCH A LINEAGE we come from! Among dancers, we still talk about those legends, and the wonderful mythology of how so-and-so performed *Giselle*, for example, is still passed along. But we cannot underestimate how much the huge strides that those choreographers took and how the rules that they famously broke have positively impacted ballet, helping to save it from obsolescence. For, while it is the dream of most serious ballet students to dance in the great Romantic and Classical ballets, and there are certainly many audience members who love to see those works over and over, revolution in the form of new ideas is crucial to the evolution of any art form, for the viewers, the creators, and the performers. We owe a great deal to Serge Diaghilev, and for that matter, to Isadora Duncan. But who knows? If Fokine, who died in 1942, could have seen the kinds of contemporary ballets that we were performing in the late 1960s, maybe he would himself be shocked, but they are his progeny.

Along with *Giselle* and *Les Sylphides*, in 1968 Boston Ballet continued to add new works to the repertory. *Scènes de Ballet*, by Samuel Kurkjian, our newly minted resident choreographer, and *Nostalgie*, choreographed by fellow Vestris Competition–winner Gyles Fontaine, both premiered this year. Former Martha Graham dancer Pearl Lang set her 1963 *Persephone* for us, a contemporary take on the mythological daughter of Zeus and Demeter. Following up on the successful performances we gave of his *Road of the Phoebe Snow*, Talley Beatty created a new work for us called *A Wilderness of Mirrors*. And Saeko Ichinohe, another Vestris winner, choreographed *Suspicion*. Both of these last two were depictions of the tumultuous times. *Wilderness* was overtly topical, with its use of projected images of the Vietnam war as well as protests against it, while the more abstract *Suspicion* hinted at the often-unacknowledged toll anxiety was taking on many people.

I'm sure that initially ballets such as these took many people by surprise. Wouldn't Fokine be proud? Certain aspects of a ballet can make it appear completely removed from reality, such as stories of dancing swan-women, which can cause some people to dislike the genre. But it doesn't mean that we, the dancers portraying the swans, are divorced from reality. Dancers go to war too and, perhaps more often, protest it. And choreographers have often made dances that tackle the wonders and the dangers of real life.

It turned out that our small community had cause to protest an issue that year as well. While not a tragic or large-scale problem, it was of dire concern to Boston Ballet and a few other local theater institutions including the

Opera Company of Boston. It was announced that the Back Bay Theater (formerly the Donnelly Memorial), which had been the venue for the past three of our Boston seasons, was to be demolished for further expansion of the Christian Science Church's buildings. The Back Bay Theater was more than just a comfortable fit for our audience base at that time; it was the only theater appropriate for the increasing professional and artistic levels the company had attained and that we could afford. In the *Boston Globe*, Margo Miller reported that the rental fee for one performance day/evening at the Back Bay Theater ran between $550 and $950 (the longer a company was in residence, the lower the rate), while other local theaters appropriate for dance charged between $14,000 and $20,000 per week. Virginia told Miller that "with a little budget like ours, rent made the difference," in terms of being able to put on the kinds of productions the company was becoming known for and the number of dancers she could hire, both permanent company members and guest artists.

With a yearly budget of just over $350,000, it wasn't an idle concern; in May, Elliot Norton wrote in the *Boston Herald* that it "could be very much within the limits of possibility that there will be no more Boston Ballet next year because there will be no playhouse available at a rent which E. Virginia Williams and her dancers can afford." Just a year earlier, members of the company had been invited to perform for the president at the White House; it may have been naïve, but it seemed incredible to me that we could have made such huge progress but possibly be metaphorically driven out of our own town. It was heartening, however, that we received the attention that we did from the press; we garnered even more attention from the public when we picketed outside the theater. Holding signs that asked whether Boston's cultural institutions could disappear, many of the dancers wore costumes, even pointe shoes. Normally ballet dancers would never risk abusing their joints and muscles on concrete—perhaps the worst surface in the world to dance on—but you can bet we pirouetted, carried our signs, and posed for reporters and passersby.

Because there was some amount of public discussion about whether the company would have to leave Boston, naturally, privately, we wondered what would happen to us as individuals. Although for many dancers, New York City is like the holy grail, the ultimate goal—"If I can make it there, I'll make it anywhere"—dancing there wasn't *my* dream. I was, and I guess I still am, to put it simply, a Beantown gal, a true blue Boston ballerina. I don't think this means I wasn't ambitious enough, but my ambition didn't lure me to New York City. It required me, like every other dancer, to be in the studio day in and day out and do the work. During the beginning of our usual layoff in the spring of 1967, I had the opportunity to guest, along with my friends Robin Adair (Dolly) and Linda DiBona, with the Garden State Ballet, in Newark, New Jersey. We were staying in the Big Apple with a friend of Dolly's and would take the bus across to New Jersey every morning for rehearsals. But we of course also took classes in the city, and maybe it was that experience that cooled my jets regarding the New York dance scene. I remember taking class at American Ballet Theatre with Bill Griffith, whose manner I would later "get" but who intimidated me at the time with his cranky, roaring tirades. It didn't help that I had some torn ligaments in my foot at the time and couldn't jump. Bill's disdain for me was loud and clear. Another lesson learned: if one is injured, it is best to let the teacher know *before* class, so no assumptions of slacking are possible.

Whether or not that experience soured me on NYC, I was clear about my feelings regarding that metropolis. When the Back Bay Theater crisis called attention to Boston Ballet's frequently tenuous financial situation, we dancers were often put in front of the press to educate more people about our predicament and hopefully boost morale and support. For an article for the *Patriot Ledger*, I told writer Pauline Dubkin that I was worried about the company's future, and thus mine, should Boston Ballet have to cut back or even fold. "As far as my own career is concerned, I don't want to go to New York. I hate New York and I like Boston. It's my home." Ouch for New York City, but I didn't let Boston quite off the hook either. "Boston is supposed to be such a cultural center; but that's a myth, the city's living on its past laurels. The only thing they really support is the Symphony, and that's been established forever." Out of the mouths of babes! Surely there was a lot of truth within the statement but expressed with that particular passion of youthful certainty.

While our local performance venue was now uncertain, we had recently made another move from our day-to-day studio home, having outgrown the sweet but now too small studios on Massachusetts Avenue. The transition was a step up for us, because now we at least had one huge studio that was commensurate with the stages we were usually dancing on. And finally, unlike our former home on Mass. Ave., there were no more poles to dance around. There was space to build out another two studios, so once again several of the dads, mine included, jumped in to do the work of building them. The layout of our portion of the building, however, was somewhat awkward; it was multilevel, and we had to go up and down staircases, and then around, to get to the other studios. These new digs were on Washington Street, located between the downtown area and what is now called the theater district. Back then, the neighborhood was infamously known as the Combat Zone; seedy and run down, the area was rife with porn shops and drug dealers, hardly befitting the stereotypical images of balletic innocence. Of course, in the 1960s and '70s, Boston, like many other big cities, had its fair share of widespread petty crime, but the Combat Zone was definitely one of the less, shall we say, idyllic areas to hang around. Nevertheless, our "delicate" images aside, we were fairly street savvy; you had to be. One day while we were rehearsing, some thug came up in the elevator and went around the corner into the big studio where he saw a dance bag. He reached right in, grabbed the wallet, and ran, but two of the male dancers, Tony Catanzaro and Warren Lynch—in ballet slippers and tights no less—flew right down the stairs after him, chased him all the way up to the Boston Common, followed him into Boylston Street Station, jumped over the turnstiles, and finally nabbed him on the subway platform.

It occurs to me now that we should have used this for marketing for the school, given the constant struggle to entice boys to try ballet. Instead of the usual "ballet is good for athletes" spiel, we could have produced a nifty "ballet is tough on crime" ad, showing how the agility and flexibility of ballet could come in handy—ballet dancers as crime busters!

Although the Washington Street studios weren't perfect, they were an improvement for us in terms of proper working space; but in the end we were only there for a few years before we had to move on again. It felt as if we had a wrecking ball following us.

8

Arabesque Voyagée

Arabesque voyagée. Origin: French. Traveling arabesque. Also called "chugs," these are small hops in which the dancer, whose gesture leg remains in a steady arabesque (the position in which the leg is lifted in a straight line to the back), can travel forward or backward in space.

THE BOSTON BALLET WILL have a Spring season."
So began Margo Miller's February 16, 1969, article in the Sunday *Boston Globe*. That capitalized "WILL" says it all: despite the company's continued artistic strides, critical acclaim, and a supportive, growing audience, our future was uncertain. Our present existence, after all, had become a frustrating choreography of two steps forward, one step back. But as the joke goes, dancers are flexible. (And, by the way, we are strong, buoyant, and creative too.) We rolled with the punches as best we could though, and our resilience usually resulted in progress.

Following the upheaval caused by the closing of the Back Bay Theater, we performed at the Orpheum Theater for our March, April, and May Boston subscription series. Though the long-ago dancing spirits of this erstwhile vaudeville house may have pleasantly haunted us, the venue was, at the time, used mainly as a movie palace. It was a beautiful little gem tucked away from the street, but it was expensive, and not fully suitable for sophisticated, modern-day dance presentations. On the plus side though, it was steps away from our new studios on Washington Street.

We also had, for the first time, a general manager, Margaret Prausnitz, who had previously worked as the assistant to the GM of London's Royal Ballet. The creation of this new position was an optimistic step toward the company's future stability, but it also in theory afforded Virginia the opportunity to focus more on the art, rather than the minutiae of running the business end of a ballet company.

For the March and April performances, guest artists again filled some of the lead roles. In March, Suzanne Farrell and Peter Martins appeared in Balanchine's *Concerto Barocco* and *Pas de Deux* (now called *Tchaikovsky Pas de Deux*), and in April, Violette Verdy and Edward Villella returned for a successful reprisal of their much-celebrated performances in the previous year's company debut of *Giselle*. Martins, who was a striking, tall, and strong dancer with beautifully classical lines, was on leave from the Royal Danish Ballet. Soon thereafter, he joined New York City Ballet where he enjoyed a successful performing career before becoming, after Balanchine's death in 1983, head of that company. Farrell was a unique specimen, moving her long limbs with what was at the time an exaggerated angularity and spikiness. As her particular physicality seemed to please Balanchine, others at City Ballet began to adopt some of those "Farrellisms." There have always been stories about dancers who, in an effort to look like Farrell, began nearly starving themselves since they couldn't literally make themselves taller or longer.

Though Farrell is now largely considered to have been one of Balanchine's most important "muses," some were initially put off by her style. Joan B. Cass wrote that Farrell's dancing "is so dominated by mannerisms and self-consciousness that it cannot come through as an artistic impression." In fact, the headline for Cass's review read, "Boston Ballet Co. Outshines N.Y. Guests." But in another review titled "Boston Ballet Opens Season: Suzanne Farrell Is Top Star," Elliot Norton called Farrell's dancing "technically faultless, all grace and style." These differences of opinion were great reminders of the subjectivity of art—or at least I tried to remind myself of that whenever I too received a less-than-stellar review.

In any event, although I was in the corps for the Farrell/Martins *Concerto Barocco* performances in Boston, I did perform one of that ballet's lead female roles that year, with Bob Steele as my partner. In January, we performed it in Ohio as guests with the Dayton Civic Ballet Company and in April with Boston Ballet in Williamstown, Massachusetts. Jerilyn Dana danced the other female lead, as she had in the Boston shows opposite Farrell. Set to J. S. Bach's well-known double violin concerto in D minor, the 1941 *Barocco* was, like *Serenade*, a ballet that Balanchine originally choreographed for his young American students, but it is no doubt a challenge for professional dancers too. We'd been performing it for several years now, and as with most everything else I ever danced, I still clearly remember where and when, and from whom we learned it. John Taras, who had performed the lone male role early on, staged the ballet on the company back when we were in the Massachusetts Avenue studios. I can still see us trying to work the choreography around the poles.

The two leading ballerinas often dance in close canon that is meant to be the physical embodiment of the counterpoint and play between the two violins; in essence, they *are* the violins. I took to *Barocco* right away, even when I was toiling away in the corps de ballet. While I, like most dancers, had ambitions and yearned for the most coveted roles, I am grateful that I went up through the ranks as I did. Sometimes young dancers shoot right up to the top and immediately begin taking on soloist and principal roles, skipping over "the trenches," as it were. But there are many invaluable lessons to be learned by working in an ensemble, both practical—keeping in exact time and line with others and maintaining spatial awareness—and metaphoric: remembering that one is part of a larger whole, which is good for one's humility and keeping egos in check.

Barocco appealed to my mathematical side because it's so geometric and everything is so crisp and clear and on the music. At least, that's the way Mr. Taras staged it on us. I have seen subsequent productions, staged by other ballet masters, that have a much softer approach. In the same way that different conductors have their own preferences of tempi, for example, the various men and women who stage the ballets of others naturally bring some of their own "interpretation" to the work. They don't change the steps—well, they're not supposed to at least, in the same way that a conductor cannot change any of Mozart's notes—although in the case of Balanchine's ballets, some dancers did learn somewhat different versions from Mr. B himself over the years and therefore passed that along in their subsequent stagings. When it comes to nineteenth-century ballets such as *Giselle* and *Swan Lake*, created when there was no video documentation and very little in the way of notation, the quest for authenticity can feel like a fool's errand. Thus, in the March program, *Swan Lake* excerpts were credited in the dance field's acceptably vague language as "after Ivanov and Petipa." Yet we have witnessed, since Mr. B died, that disagreements over what is the "correct" version of a Balanchine ballet can get pretty heated. There are fairly strict standards in place as to who can perform his works and, more importantly, who can stage them. Before he passed away, he split up and "gave" his ballets to several different people. Subsequently, the George Balanchine Trust was set up to allow other companies to license them—in effect, to borrow the ballets, like art museums temporarily acquiring works from other museums' collections.

Though people disagree on whether the version they remember should be the gold standard, the circumstances that led to the trust's existence sparked an important conversation that continues today about "legacy" in the dance world. Some choreographers have since made very clear plans about how their works should be staged after their deaths. In the case of the great modern choreographer Merce Cunningham, who died in 2009, he too set up a structure for his works to be staged only by qualified people assigned by his own trust. Cunningham took one interesting step further: he decreed that two years after his demise, his eponymous company would be dismantled. Though many fans are dismayed by the loss of this great troupe, Cunningham was able, to a certain extent, to keep the integrity of that aspect of his legacy intact. In an unfortunate contrast, no such structure was in place in 1991 when Martha Graham died. For years afterward, the dancers and directors of her company battled with Ron Protas over who had the right to perform her work. He was a nondancer who had become close with Graham toward the end of her life. She had named him associate director of the company, in the hopes that he would administer her legacy after her death. After a messy, drawn-out, and very public war, the company finally won out, but the fight took a big toll. This international treasure of a modern dance company continues to struggle to stay afloat. Over and over again in the dance field, the word "relevant" is parsed along with "legacy."

FOR THE MAY SEASON CLOSER, Virginia proved that her home team could do the whole job just fine. Even the *Boston Herald*'s Elliot Norton —never one to mince words when Boston Ballet came up short in his estimation—cheered for us. "We can be very proud of the Boston Ballet Company. Although they are facing fiscal crisis every few weeks, they manage to survive and in the process continue to develop artistically as if they hadn't a worry in the world," he wrote. He added that what made the performance he was reviewing "most impressive is that they managed to produce two new ballets . . . and did it all without going beyond their own ranks."

The program included a new ballet by Sam Kurkjian, *"Là ci darem" Variations*, and guest choreographer Geoffrey Holder's *Valse Creole*. As always, Sam's creation was musical and physically "organic," a pleasure to dance, and *Valse Creole*, a celebration of Trinidad, was as spirited and big-natured as Holder himself. Saeko Ichinohe's *Suspicion*, which the company had premiered at Jacob's Pillow the previous summer, had its "official" Boston debut then too. For two of the three performances, we presented our old friend *Scotch Symphony*, with Bob Steele and me in the leads. In her review, Joan B. Cass wrote, "The high point of the concert was Balanchine's 'Scotch Symphony' . . . soloists Laura Young, Robert Steele and Geraldine Gagnon, as well as the corps, brought the necessary spirit and precision to their roles." *Scotch* was swapped out in one of the programs for *Symphony in C*, in which Bob Steele and Edie Toth performed the leads in the second (adagio) movement while this time I led with Robert Pierce, the first (allegro vivo) movement. Finally, a chance to show I was more than just an adagio dancer!

In Norton's review—in which he offered particularly warm compliments for Jerilyn Dana, David Drummond, and Rose (Anamarie Sarazin)—he wrote, "In most of the best and biggest programs so far, they have relied on visiting stars from New York City Ballet. On Saturday evening, all the top roles were danced by their own performers, and for the most part with stunning success . . . while they are fighting for survival, they are dancing with so much skill . . . that everybody is going to have to take cognizance, take action, to make sure the company is preserved and protected. In a city as rich as Boston, that most surely can be done."

———————

GENEROUS THOUGH Norton's words were, this "rich city" wasn't able to fully protect us. The Boston Ballet continued to have support from many corners, but it was never nearly enough; our struggle and insecure existence continued. In July, after another successful stint at Jacob's Pillow, we scattered for the postseason break. This in itself wasn't unusual, or indicative of the company's instability; it is standard for dance contracts to be "seasonal" rather than year round. This usually means that dancers are free during the summers, and while we try to get some R&R for our tired bodies, we also seek out guest appearances or, as I'd done in the past, summer stock work. That August, Ginny Zango and I performed throughout Massachusetts and in upstate New York in the chorus of a production of *Milk and Honey*, choreographed by Joyce Trisler. In addition to the much-welcome paycheck, working in these summer stock productions broadened my experience as a dancer and an actress, and in this one I had to sing too. By now, Trisler knew me well from an earlier summer's production of *Brigadoon* and from when we worked together at Garden State Ballet.

That September, however, half the company, myself included, didn't return to Boston. We were offered work with the Chicago Lyric Opera for three months because the opera's own dancers were on strike. We didn't have much choice in the matter. The impression we got was that, once again, BB was on rocky footing and that Virginia and our new general manager felt this opportunity provided them a way to keep all of the company members employed that fall. At the time we didn't realize we were technically "scabs"— as we saw it, it was part of our job. At twenty-two, I was old enough to know that I needed the work but still young enough to be able to experience it as an adventure along the way.

So, my roommate Diane and I let our Beacon Street apartment go, and I took off for Chicago. But, oh boy, we worked hard during that three-month "adventure." We performed in the opera *Khovanshchina*, with choreography by Ruth Page, and in *El Amor Brujo*, choreographed by the flamenco dancer Antonio Gades, who also starred in the run. This time around, Sam Kurkjian got to dance versus choreograph, so his expressive abilities as a character dancer were on sparkling display in *El Amor Brujo*. For myself,

Page's choreography took quite the toll on my Achilles' tendons because she required all jumps to land on demi pointe, with the heels up, instead of lowering them to the ground, which is how the tendons and calves get a necessary stretch between jumps. Toward the end of the run I could hear my tendons squeaking over the music! I had severe tendonitis in both ankles by the time we got back to Boston.

But there was no time to rest when we returned from Chicago in December. We and the other half of the company that had remained in Boston had one week to rehearse together before *Nutcracker* performances started. I moved into a studio apartment, all by myself, on Hereford Street in the Back Bay and dove into the frenzied schedule. In some ways it was back to business as usual, but in other ways it seemed as if we'd been away much longer than three months. There were several new dancers, many of whom would become longtime Boston Ballet "family," including Stephanie Moy, James Reardon, and Leslie Woodies.

More than my professional curiosity was piqued, I must confess, when I met another new face, Tony Catanzaro. Dark-haired and dark-eyed, he brimmed with vitality and pizzazz. Apparently we had been at Jacob's Pillow at the same time over the summer, but if we met then, I don't remember. Mostly trained as a modern dancer, he was at the Pillow with Norman Walker's company (Walker was the modern choreographer who'd created *Reflections* on us back in 1965) but was teaching rather than performing there. Meanwhile, I apparently was solely focused on performing because I didn't notice him then. Virginia did, however, and invited him to come and join the company. This time though, when we crossed paths, I did take note, and he seemed interested in me too—but also seemed interested in my friend Ginny Zango. I wasn't quite sure what to do, but in the end it was Ma who gave me a helpful push. "How come he's talking to Ginny?" she asked me one day, noticing that Tony and Ginny looked rather chummy. "What's wrong with you? Get over there!"

So I did, and by March, Tony had moved into my little studio apartment. He was there on the morning of April 23, when we awoke to someone rapping on the window of my ground-floor apartment. It was my brother Jim, saying in a low voice, "Open the door; I know you're in there." We hadn't told my family that we were living together yet. "Oh, my God, that's your brother?" Tony whispered—naturally he and I were a bit panicked, but when we finally opened the door, Jim just looked at him and said, "Don't worry about it; it's got nothing to do with you. Phyllis just gave birth to a baby girl." I hope we had the presence of mind to cook the new father some eggs, but I was so unnerved at being found out, I really don't remember!

Jim's Aaron now had a little sister, Bridget, and so now I was an aunt twice over. Six months later, Tony and I were married and on our way to New York.

9

Fouetté

Fouetté. Origin: French, from *fouetter*, to "whip." Usually executed by female dancers, fouettés are a series of "whipping" turns performed on one leg, and ideally, "on a dime," that is, without the ballerina traveling. Fouetté sequences are often showstoppers in ballets such as *Swan Lake* and *Don Quixote.*

IF MY WHIRLWIND ROMANCE with Tony made my personal life positively dizzying that year, I was flying rather high professionally too. In February, during the company's first subscription performances of 1970, we performed *Les Sylphides* in Boston's Savoy Theater. By this point we were really feeling nomadic and wondering if we'd ever have a theater that would satisfy our artistic needs that we could call our own. Though *Les Sylphides* was a company staple by now, this time around our performances were elevated by the presence of guest artists Richard Cragun and Margot Fonteyn. The intensely dramatic Cragun was on loan from the Stuttgart Ballet; Dame Margot, though affiliated for most of her career with London's Royal Ballet, seemed to belong to all of us in the dance world. What a beloved, iconic, and positively towering—though petite—figure she was!

Although dancers are performing longer than they used to, it's still fairly rare for ballet dancers to continue performing into their forties today, but I believe Fonteyn was *fifty* when she danced with us—practically unheard of at the time. She had been famously plucked from near retirement years earlier, when the great Russian dancer Rudolf Nureyev sought her out.

Nureyev, who had defected from his country in 1961, held Fonteyn in great esteem despite their differences in age, background, and training. Regarding the age gap, Fonteyn once wittily remarked that she worried their partnership would be like mutton dancing with lamb. The epitome of elegance and classicism, Fonteyn, who passed away in 1991, is regarded as one of the finest ballet dancers in history. Nureyev—who died only two years after that, a victim of the AIDS epidemic—shares that prestige. In contrast to Fonteyn's "ladylike" cool, however, he was known for his fiery passion. But Nureyev was prescient in his desire to dance with her: audiences flocked to witness this great artistic match, and their legendary partnership is still celebrated today.

Fonteyn was as gracious with us in person as she was in public and on the stage. It still thrills me to remember that I got to dance opposite her, in the Nocturne of *Les Sylphides*. In time, Boston Ballet would embark on an important relationship with Nureyev; I never dreamed that I would one day get to dance with that artistic giant too.

————

IN MARCH I CELEBRATED an important milestone in my career when I performed the lead role of Odette in act 2 of *Swan Lake* with Bob Steele as my first Siegfried, at the Boston Conservatory. It would be a few years before the company performed the full-length ballet, but we had performed sections of it several times already, always still with guest artists in the leads. That April, in fact, guests Melissa Hayden and Jacques d'Amboise returned to perform Odette and Prince Siegfried. Although my debut wasn't part of the more prominent subscription series, it was nonetheless momentous for me—and, if the truth be told, quite a relief to have a first crack at such an important role in a less prominent setting.

Swan Lake's structure and choreography reflect the great strides in technique that had been steadily evolving over the decades. Among the most striking advances by 1895—when choreographers Marius Petipa and Lev Ivanov created their version of *Swan Lake*—were the ways in which pointe work was executed and incorporated in ballets. Pointe work had come a long way from its official introduction in the 1832 premiere of *La Sylphide*. Although Marie Taglioni, the first Sylph (and that "grande dame" that I played in *Pas de Quatre*), caused a sensation when she seemed to hover on the tips of her toes, we now know that the shoes she and other early pioneers wore lacked the kind of support necessary for sustained dancing en pointe. Of course, although Taglioni and others may not have been able to do much more than rise up fully en pointe for the briefest of moments, it was still thrilling for audiences of the time and added to the ethereal quality with which the Romantic ballerinas were associated. But over time, pointe shoes became sturdier—as did the women's technique—and thus ballerinas were able to dance en pointe for longer sequences.

And choreographers, particularly Petipa, realized that the women could stay up en pointe even longer if they had the support of another, and almost always male, dancer. Indeed, in Petipa's 1890 *Sleeping Beauty*, in the "Rose Adagio" section, he famously illustrates the ballerina as idol and the ways in which male partners can assist in this exalted status. Princess Aurora strikes one gorgeous pose after another, and with the chivalrous aid of her four potential suitors, the scene's drama builds as she remains on the same steady pointe-shoed foot for long periods of time. Finally, though the ballerina absolutely requires the help of those men who take turns turning and holding her up, Aurora demonstrates her independence and strength by triumphantly letting go of her suitors' hands and balancing all on her own. It's as if even Petipa was bowing to the notion of the female ballet dancer's superiority to her male counterparts. *Beauty* is considered by many to be the crowning achievement of ballet's Classical era and the most precious jewel of the several Petipa/Tchaikovsky collaborations. And this was the one full-length ballet that always engendered serious nerves in me, as it required impeccable technique and clarity. There were no props to hide behind.

What a funny history men have had in ballet. During the early days of ballet (in the seventeenth- and eighteenth-century courts of Italy, England, and France) men were the main practitioners and performers of the genre. Women were sometimes even banned altogether from performing in a ballet; in many instances, if a ballet included female characters, those were performed by men *en travesti*. But as ballet transitioned from a court entertainment offered by and for the nobility only into a theatrical spectacle performed by professional dancers in public venues, women not only were "allowed" to dance but also became the overwhelming majority. Whether or not some of the audience's enchantment with female dancers was because—as has often been winkingly noted—their costumes were shockingly scanty is now unimportant. What is stunning is just how quickly women became synonymous with ballet and how precipitously men fell from the ranks. Oddly, the desire to further develop pointe work in ballets meant that a greater male presence began to reappear; as partial reward for lifting and supporting the ballerinas, men were also given more solo stage time. However, the population never balanced out gender wise. Visit almost any dance studio today, and you'll unfortunately find a huge disproportion of female to male students—and don't be surprised if there are no boys or young men at all.

In any event, *Swan Lake* may well be the quintessential Classical-era ballet; even people who know nothing about ballet have heard of it. This may not have been the case, however, if Petipa and Ivanov hadn't made their version, since an 1877 version created by the largely unknown choreographer Julius Reisinger was roundly condemned as a failure. Alas, Tchaikovsky died before the Petipa/Ivanov production premiered, so he never benefitted from that reversal of fortune. The story is reminiscent of the fantasy worlds that infused ballets from the previous Romantic era. A young prince, Siegfried, comes of age and is reminded he must choose a bride, but he is resistant to the idea of marrying without love. Restless, he wanders by a lake and comes upon a flock of swans, who are actually women under the spell of an evil sorcerer, Von Rothbart, who is in love with their "queen," Odette. Because Odette doesn't return his love (well, he is an "evil sorcerer" after all), Von Rothbart has in essence made it impossible for any other man to "have" her. Siegfried is transfixed by Odette, who explains that Von Rothbart's spell, in which she and the others only return to their human form at night, can be broken if another man promises his eternal love to Odette. This Siegfried gives quickly but soon after is tricked by Von Rothbart and his daughter, Odile, who has been made to look like Odette. At Siegfried's grand birthday gala, he triumphantly presents Odile to his mother as his soon-to-be-bride, declaring his love. His promise to Odette is thus accidentally but tragically broken.

It's a deliciously dramatic ballet that also happens to contain some of the most beautiful "ballet blanc" scenes in ballet. While Petipa is overall the more familiar figure from the Classical era, the lakeside scenes were choreographed by *Swan Lake*'s co-creator, Ivanov. They're moonlit and melancholic and set to Tchaikovsky's stormy, passionate score, and Ivanov heightened the sculptured beauty of the balletic lines by creating stylized arm movements for the hybrid swan-women. These arm movements—port de bras—must emanate from the dancer's back and must ripple sinuously as if her arms are wings, and boneless at that.

What ballet dancer doesn't want to perform that poetic second act of *Swan Lake*? There are those beautiful port de bras, but what I especially loved was the emotion, the acting. Yes, technically the ballet is earth-shatteringly challenging—especially when the ballerina performs as both Odette and Odile, a practice that has become traditional with many productions and something I would do a few years later—but the storytelling was always my favorite aspect of performing *Swan Lake*.

———

WHILE IT IS COMMON PRACTICE for choreographers to create plotless dances, thanks to earlier pioneers such as Fokine and Balanchine, new "story ballets" are also still made. In addition to those wonderfully energetic and musical dances he continued to make for the company, Sam Kurkjian choreographed his own version of *Peter and the Wolf*, set to the playful score by Sergei Prokofiev. Sam, perhaps in his own playfully coy way, cast Joan Kennedy, wife of Senator Ted Kennedy, as the narrator. In a town noted for its politics, sometimes divisive, the liberal Kennedys were certainly one of Massachusetts' most famous political families. "Joan Kennedy made a big hit with the audience as a pleasant voiced, low-keyed narrator," Joan B. Cass noted in her *Herald Tribune* review, although she reserved her biggest praise for Tony, who was also having a professionally successful season in this, his first year with Boston Ballet. "While the whole cast was fine, I liked Tony Catanzaro best as Peter," Cass wrote, "bouncing about, leaping into a backward somersault, or casually tossing off a first rate air maneuver with careless charm."

Although Tony had been a trainee at New York City's Harkness House and thus had a strong ballet background, he had primarily worked as a modern dancer and was an acrobatic, limber mover. He was cast in another title role that year, as the "Minotaur" in the ballet created for the company by guest choreographer John Butler. The work frankly depicted one of the many Greek myths involving violence, incest, and power. Butler, himself a former modern dancer most closely associated with the Graham company, had also trained seriously in ballet, and most of his work as a choreographer was set on ballet companies. As the Minotaur who was born from the bestial union between Pasiphae, the queen of Crete, and a bull—and who was cursed with loving his own sister Ariadne—Tony was on full display, both choreographically and sartorially. His costume consisted, as Gerald Fitzgerald wrote in the *Patriot Ledger*, of "a crown of horns and a few leather straps (amounting to a stylized phallus)." Butler was likewise explicit with his Minotaur's movements: "Anthony Catanzaro," Fitzgerald wrote, "plays the bull-brother, every muscle quivering with desire and aggression. Butler uses a crotch-splitting pelvic thrust-squat as the bull's motif."

I don't know if it's funny or perverse—or maybe bit of both—but *Minotaur* was paired with *Coppélia*, the well-known comic ballet from the Classical era. It was first choreographed in 1870 by Arthur Saint-Léon; our version, staged by Virginia, was a composite of choreography by Ivanov and the great Italian teacher Enrico Cecchetti, with a bit of Sam's choreography also added into the mix. Set to Léo Delibes's infectious, mazurka-filled score, the title character is one of the doll maker Dr. Coppélius's life-sized creations. One day, the real-life heroine of the story, Swanhilda, notices her fiancé Franz flirting with her neighbor, a mysterious, beautiful young woman sitting in an upstairs balcony, very quietly reading a book. Great hijinks ensue when the indignant Swanhilda tries to confront the neighbor, only to discover that she is a doll. It's a silly, fun ballet to perform, and although I loved all of the "serious" roles too, I was always especially drawn to those requiring me to flex my comedic muscles. Later, when I danced Swanhilda—who has a bit of fun with Franz by pretending, briefly, to be Coppélia—I looked to the popular mime team Shields and Yarnell for thoughts on how to interpret Swanhilda's purposefully stiff "doll" solo. The way they held their hands, with the fingers and wrists crooked and a bit hyperextended, created just the proper dolly look for my interpretation.

TONY WAS ALSO a really adept dance partner, so in addition to the early favorable response from critics, the women in the company appreciated him right away too. Although at five foot six inches, he was a little short to be an ideal partner for me, he was strong and quick, and thus extremely reliable. With my being just shy of five foot three, and when one factors in the extra inches of height a woman gets once she's standing on pointe, certain partnering bits had to be modified. Therefore, if we had to do something like a "finger turn," in which the woman's arm is stretched above her head, holding onto one or two of her partner's fingers, I had to shorten my arm position while Tony had to rise up to demi-pointe. But, boy, was he charismatic, and we had a fabulous time dancing together, our sizzling onstage chemistry a gift to both of us. In his first year with Boston Ballet we were only paired in the company's revival of Talley Beatty's *Road of the Phoebe Snow*, but it was a profoundly rewarding experience. For someone who had been typecast into lyrical roles, this was a huge departure for me in my growth as a dancer. Our relationship also provided us with built-in personal coaching, as we would analyze the day's rehearsals over dinner.

ON SATURDAY, SEPTEMBER 26, 1970, Tony and I were married at St. Thecla's Church in Pembroke, located a few towns away from my childhood home on Boston's South Shore. Attendees included my immediate family, my sister-in-law Phyllis—who was one of my bridesmaids—and my nephew Aaron, who was our ring bearer. Many of our fellow dancers were there, as well as Virginia and Sydney. How proud I was to have them there and how sweet the memory.

And where did we go on our honeymoon? Well, after our wedding night —in the Lenox Hotel, one of Boston's most iconic landmarks—we packed our belongings into a U-Haul truck and drove straight to New York City through a blinding rainstorm. No rest for the weary. Though it seems a bit farfetched now, Tony had to be at City Center, where the Joffrey Ballet was performing *Petrouchka*. Mr. Joffrey had contacted Tony to see if he could be "on call," to fill in for Gary Chryst, who was unsure if he would be able to perform in that evening's show. Yurek Lazowski, the great character dancer/teacher, who knew Tony well from his days at the High School of Performing Arts in New York, knew that Tony could fill the bill in the Russian character role as one of the grooms in *Petrouchka* with little or no rehearsal. Because of the bad weather we rolled up to the theater on West Fifty-Sixth Street so close to curtain that I had to sit in the truck and pray that no NYC police officers would try to tow us while Tony ran in to the theater. As it turned out, Gary was in costume and ready to perform, so our mad dash to New York City seemed to me to have been in vain. But Tony really wanted to join the Joffrey Ballet, and so for him, it was no fool's errand; it got us to New York City and eventually a full contract for him. I had hopes as well, but . . .

I, of course, did have a job—in Boston, as one of the proud founding members of Boston Ballet, a dancer who had risen from an eager student through the ranks to my place as principal dancer. It's easy to look back and wonder if I was just another woman giving up her hard-won job status too easily for a man, but at the time, it was simple: I was in love.

When I spoke to Virginia about leaving, kind of mumbling something along the lines of "well, you know, my husband has work in New York . . ." she told me that we could always come back and that I didn't have to stay there the whole time. And in fact, I did go back in December, to perform with the company in its *Nutcracker* shows at Boston's Music Hall. Ironically, now that I was dancing as a guest—or "featured artist," as the program stated—I finally appeared at the top of that *Nutcracker* stairway, as the Sugar Plum Fairy, in front of our Boston audience, with Tony Williams as my Cavalier. I shared the role with two other Sugar Plums, Patricia McBride once again on loan from New York City Ballet, and Boston Ballet's young prodigy Edra Toth. I also performed the role of the Snow Queen for some of the shows with Bob Steele as my King, performances that Gerald Fitzgerald's *Patriot Ledger* review described as "pure and elegant." We were blessed, by the way, to have none other than Arthur Fiedler, the beloved leader of the Boston Pops and practically a one-man Boston institution himself, as our conductor.

———————

LIKE US, Boston Ballet had to move yet again. I believe we lost the lease to the Washington Street studios, so the company struck its tents and moved to the recently opened Boston Center for the Arts, on Tremont Street in the South End. Today the BCA is a lovely place, and much of the South End has become a hip, revitalized urban center, but this was hardly the case in 1970. The Tremont Street studios were, well, simply horrible. Two of the studios were small, very narrow, and cigar-shaped, so you couldn't do a manège (a series of turns executed in a circle) as there was no way to turn the corner. There was one big studio upstairs, but like our first studios on Massachusetts Avenue, it had huge poles to deal with. It seemed an apt metaphor for the obstacles I faced, as I tried to figure out if I could navigate my life and career between Boston and New York City.

10

Tour Jeté

Tour jeté. Origin: French. In a tour jeté, the dancer jumps up, kicking one leg up in front, and then midleap turns halfway around while kicking the other leg to the back; at the end of the jump therefore, the dancer is facing the opposite direction.

WELL, IT'S A GOOD THING we *were* newlyweds in love, because we did indeed struggle professionally at first. Although I had received an offer to take daily company class at Joffrey and learn and rehearse parts from the ballet *Petrouchka*, I got the distinct message that Mr. Joffrey didn't want to have to "deal" with someone who'd already been a principal dancer elsewhere. At age twenty-three, I was too old for his current roster, whose company had ostensibly been the reason we'd moved to NYC. Tony did finally secure a full-time contract with them by the spring of 1971, after months of sporadic performances as one of the grooms in *Petrouchka*; he drove a cab on the side to help make ends meet, the quintessential New Yorker blue-collar job if ever there was one.

The 1911 ballet, choreographed by Michel Fokine and set to Igor Stravinsky's score, tells the story of the title puppet who falls in love with a ballerina doll and is mocked and ultimately killed by his rival, the Moor puppet. It was one of the original Ballets Russes' signature works, and another vehicle for the great Nijinsky, who famously brought tremendous pathos to the main character. The vibrant set by Alexandre Benois colorfully captures a bustling village celebrating during a Shrovetide (the period just before Lent) fair. As a groom, Tony—like the Joffrey star Gary Chryst, whom Tony filled in for when necessary—had the powerful legs able to both drop into the dance's many deep knee squats and pop effortlessly out of them into a hitch kick or an aerial split. The two men also shared a visceral charisma that heightened any role they were dancing; in something like the "grooms" section, their energy was irrepressible.

Although the Joffrey Ballet had garnered attention for its very contemporary presentation of ballet—particularly in works such as *Astarte*, often called the first "rock" ballet—the company also staged gems from earlier periods, some that weren't often seen elsewhere. Ballets such as *Petrouchka* had a special place in Robert Joffrey's heart: as a young boy he saw a touring branch of the Ballets Russes perform it and other iconic works. Looking at the repertoire that he and his partner and cofounder Gerald Arpino developed over the years, Ballets Russes' "exotic" and bold ballets, music, sets, costumes, and of course dancers seem to have made a lasting impression upon him. But the Joffrey was, and continues to be, first and foremost a ballet company, with classically trained dancers who must also be able to move in decidedly nontraditional ways when need be. Though the Joffrey Ballet certainly made its mark early on with its chameleon-like dancers and its eclectic repertoire, today the same kind of technical and artistic flexibility is expected of ballet dancers at most companies. Thus, ironically, in our first experience with the often radical Joffrey, the ballet we were working on was relatively traditional, while back in Boston, the company was getting ready to present its own first "rock" ballet, *Gamete Garden*.

Choreographed by Louis Falco, *Gamete Garden* was set to an original score by composer Michael Kamen. Some of the music was played live by the Boston Ballet orchestra, while some was on tape, prerecorded by the New York Rock Ensemble. Like Tony, Falco was a modern dancer who had graduated from the High School of Performing Arts. He performed in the company of José Limón, one of modern dance's great innovators. Led by Anamarie Sarazin and Bob Steele, the dancers were costumed in nude unitards overlaid with draping macrame, handmade by Boston Ballet member Clyde Nantais. The effect was movement with a kind of creaturely wildness. "All the dancers were constantly *being*, throbbing life-forms," Valerie Restivo wrote in the *(Boston) Phoenix*, stating that Rose and Bob "were consistently brilliant." The set was composed of a series of cages, some of which had live birds in them, as well as bare light bulbs with a pull chain that the dancers turned on and off randomly. "I couldn't help thinking that the birds may have been terrified by the high-decibel portions of the score," noted Restivo. In fact, the birds were later relieved of duty, which was probably a good thing. "But," Restivo reported, "they performed admirably and none evidenced panic." As for the human creatures, there was equal praise. In the *Christian Science Monitor*, Kathleen Cannell wrote, "The young Boston Ballet dancers performed the difficult multi-moving steps superbly. In fact, for the first time they appeared to have completely encompassed the modern dance technique."

Although I did appear on the same February program, I wasn't around when *Gamete* was created. Instead, I performed the peasant pas de deux in act I of *Giselle*, which didn't require me to be in Boston for very long, which was helpful since I was shuffling back and forth from NYC. The typical pas de deux—dance for two—consists of the couple's spirited entrance that segues into supported adagio work, followed by solos and, finally, a rousing coda. This particular one—usually just referred to, simply, as "Peasant Pas"—is a familiar favorite, lovely and musical but demanding. Though the company was presenting the full *Giselle* again, it's often performed, as are many pas de deux from famous ballets, as a stand-alone piece, a balletic showcase. My partner and friend David Drummond and I were able to work on our solos separately, and since we'd danced enough together previously, the partnering sections fell into place quite nicely. Of course, we worked hard at it in our compacted rehearsal time; I still remember David, a meticulous, beautiful technician, drilling the two of us in the many cabrioles. These jumps, in which one leg is lifted behind in arabesque while the other leg beats against it, often transition right into another movement; in the peasant pas opening, however, the couple's series of cabrioles are held briefly on the landing leg before the dancers move on. A bobbled cabriole here is thus nearly impossible to hide, so David kept us honest.

This time, only the male lead, Count Albrecht, was handled by a guest artist. New York City Ballet's Earle Sieveling—who had trained and begun his career with Virginia and had returned several times to guest with us —partnered Edra Toth (Edie), the wunderkind whose technical prowess was beginning to be flavored beautifully with artistic maturity. Cannell, explaining how, at Jacob's Pillow the previous year, Edie had stepped into the role as an emergency replacement, wrote in the *Christian Science Monitor* that "since then she has researched and studied the role and this time she gave her finest performance to date. . . . Miss Toth had discarded all her mannerisms. . . . Her bewilderment in the mad scene was ineffably pathetic."

David and I also performed another treasured pas de deux on that program, this one from the 1858 *Flower Festival at Genzano*, choreographed by the Danish master August Bournonville. We learned it from Rochelle Zide, a talented woman who had danced with, taught at, coached for, and directed many reputable troupes including the Ballet Russe de Monte Carlo, Joffrey, and Netherlands Dance Theater. Although a series of injuries and accidents forced her to retire from dancing prematurely, Rochelle continued to inspire students and dancers for decades, with her keen eye and vast experience. She had received her early training with Virginia and another famous Boston teacher from earlier days, Harriet Hoctor. Rochelle was a terrific ballet mistress. She had a full body of knowledge and she was exacting; she knew just what she wanted and was expert at conveying the "how-to" that propelled us forward technically. I credit Rochelle for the positive reviews we received, as her suggestions and corrections, both broad and minute, had expanded and fine-tuned my, and our, artistic growth.

———

DESPITE THE GOOD PRESS we received and how wonderful it was to be back in Boston, I wasn't with my husband, who was back "home" in NYC. So, at the end of the February run, Virginia and I had another talk, which was quite different from the last one. It was a cheerful conversation but frank. "Virginia," I said, "I just can't do this anymore. I can't keep coming back. I just got married, and this is not good for my marriage." So, back I went to New York, where there were no professional opportunities on my horizon but where Tony awaited my return. My only regret is that I wasn't in Boston when, later that season, Virginia scored a big coup by bringing Natalia Makarova in as a guest. The great ballerina who had recently defected from the USSR and American Ballet Theatre's Ted Kivitt danced excerpts from *Swan Lake* in the May program. Makarova, impeccably trained and a graduate of the world's most hallowed ballet institution, St. Petersburg's Vaganova Academy of Russian Ballet, was the epitome of the Russian ballerina. Despite the Kirov's exalted status, dancers such as Makarova felt professionally stunted back in the days before Russian citizens could travel freely; hers was among a handful of highly publicized defections that also included Mikhail Baryshnikov and Rudolf Nureyev. While these three found semi-permanent "homes" with various companies in the West, they were in great demand for guest appearances around the world, their fame casting stardust wherever they danced and with whomever they danced. In 1972, the seeds of the Nureyev/Boston Ballet venture that I mentioned earlier were planted when Rose, Edie, and Jerilyn (Dana) toured briefly with Rudolf, the three "muses" to his Apollo in Balanchine's great 1928 ballet of the same name.

AT CHRISTMASTIME, Tony and I drew on our poise and performance skills when we worked temp jobs as "bow maker" demonstrators at Macy's, showing potential buyers how to make the perfect bow, over and over and over again. Ah, years of training.

But our early days in New York City weren't all doom and gloom. While our meager finances meant we couldn't often take advantage of the city's many cultural offerings, we did have fun hanging out with friends. Our closest pals in those days, Jimmy Dunne and Dana Sapiro, Joffrey dancers, were a couple who lived on 181st Street. Tony and I would frequently hop on Tony's motorcycle—then, as now, it's nearly impossible to keep a car in Manhattan—and head up the West Side Highway to their neck of the woods. What were we thinking? Getting in an accident on that motorcycle could have been a career ender right there. Ah, youth.

Of course, it's usually true that home is where the heart is, and even our little apartment on West Fifty-Sixth Street near Hell's Kitchen was becoming a cozy nest. One day Tony came home, his chest looking a bit puffier than usual; from the top of his zipped-up jacket, out popped an adorable little furry face, a six-week-old pup he'd brought home from the pet store on the corner. "Honey, look!" he said, knowing that although he hadn't consulted with me as to whether I too wanted a dog, there was no way I was turning down this little cutie. We named her Tache, which I knew meant "spot" in French, and we thought we were pretty clever with that name until my grandma said, "No, no, it's 'spot' as in, something you've spilled on your tie!" Oh well, no matter. Sweet, mixed-breed Tache was the first addition to our new little family, and she stayed with me for a long, long time, living twenty-two years. About a year after we first got her, Tache got a brother, whom we named Czar. Tony had long wanted a Siberian Husky, particularly one with blue eyes. This time we went to the pet store together, and somehow, in that irrational, giddy state one can get into when falling in love, we neglected to notice one detail. When we got home with our beautiful Siberian Husky, it turned out he had brown eyes. Too late—he too was already a member of the menagerie.

In addition to all the joy they brought to our lives, the pups helped fill my otherwise "underemployed" life in more practical ways: I spent a lot of time in Central Park, walking the dogs.

––––––––––

IT WASN'T LONG, however, before I began to sink into depression. I was clearly *not* "making it" in New York City. I knew the Joffrey was a dead end, and even though Boston Ballet had had such a connection with Balanchine, I knew I didn't have the right body type for City Ballet. And, scared off years earlier when I took class at American Ballet Theatre, I didn't even *try* auditioning there. Demoralized, I stopped going to class, the dancer's daily "must do" in order to stay in proper shape and maintain technique.

Clearly adrift, what good fortune it was when I heard from Nicolyn Emmanuel, whom I'd known when I was a young student. Nikki had been one of Virginia's "older girls" when I started, and now she was the dance captain for the Metropolitan Opera. I had run into her at some point in New York and must have told her I was jobless. She called to let me know that the Met was hiring and warmly encouraged me to come. "We're having auditions for the Opera Ballet and you should come, you should absolutely come!" I went, and at the end of the audition we were told to put our pointe shoes on. At this point, having not had class in nearly six months, I was already discombobulated enough—I felt as if my right eye was winking and my left eye was blinking. It's amazing how quickly the body "forgets" how to work, or at the very least struggles to do what it had so recently done so easily. In any event, though I felt I was going to die, I put my pointe shoes on. I didn't get the job right away. There were two spots available, and I was the third auditionee they were interested in. However, one week later, when one of the two other women decided to not pick up her contract, it was offered to me. As far as dance contracts go, it was a sweet deal: thirteen months with nine paid weeks off. But that was a rarity that only occurred once because the Met was going on tour for three months and weren't taking any operas with ballet in them.

In some ways, life at the Met was like life in any other ballet company. We had daily company class and then went from one rehearsal to the next. We had excellent teachers, particularly the fabulous Hector Zaraspe, whom I can still see in my mind: tapping his cane along the floor as he walked among us, wearing either his black outfit with the blue scarf or the blue outfit with the black scarf. If it works, you stick with it, I guess. These days, I have my own simple teaching outfit—black on black with black shoes. No more pink tights for this woman.

But dancing at the Met was a far cry from the rigorous standards I'd been used to at Boston Ballet. Other than at the end of my audition, I only danced on pointe at the Met once. That, by the way, was a particularly memorable occasion: the "Bingala," as we called it, the giant fete thrown for the opera's inimitable general manager, Rudolf Bing, who was retiring after twenty-two years. In one of the gala's performance excerpts, they needed someone who could pull off a series of fouettés. That was right up my alley, so I strapped on my pointe shoes and got 'er done.

Don't get me wrong—one had to be, and still must be, an excellent dancer to get into the Met; it's just that, while the management expects the same level of excellence from those dancers as they do from the singers and musicians, it's primarily an opera company. The dancing is not the focus and is relatively sparse. I liked to joke that my job there was really "advanced costume wearing" more than anything else. Oh, but those costumes were extravagant and heavy too! Though surely my body was maturing, I do wonder if some of the nearly twenty pounds that I lost during my years in New York City were shed simply because of the weight of the costumes I wore.

There were times at the Met when we were challenged to put our training

My mother and I on
pointe together, 1959.
Author's collection.

First *Swan Lake*, 1961.
Author's collection

Above
George Balanchine and
E. Virginia Williams rehears-
ing *Scotch Symphony* on stage,
1965. Choreography by George
Balanchine. © The George
Balanchine Trust. Photograph
by Al Schroeder.

Right
Virginia helping to glue my
necklace for my first principal role, Taglioni in *Pas de
Quatre*, 1965. Photograph
by Al Schroeder.

Above
Concerto Barocco, Laura with Mark Hudson and, *left to right*, Linda DiBona, Jerilyn Dana, June Perry, and Phyllis Heath, 1965. Choreography by George Balanchine. © The George Balanchine Trust. Photograph by Al Schroeder.

Left
Helping make *Nutcracker* headpieces. My head was the drying rack. 1968. Photograph by Al Schroeder.

Above
Dad and me, 1968.
Author's collection.

Right
With Anthony Williams,
center, backstage after our
first *Nutcracker Pas* with
David Drummond. 1970.
Author's collection.

Tarantella, 1975. Choreography by George Balanchine. © The George Balanchine Trust. Photograph by Frank Derbas.

Scotch Symphony with Tony Catanzaro, 1976. Choreography by George Balanchine. © The George Balanchine Trust. Photograph by Abe Epstein; courtesy of Ed Epstein.

Right
Head shot for Fortuna in *Carmina Burana*, 1977. Photograph by Béla Kalman; © Studio 350.

Below
With John Meehan of American Ballet Theatre in *Giselle*, 1978. Photograph by Abe Epstein; courtesy of Ed Epstein.

Act 1 of *Sleeping Beauty*, 1979. Photograph by Abe Epstein; courtesy of Ed Epstein.

With Nicolas Pacaña in *Donizetti Variations*, 1979. Choreography by George Balanchine. © The George Balanchine Trust. Photograph by Abe Epstein; courtesy of Ed Epstein.

Act 3 of *Sleeping Beauty* with
Woytek Lowski, 1979. Photograph by Abe Epstein; courtesy
of Ed Epstein.

Sugar Plum with my Cavalier,
Bruce Wells, 1979. Photograph
by Abe Epstein; courtesy of
Ed Epstein.

Act 1 of *Sleeping Beauty*, 1979. Photograph by Jaye R. Phillips.

Cinderella in Beijing, China, with Augustus van Heerden, 1980. Photograph by King Douglas.

With Elaine Bauer in *Cinderella*, 1981. Photograph by Abe Epstein; courtesy of Ed Epstein.

With Anamarie Sarazin (*standing*) in our dressing room in Beijing, 1980. Photograph by King Douglas.

Above
With Ron Cunningham as Mother Simone in *La Fille Mal Gardée*, Shanghai, 1980. Photograph by King Douglas.

Left
Backstage in Shanghai with, *left to right*, Ma, Bruce Wells, Nicolas Pacaña, me, and Dad 1980. Photograph by King Douglas.

Catching some *z*'s on the train from China to Hong Kong, 1980. Photograph by King Douglas.

As the Cowgirl in *Rodeo*, 1985. Photo © Bernie Gardella.

An impromptu moment of having fun with Marie-Christine Mouis (*left*) during a photo shoot to promote *Don Quixote*. Photograph by Jean Renard.

In rehearsal with Rudolf Nureyev, where he is telling me to "use the fan like you are spreading butter on your leg!" Photograph by Peter Southwick.

Stage rehearsal with Rudolf Nureyev in Atlanta, 1982. Photograph by my cousin Bill Young.

As Kitri in *Don Quixote* with the fright wig that later got tamed down. 1982.
Photo © Bernie Gardella.

Madrilene with Donn Edwards, Twentieth Anniversary Gala, 1984.
Photograph by Jennifer W. Lester.

to good use. When the great American choreographer Alvin Ailey came in to choreograph a production of *Carmen*, it was a huge breath of fresh air for us. It was fabulous! Finally, meaty choreography. We were challenged—real pirouettes. We were excited . . . until we got the costumes, which seemed to weigh the requisite twenty pounds. In order to do a double pirouette, one had to take hold of the costume, kind of fling it, and then grab it again to stop it from swirling or it would just keep taking you around. What had seemed like great choreography became a major effort to get through without falling over, and as usual, we dancers were more or less just a pretty background for the singers. Ailey, who was so wonderful to us, was just as disappointed as we were. After the dress rehearsal, he came up to us and said, "I just figured it out. You're supposed to dance wherever the light *isn't*," meaning, we dancers were literally and figuratively in the shadows at the opera. In the end, we could have just worn skirts and flung them around for effect.

The makeup and wigs were often extravagant too—and sometimes messy. At least, when we had to wear body paint, we got extra money for it, because of the extra time and effort it took to put it on and take it off. When we performed as Bedouins in *Aida*, we had to cover ourselves with blue body paint from our bare feet up to our necks, and then use blue grease paint on our faces. We looked like precursors to the Blue Man Group. Afterward, you'd scrub and scrub and scrub and still find little bits of blue everywhere, including on your bed sheets in the morning.

Well, at least with such pomp and extravagance some hilarious accidents are bound to happen. Once, when we were performing as angels in the serene lullaby scene from *Hansel and Gretel*, I was standing, posed, center stage with another dancer, Marilyn. At this point there were other additional dancers, "supernumeraries" costumed as angels who would "fly" across the stage behind us. Each of those supers was attached to a nonvisible harness manipulated by a stagehand; they'd push off from the wings, "fly" to the other side, and then grab a rope behind the wings and park until the next flyby. As protection from rope burns, the flying angels wore a large, gray glove on the hand that grabbed the rope, which they kept hidden behind while flying across. On this particular evening, the angel in Marilyn's sight line made a critical error. Marilyn whispered to me, "Oh my God! She missed the rope," and because my back was to the comedy unfolding behind me, she further reported that the angel had managed to grab the curtain and was now swinging from it. She finally decided to just let go, right at the exact time the stagehands decided to lower her, so she came wildly winging in, heading straight for me. Ever the professionals, of course, Marilyn and I held our ground, though Marilyn at least kept me updated. "Look out, she's gonna hit you," she hissed. I leaned upstage and luckily, she just missed me. There were the three of us now, frozen, center stage. Our misguided angel, who figured she'd try to save some face by exiting, for some reason led with her large gray glove, looking like Mickey Mouse mimicking a "pedestrian crossing" sign. Oh, the poor dear, she'd almost made it into the wings when she realized the wire attached to her harness wasn't quite long enough. She proceeded to turn and walk completely across the stage with her gray glove while we were all standing still. Eventually we all hissed, "Stand still!" Curtain.

In my second year at the Met, I was apparently doing well enough that they actually gave me the lead in the Pastorale of Tchaikovsky's *Pique Dame* with the veteran Met dancer Jack Hertzog. While a wonderful boost to my morale, wouldn't you know that I had to do a series of little steps with beats called brisés—in heels and in yet another twenty-pound costume and wig. Lesson 489: make the brisés high and clearly beaten to the side or your ankles will be bloodied.

At least that generous contract meant I could take advantage of other performance opportunities when they arose. One "runout" that Tony and I did was extra special because he choreographed a pas de deux for us to perform in Sarasota, Florida, where my parents had moved recently. My mother's asthma had gotten worse, and my dad took an early retirement so they could move to a better climate. Since they had gotten so used to being involved with a ballet company, they joined the Florida Ballet Company's board of directors, and my father even did some character roles with the group. At the time he had a "Colonel Sanders"–like mustache and beard so someone thought he'd make a good Burgomeister in the company's production of *Coppélia*. And so he did and, drawing on his "end man" experience, had a ball.

———————

ULTIMATELY, the endless "advanced costume wearing" took its toll, and I found myself once again demoralized. Tony eventually became disillusioned too when he felt he was being typecast into specific roles at Joffrey. Finally, when he was cast as Bottom in Sir Frederick Ashton's *The Dream*, Tony was done. In Ashton's version of Shakespeare's *A Midsummer Night's Dream*, Bottom dances on pointe. "These feet are not going up on pointe," Tony declared. So, while my one pointe experience at the Met was not enough for me, once was one too many times for him. We decided it was time for us to go back home to Boston.

II

Ballon

Ballon. Origin: French. A dancer with good ballon appears to hover in the air midjump before briefly touching down and rebounding, seemingly effortlessly, into the air again.

DESPITE THE MEAGERNESS of technical and artistic challenges I'd experienced during my time in New York City, I returned to Boston a much stronger dancer. While I had lost weight from hauling those ponderous costumes around (and the natural slimming that often comes with adulthood), I had gained a lot of understanding. Maturity plays such a big part in how an artist digests, interprets, and puts information to use, whether it's new or something you've already heard before. Prior to leaving for New York, Virginia had more or less typecast me as a "lyrical dancer," which is certainly a lovely thing to be but limiting, if that's *all* you're seen as. As a result, she rarely put me in any roles with "pizzazz," even though I was itching to prove my versatility. When I returned, however, she began to see me differently. Had I indeed changed so much? I don't know. But I do know that while in New York, I took advantage of one of the few perks that Tony's Joffrey gig offered: free tickets to Joffrey performances. I remember sitting in the audience, night after night, drinking in the enormous vitality just spilling out of the dancers in those contemporary, energetic works. They were performing in all the ways I wanted to, if only I could get a chance. And so I did, once back in Boston, and I got many chances right away.

Although Boston Ballet had continued to grow, and some dancers were garnering increasing attention from critics and audiences while I was away, Tony's and my return received rather favorable press, saying it was a positive step for the ballet, which was admittedly rewarding to hear after our struggles in New York. Our arrival coincided with an important milestone: it was the company's tenth-anniversary season. Our return was particularly exciting, given the fact that among other new company members, one was being heralded as a bona fide star. The Polish-born Woytek Lowski, who had received some of his training from Russia's legendary Vaganova Academy, was a beautiful, internationally respected dancer who was recruited to Boston with the hope that by having him as a "regular" member, Virginia could finally move away from the need to find big-name guest artists to sell tickets. Of course, the overall quality of the company had steadily grown over the past decade, and the majority of the repertoire was indeed now handled with aplomb by Boston's own dancers. But had audiences gotten so used to the idea of guests that there was now a catch-22 scenario? Were the "stars" still the main draw?

In any event, Michael Judson, Boston Ballet's new general manager, had hopes that Woytek's star presence would help bring more men to the ballet. In an interview, while discussing one area that had *not* changed—the ever-tenuous fiscal situation, now exacerbated by diminished ticket sales—Judson suggested that a factor he considered to be a "weak area" was "the male dancer" in the school and company. "That weakness is one reason we have trouble building a male audience," Judson claimed. While Judson was certainly correct about the ongoing disparity between the number of female and the number of male ballet students, his comments were, if inadvertently, something of a slap to the men we did have. If the company men were at all put out by Judson's public statements, Woytek himself didn't add more fuel to the fire: he was a lovely man whose undeniable talent and artistry was balanced with a good-natured, hardworking, and humble professionalism. He was, as the best colleagues are, quick to share ideas; I've confessed that I was never a sensational turner, but he was the one who finally enabled me to pirouette consistently. I took the high retiré that former company member Susie Magno had taught me to use in pirouettes years earlier and added Woytek's simple rule: "The only thing you have to think about is that everything has to happen at the same time," the relevé on the standing leg, the lift to retiré with the working leg, the closing of the arms, and the snap of the head. Otherwise, Woytek told me, it's not going to work. And even if a triple or quadruple pirouette wasn't in my wheelhouse, my modest double pirouette became more reliable.

His classical lines and good technical "breeding" aside, Woytek was versatile, having danced with two of Europe's most contemporary ballet choreographers of the time, Roland Petit and Maurice Béjart. His debut with the company amply proved his range: he performed *Le Cygne*, an avant-garde solo created for him by Béjart; as the lead male in Balanchine's quicksilver *Donizetti Variations*; and as Franz in Sam Kurkjian's restaging of the comedic *Coppélia*, a ballet that demonstrated his acting skills.

Rodeo, Agnes de Mille's 1942 masterwork, was also on the November 1973 program. Aaron Copland's now-famous score was written specifically for the ballet. Both the music and the dance were immediate hits when *Rodeo* premiered and continue to be audience favorites. It also put de Mille, until then a relatively unknown name, on the map; she became a sought-after choreographer, the recognition especially meaningful in the largely male-dominated field of choreographers. Her success went beyond the ballet world as she choreographed for many hit Broadway musicals including *Oklahoma!*, *Carousel*, and *Brigadoon*.

At times infectiously rambunctious—who can resist that toe-tapping, knee-slapping "Hoedown" music?—*Rodeo* is also by turns tender, even wistful. It is often seen as a sweeping ode to one slice of Americana: that oft-romanticized "home on the range." Boston Ballet had premiered *Rodeo* the previous year, and although I wasn't in it this time either, the lead female—the tomboyish "Cowgirl"—would become one of my favorites, a role that fit me emotionally and comfortably as the costume of jeans and cowboy boots fit my skin. That the ballet doesn't tip into sentimentality is thanks to de Mille's famously crusty nature, which was laced with her sharp-as-a-tack wit. Although by the time I debuted as the Cowgirl years later de Mille had been nearly paralyzed by a stroke, she was still feisty as ever. Oh, my word! When she would authoritatively rap on the mirror with her ring to stop rehearsal, we were transfixed, wondering what faux pas we had made.

We were terrified at the thought of doing anything wrong in front of her in rehearsals. She liked things to be exact, but as I discovered, what she was really after was not a pedantic correctness but instead emotional and physical truth. William Pizzuto (Billy), the Champion Roper to my Cowgirl, and I unintentionally altered a moment in one scene. One day in rehearsal, Billy grabbed my arm, spun me around, and wound me up in a hammerlock to give me a kiss—not exactly what de Mille had choreographed, but it just happened, and we liked it. But would de Mille? Well, when we traveled to New York to rehearse with her, we took a deep breath before running that section and decided to go for it; for a moment or two she was silent, sitting in her wheelchair, just looking at us with her mouth open. "Where did that come from?" she demanded, and when we confessed that it had "just kind of happened" in rehearsal, she bellowed "I *love* it!" And so it stayed in. Thank you, Agnes.

It was such a thrill, and even in the brief time that I was fortunate enough to work with her, I learned so much about what she was all about—honesty of emotions and true reactions—and why so many of her highly dramatic ballets resonate with performers and viewers alike. Her 1948 *Fall River Legend*, with music by another American composer, Morton Gould, is an example of de Mille's deftness with the tricky genre of "psychodrama" ballets. Could anyone else have created such a gripping ballet—a ballet!—with no words to "explain" the unfolding story, about the infamous Lizzie Borden, the New England woman who was believed to have brutally axed her parents to death in 1892. The company, after first performing it later in that '73–'74 season, presented it many times over the years. In the company's premiere, Rose earned praise from all corners for her interpretation of Lizzie. In the May 1974 edition of *Dance News*, Walter Terry wrote that "Anamarie Sarazin, a vivid dancer and the special pride of the Boston Ballet" offered "a performance of shattering dramatic intensity which made Lizzie at once terrifying and sympathetic, an angel of destruction and a pitiful victim."

———————

IT WAS IN *Donizetti Variations*, with Woytek, that I made my "official" Boston return in November 1973. Choreographed in 1960 by Balanchine, the abstract ballet is by turns playful, romantic, and quite technically challenging. Some of the passages are distinguished by soaring allegro steps cut with lightning-quick changes of direction. As it often is with Mr. B's ballets, the supreme musicality of the choreography made these challenges not only possible but also pleasurable. Our years with so much Balanchine repertoire certainly helped since it takes time to acclimate to the specifics of the Balanchine style. Gerald Fitzgerald wrote in the *Patriot Ledger*, "Like many European dancers, [Lowski] found the speed of a Balanchine ballerina (in this case, Laura Young) hard to keep up with." If there was any doubt in Virginia's mind about my ability to be something other than "lyrical," I think these performances erased them. Fitzgerald went on to say about me that "to be worthy of Balanchine's choreography seems high praise; she was and it is."

Woytek's qualities as a partner were also noted. He had a great way of conveying emotion while performing; we'd look each other in the eyes and really connect. It's so important: if you don't actively communicate with your eyes during a duet, it's difficult for viewers to sense the emotional connection between the dancers, and thus the overall "feeling" of the ballet can't be fully conveyed to the audience. Fitzgerald wrote that Woytek "partners attentively with so great a concentration that his face transfers energy to the girl." (Yes, I was "the girl" in question.)

Tony was hailed as an important addition to the male ranks too. Referring to Woytek and Tony, Elliot Norton wrote in the *Boston Herald-American* that "two men stars, both added to the company for this anniversary year . . . helped make [the performance] spectacular." Meanwhile, referring to Tony in the *Real Paper*, Laura Shapiro noted, rather shrewdly, "I hope Lowski's arrival doesn't overshadow the importance of his return to the company. . . . Catanzaro is very different from the European; springier, more athletic, tough without being brash; and he enlivens the whole company without standing out quite so startlingly as Lowski." But indeed Tony was well received in the ballet he performed in during that season's first Boston series. He was paired with Rose in Norman Walker's *Baroque Concerto*, a modern ballet that was created for him when he was a member of Walker's company. As fun as it would have been to dance with Tony in those November performances that marked our return to Boston, I think it was important that we triumphed as individuals first. Besides, just a month earlier, on tour in Texas, Tony and I had had great fun dancing in another Balanchine ballet, the 1964 *Tarantella*, a giddy pas de deux set to music by Louis Gottschalk. Whatever sparks brought us together as a couple fairly crackled onstage, especially in something as rousing as *Tarantella*, another of Mr. B's speed-demon works and this one with tambourines. We were part of a small group of Boston Ballet dancers who'd traveled down to McAllen, Texas, to perform as guests of the Rio Grande Valley Ballet Foundation. It was during this runout that I got to know Elaine Bauer (Lefty), who had joined her husband, David Brown, as a member of the company while I was in New York. It was a short tour but a memorable beginning to what has ended up being a lifelong friendship. We are now living on opposite coasts but strive to visit each other as often as possible.

A handful of months later, in March, the company embarked on its first "real" tour. So, compared to those runouts that consisted primarily of a small group of dancers appearing in one location, a larger group of us performed in several venues, traveling to Arizona, Wyoming, and California. Touring companies were still the main exposure to ballet many communities had then, but now it was often regional troupes such as Boston Ballet, rather than well-known international companies, that could meet the increasing demand for ballet performances. Indeed, a great trickle-down effect was happening; sometimes our performances were sponsored by a community's own "ballet society," a group of patrons hoping to increase awareness of the art form and ultimately the ability to support its own homegrown company. It was heady to realize that by appearing in their communities, or sometimes as guest artists on their programs, we were now helping fledgling companies gain prominence, in the same way that others helped us in our early years.

But the tours and the runouts were exciting for us too. In April, eight company members performed in Fort Lauderdale, Florida, in what was called the "Scrambled Legs Tour" by organizer Aloysius Petruccelli (Al), BB's stage production manager—and Rose's husband—and sponsored by the Fort Lauderdale Civic Ballet Company. The performance was officially billed as "Edward Villella and the Principal Soloists of the Boston Ballet." Just a few years earlier of course, Villella was one of the stars brought in to lend authority to Boston Ballet's home performances, and now we were capable of sharing almost equal billing with him. As it turned out, there were some "behind-the-scenes" dramas that made the experience downright terrible. Villella was injured in the period leading up to the performance date, and so those of us dancing directly with him in any of the ballets on the mixed program failed to get any rehearsal time with him. But the show must go on, and so it, and we, did. Any difficulties on our end were thankfully not apparent to the audience, or to the critics who reviewed the show. "The highlight of the evening was *Apollo*," wrote Jack Zink in the *Fort Lauderdale News*. "Here Villella teamed expressively with Edra Toth, Laura Young, and Miss Sarazin." Of our appearance together in Balanchine's *Stars and Stripes*, Bob Freund wrote, "Villella was teamed with Miss Young for a whirling and leaping tribute to Americana, and the star's humor and versatility was demonstrated.... Miss Young was a stunning and technically expert partner." Naturally, it was thrilling to know that whatever growth I'd achieved while away was recognizable to the outside world too, and I was dancing something with "pizzazz."

IF I HAD CHANGED while in New York City, what had changed at Boston Ballet while I was away? In addition to new general manager Michael Judson, the company hired its first music director, Michel Sasson. In the same way that acquiring Woytek was meant to eliminate the need for so many guest dancers, Sasson's appointment was another positive indication of Boston Ballet's growing independence. The company and school had moved, yet again, but though the new quarters were just around the corner from the previous studios on Tremont Street, they were a big improvement, at least in terms of space. Now there were enough studios—four, two of them quite big and only one with poles!—so that we didn't have to break up our days to accommodate the school's classes. Previously, we had class from 10:00 to 11:30, rehearsed from 11:30 to 3:30, and reconvened at 6:30 to 9:30 for further rehearsals. This new home at 19 Clarendon Street was, however, a rather dilapidated old warehouse. There was a huge loading dock with a ramp, where they had to put in a staircase so we could get to the front door. The boiler would break down periodically, and we'd be at the barre in our coats and mittens. There were critters galore, but this was hardly surprising to us; we even decorated a mouse hole in one of the studios and called it (after Walt

Disney's famously cute little rodent) "Mick's Place." Years later, the building was demolished and a new, gorgeous, three-story building with seven dance studios was erected in its place. If only the young dancers of today's Boston Ballet could have seen the old studio—they would never believe it.

Then again, the whole neighborhood, Boston's South End, has also metamorphosed dramatically since the mid-1970s. The cold we dealt with wasn't only because of that temperamental boiler: there were bullet holes in some of the windows, with outside air constantly coming in through them. The side streets then were filled with boarding houses that rented out the basics of a bed and a toilet; most of these houses, many of them brownstones, have since been rehabbed into beautiful and very, very expensive three-story homes or separated into condos. Now there are hip little shops, trendy cafés, organic bakeries, and a host of fabulous restaurants. Back then, however, there was little in the way of decent food, so we usually just brought our own food to work. There was one donut shop — "The Dip and Sip"— and one little restaurant that we simply called "The Greasy Spoon." We didn't know its name, but you could get a plate of greasy eggs there in the morning, if you so desired.

Boston in those days was much grittier compared to the kind of "small town" quaintness that permeates it now. Muggings were not uncommon, but that was the story in many cities, including of course New York, which was especially treacherous. Thankfully I was never robbed or assaulted in either city, but I always had my guard up when I was out and about. It could be nerve-racking, but it was also just how it was; we learned to be aware so that we could live and enjoy our lives. And we did have a good time, Tony and I, dancing, and yes, living right there in the South End. We had a sweet little one-bedroom apartment in a brownstone on the second floor on Hanson Street with the airy, high ceilings those buildings are known for and that make even tiny abodes seem relatively spacious. Indeed, we were the picture of domestic bliss in a March 5, 1974, *Boston Herald-American* feature about us. "Now they're back in Laura's home country, amid an apartment that's part Tony, part Laura," wrote Bonnie Selway, "scattered with Laura's needlepoint pillows and Tony's pony-skin rugs. Tony's learning to like Yankee cooking and Laura sometimes experiments with Italian cooking."

Outside our cozy home, however, the entire city was about to enter into one of its most troubling eras, what became known as the Boston busing crisis. The student population of the city's public schools was at that time racially imbalanced, so much so that the school system was finally put under a court order to desegregate or lose state funding. In the first year of the mandate, some students from the mostly white South Boston High were bused to the mostly black Roxbury High School, and vice versa. Reactions to the order were vehement and divisive; on one side were proponents of equality who were working to continue the progress that had begun under the civil rights movement of the previous decade. Some opponents were simply fearful, uncertain of the unknown, but there's no way around the fact that some of the opposition was rooted, appallingly, in racism. The situation affected individual families, whose children were either bused to schools in other neighborhoods or whose newly diversified classrooms were under intense national scrutiny, but the division was also seen all the way up to the government level. The issue was at the heart of the mayoral race in 1967, when Kevin White ran against Louise Day Hicks, a member of the Boston School Committee who was opposed to desegregation. Though White won—and went on to become one of Boston's most celebrated political figures, serving as mayor for four terms—the bitter fight and the highly publicized violence that rocked the city during the worst of the crisis left a deep stain on Boston's image.

The issue surely helped people wake up about diversity—or the lack thereof—in other avenues. Although most ballet companies in the United States today still fail to reflect the racial makeup of our country, the situation in 1974 was downright bleak. "One notes that there are no black dancers in [Boston Ballet]," wrote Ella Jackson in the February 19, 1974, edition of the University of Massachusetts' *Mass Media*, going on to note that "Stephanie Moy, the only Oriental in the company, has never danced a featured role. Hopefully, this inexcusable situation will correct itself soon." Jackson's use of "Oriental" aside—universal adaptation of the proper term "Asian" was a few decades away—the fact that people were noticing the disparity was heartening, and by the end of 1974, we would have two black dancers from South Africa, when Augustus van Heerden and Sheridan Heynes joined the company.

WHILE THE WORLD around me tossed and turned and grappled with these crucial issues of equality, my return to Boston Ballet marked the beginning of a tremendously favorable period in terms of my own professional opportunities. In quick succession, I danced the leads in *Giselle* and *Swan Lake* act 2 during that tenth-anniversary season. Though it would be several years before the company did a full *Swan Lake*, and although Bob Steele and I had performed act 2 at the Boston Conservatory a few years earlier, it was affirming to be given the chance to dance it in front of our subscription audience, with Bob once again my Prince Siegfried. Ten years after the company's inception, families were still part of the organization as volunteers. Needing a parade of swans to cross behind the ground row of lights for act 2, my brother, Jim, proceeded to take on the task. His knowledge from when he was a project engineer for Boston Whaler (the Fisher-Pierce Boat Co.) gave him the unique ability to create swan molds out of fiberglass. He still has Odette's head and tiara from that production.

Tony and I also got the chance to reprise *Tarantella* for the Boston audience, which was received as gleefully at home as it had been on the road. Waxing quite enthusiastically about our performance of it, Walter Terry wrote that Tony and I were "both on the threshold of what could be major careers in ballet."

For my first-ever shot at the title heroine of *Giselle* I was once again paired with Woytek. Edie Toth and I shared the lead over the course of three performances and alternated in the Peasant Pas as well. Along with the coaching that one usually receives when taking on an important role, I had benefitted over time, from simply being in the studio when others—not just Edie but also Violette Verdy and later Elaine—were being coached for *Giselle*. Even if you aren't "officially" called to a rehearsal because you're in one of the casts or are an understudy, it's an amazing opportunity if you can be in the room anyway. This was one of Virginia's mantras, and it served me well. I did just that over the years and absorbed as much of others' coaching as I could. So, when my chance came, I was ready to seize it. One can never know, definitively, if one is "ready," but I felt up to the challenge. "After watching lovely Laura Young dance exquisitely in the not only technically demanding, but dramatically demanding role of *Giselle* my faith in the Boston Ballet Company was amply restored," wrote Ella Jackson in *Mass Media*. "After spending the last two years with the Metropolitan Opera Ballet Company... Laura has returned a more polished and expressive artist."

If there's such a thing as karma, perhaps the dance gods decided that I'd more than paid my dues while in New York.

12

À Terre; en l'Air

À terre; en l'air. Origin: French. On the ground; in the air.

A WRITER ONCE DESCRIBED Virginia as "plumpish, smiling, and almost neighborly," but this unassuming appearance notwithstanding, she could be quite bold. Her opening program for the company's eleventh season included two works by one of dance history's most unconventional modernists, Merce Cunningham, his 1958 *Summerspace* and 1964 *Winterbranch*. Cunningham, who had gotten his start with Martha Graham's company before striking out on his own, often made works in which the various elements—movement, music, costumes, and decor—were created somewhat or even fully independent of each other. His legendary use of "chance" procedures sometimes meant that he tossed a coin to determine the specifics of a dance. The movement he created, however, was razor sharp in its precision and often quite demanding; though much of it employed modern dance hallmarks such as parallel legs and weighted, grounded movement, ballet vocabulary is also clearly imprinted in Cunningham technique. His works are peppered with long balances, high extensions, and springy jumps, and although he thus required dancers who were superbly trained in ballet as well as modern dance, he rarely worked with ballet dancers outside of his own company.

Of course, Virginia had long been engaging modern choreographers to create or remount works on us. Indeed, as Carole Mazur recounted in the *Patriot Ledger*, Cunningham expressed "satisfaction with the performance he is getting from the Boston Ballet dancers and notes their ability to be flexible because of their previous work with various choreographers." Our audiences were therefore also used to—and usually embracing of—the nontraditional fare. Then again, Cunningham's *Summerspace*, one of his more lyrical, "accessible" dances, wasn't such a hard sell. The dancers—costumed in beautiful, pointillist painted unitards whose impressionistic patterns were mirrored and enlarged in the backdrop, all designed by Robert Rauschenberg—moved like fey, exotic creatures, pausing contemplatively or silently swooshing along the stage. Morton Feldman's score is by turns spacious and tranquil, reminiscent of nature.

And then there was *Winterbranch*. Unlike *Summerspace*, no company other than Cunningham's, ballet or otherwise, had ever performed it. The lighting design was random and murky at best; it took a while for viewers' eyes to discern the crawling figure, slowly inching all the way across upstage from left to right as the piece began. Occasionally, a jolt of shockingly bright lights would shine directly at the audience. The score, by La Monte Young, was composed of sounds that were as piercing as those lights. *Winterbranch* was as jarring as *Summerspace* was serene, and reactions were all over the map. Tony—the crawling figure costumed in a neck-to-foot black wool tube and a black knit hat, with black slashes of makeup applied under his eyes like a football player—finally made it downstage and held a push-up position for what seemed an interminable amount of time. At that point, he was directly in line with the aisle and staring straight ahead. All he could see were people's backs as they headed for the lobby in droves with their hands over their ears. Company lore credits *Winterbranch* with over-the-top champagne sales during that run.

One writer compared the opening night to the infamous May 29, 1913, Paris premiere of Vaslav Nijinsky's ballet *Le Sacre du Printemps*. That audience was largely split into two factions: those who were vehemently opposed to the Ballets Russes star's starkly modern choreography and Igor Stravinsky's likewise groundbreaking score, and those who championed the innovations that the ballet and the music represented. Well, some sixty-plus years later in Boston, there were those who indeed applauded Virginia's spunk, arguing that the local audience needed an occasional kick in the pants. Others protested bitterly, suggesting that Virginia had betrayed their loyalty. By the way, those audience members who had walked out on the performance made sure to come back in time for the bows at the end, so they could express their displeasure. Oh, how they booed.

———————

HAVING NOT BEEN CAST in *Winterbranch*, and busy downstairs readying myself for my own performance, I missed out on all of that excitement. I admit that I didn't really mind though, since as you can imagine, being booed at is no fun, even if it's not exactly your "fault." I also wasn't surprised that I was sometimes passed over by the likes of Merce Cunningham. There were others in the company, such as Rose, Stephanie Moy, and Leslie Woodies, who'd had prior modern training and were really, really good in those dances that required serious modern chops. Certainly by working with the abundance of guest and in-house choreographers over the years, I picked up a lot of information and was able to develop versatility over time. Nowadays, it's a given that even the most ballet-centric of professional dancers need training in other forms of dance: modern yes, but something like hip-hop also comes in handy with the fluid, cross-genre movement used by many choreographers today.

But then, as now, it's not always a deal breaker if one is unfamiliar with a specific style; sometimes a choreographer will just like the way a dancer moves and will be willing to work with that dancer, to help him or her physicalize the particular movement to satisfaction. And so, while my colleagues were dancing in the Cunningham pieces, I performed in the great Swedish choreographer Birgit Cullberg's 1951 *Medea*. Set to a compilation of orchestrated Béla Bartók piano pieces, this choreodrama depicted the Greek myth of the title sorceress and her husband Jason. I was cast as Creusa, Jason's lover. Cullberg, who founded the company that bears her name, and her son Mats Ek, who also directed that company for many years, are both looked to as masters of the early ballet/modern hybridization that continues to transform. *Medea* was definitely a perfect transition ballet for me by melding dramatics, ballet, and modern into my own personal repertoire.

In addition to the flow of works from outside choreographers—including our steady, and by now considerable, diet of Balanchine ballets—repertoire from in-house choreographers increased. *Speed Zone*, a ballet Sam Kurkjian made for the company, was fun to do and rather cutting edge for its time. An audience favorite, it became a signature piece that was performed a good deal on tour. I was really impressed by Sam's daring; his dances before that were noted for the poetic, impressionistic way he used the ballet vocabulary, whereas *Speed Zone* was percussive and quite modern. Sam, who passed away in 2013, was a much in demand teacher and choreographer both abroad and locally. He was a longtime and beloved figure at the Boston Conservatory and Walnut Hill School for the Performing Arts, and although he moved on from his full-time status with Boston Ballet after that tenth season, he remains an integral part of its history.

Ron Cunningham (no relation to Merce, and currently artistic director of Sacramento Ballet), who ultimately danced with Boston Ballet for many years, was another choreographer-in-residence just coming up during that time. While he created a variety of dances over the years, both story ballets and contemporary works, he had a talent, as did Sam, for creating children's ballets too. Virginia usually had one "child-friendly" program per Boston run, specifically geared for the matinées, and before you know it, Ron had made several charming ballets: *Raggedy Ann 'n' Andy*; *Tubby the Tuba*; and *Hansel and Gretel*. It's a smart move to appeal to the little guys: what a great way to introduce them to this beautiful but unfamiliar art form. At the same time, it's also a clever way of winning over the adults who have to bring them to the theater. The ballet world is always looking for ways to build its audience.

Lorenzo Monreal, who came to the company at the same time as Woytek Lowski, was still performing when he was first hired into the company but eventually became resident choreographer and created several ballets for us. Like Woytek, Lorenzo had trained in St. Petersburg and was an excellent teacher. His company class was mostly based on that demanding Vaganova technique, and while we had many wonderful teachers over the years, Lorenzo's consistent attention to specifics bumped us all up a notch technically. Another asset he brought was his ability to expertly stage and coach dancers in international repertoire. His breadth of knowledge was initially put to use in his staging of bravura "showcase" pas de deux such as the Classical-era staples from *Don Quixote* and *Le Corsaire*. Soon, his expertise would be put to use in a much bigger undertaking, when he was called upon to assist in the staging of Boston Ballet's first full-length *Sleeping Beauty*.

Between Virginia and Lorenzo, they staged the most devilish version possible with all the hardest and most cherished parts of the Kirov's and Royal Ballet's productions. There were no kneeling pages to lend their shoulders for support to Aurora for her penchés arabesques in the Rose Adagio; she was all on her own. And the promenades in the Vision Scene were what one might think one-handed, but hands were not actually involved in this version. The princess placed her wrist on top of the prince's, making it the only means of support as he walked completely around her while she was on one pointe. There were many more fiendishly difficult instances such as this throughout the production, and yes, we accepted the challenge and rose to it. Through this grueling version, we all grew stronger and more willing to take the requisite risks.

Years later, when we finally put on a full-length *Don Q*, the lead role of Kitri would become one of my favorites—good thing too, because we performed it a lot!—but at this point the sassy, stylized excerpt was performed by Edra Toth with Woytek as her partner.

Another "showstopper" duet that Lorenzo staged early on was Asaf Messerer's 1949 brash, spectacular *Spring Waters*. Messerer, who came of age in postrevolution Russia, trained and danced at the Bolshoi Ballet in Moscow. The Mariinsky and Bolshoi are sometimes thought of as two very different sides of the same coin; they are both revered as keepers of the Russian ballet flame, with equally demanding training but dissimilar stylistically. It's often noted that "Bolshoi" means "big," and the Muscovite dancers are known for their bold, muscular way of moving versus the St. Petersburgers' serene elegance.

The movement for the *Spring Waters* duet is drawn from standard ballet steps, but the emphasis is on abandon. The female tears across the stage and hurls herself into the air, yards away from her partner; later, he pitches her way above his head, where she twists twice before coming back down. He catches her each time, of course, but oh, how breathtaking it is to see every time. A crowd pleaser for sure! I didn't dance that one, but Jerilyn Dana (PeeWee) did, partnered by Lorenzo himself, complete with the requisite and exhilarating encore.

(As it turned out, it was to be Jerilyn's last season with BB, because she left soon after for a principal contract with Les Grands Ballets Canadiens.

We continued to stay in touch though and were always aware of each other's proximity. When both companies were on tour in Europe for festivals in the same city, we would leave notes in the dressing room for the other to find upon arrival. Although we never actually saw PeeWee while on tour, it became a fun tradition that let her know she was missed. Twelve years later, Lefty, Rose, and I drove to Montreal for PeeWee's retirement from the stage. We were heartened to know that our dressing-room banter was still intact. When we arrived at the stage door during her rehearsal, we were ushered into her dressing room to wait. When we heard her coming close, all three of us immediately put hands to cheeks to mimic a "facelift." As she opened the door and saw us, without missing a beat, she dropped her armload of pointe shoes and did the same, saying, "Great to see you guys!" Years later, having made the decision that she had no desire to teach and was ready to try a new career, she returned to Boston Ballet in a major way, as Bruce Marks's administrative assistant.)

Lorenzo had a talent for original creation as well. He choreographed two big ballets for us in 1975, *Hamlet*, a dramatic yet spare one-act based on Shakespeare's play, and *Carmina Burana*, whose lusty, intense choreography was a great match for Carl Orff's popular, flamboyant score for orchestra and chorus. It's a shame that neither it nor Sam's version of *Carmina* have been revived; for years, people would ask me when the company would perform either one again. But like so many ballets over the years, and prior to the advent of videography as a regular tool used for documentation, once they are out of the repertory for too long, few dancers remember them. The footage from old reel-to-reel videotapes is often so poor that it is difficult to tell who the dancers are, or even how many dancers there are, never mind what the individual steps may be.

ALL IN ALL, it was a healthy time for new choreography, for dance makers, and for us dancers too. It doesn't matter how thrilling or challenging it is to dance in ballets from *Giselle* to *Serenade*, without fresh material, dancers can go a little stir crazy. Fortunately, Boston Ballet was often proactive in seeking out and providing opportunities for choreographers. Sam, after all, had been "found" through the Vestris Competition back in 1967. In 1975, the company presented a program called "Experiments in Dance." Known in subsequent years as the Choreographers' Festival (as well as the Choreographers' Series, or Showcase), this iteration was largely a platform for company members to present their works by not only giving them a chance to test their skills but also seeking to identify and develop talent from within. For the first series, Robert Steele, Larry Robertson, and Alfonso Figueroa each offered a dance. The *Corsaire* pas de deux showed up on that program as well and became a showcase for a lovely, up-and-coming corps de ballet member, Dierdre Miles (later changed to Myles), partnered by Woytek. Going forward, the Choreographers' Festival/Series/Showcase included both in-house and guest choreographers and eventually blossomed from a national into an international event.

If, through our experiences with so many styles and choreographers, we developed our technical and artistic range, it's inspiring to think that perhaps the reverse was true as well. When Agnes de Mille created *Summer: Death and the Maiden* for us in 1975, a shift in *her* usual style was noted. Set to a handful of Franz Schubert lieder, the abstract ballet's various scenes portrayed a potpourri of moods, from the comic to the tragic. In the *Boston Globe*, Christina Robb wrote that de Mille's "idiom has never been so classical," while in the *New York Times*, Clive Barnes commented that *Summer* was "far more classical in feel than most of Miss de Mille's work."

OUR "REAL LIFE" SUMMERS those days were spent making new connections and reestablishing old ties. In 1974, Mayor Kevin White created "Summerthing," a program devoted to bringing the arts to outdoor locations throughout the city. For Boston Ballet's part in this ambitious project, we danced in parks and on closed-off neighborhood streets around the city, hoping to grow our local audience base. We were provided with a mobile stage, comprised of a semi truck that opened outward on the side from the bottom, creating an eight-foot awning over the back of the stage, which meant that any lifts had to be done toward the front. The stage itself was created with tables overlaid with a marley floor across them. The tables had adjustable legs to accommodate the uneven ground, but they would still shake from our movements. And our dressing room was an old school bus,

invariably placed right next to the generator providing our power. In eighty-
to ninety-degree temperatures, we had to keep the windows closed to avoid
inhaling the exhaust, so no sooner had we put on our makeup than it would
begin to melt!

I remember trying to dance *Tarantella* under the awning as the rain came
down. That was interesting! But we pulled if off by dancing in the rain only
when absolutely necessary. We had our share of mishaps at these venues,
including rocks thrown at us by kids, and the jets taking off and landing
at Logan Airport would drown out the music, forcing us to become quite
adept at keeping our tempi so that we'd be in sync with the music when
we could finally hear it again. This was when we coined the term "guerilla
ballet" for our intrepid performances. We would arrive, set up, rehearse, do
the show—and we'd be gone.

As an adjunct to "Summerthing," the company also offered ten free performances on Boston's famous "Hatch Shell" stage on the Esplanade, the
future site of the city's hugely popular Fourth of July Boston Pops concert
and extravagant fireworks display. The Esplanade runs all along the banks of
the Charles River. These "Ballet on the Esplanade" performances became an
important tradition for the company and eventually for its junior company,
Boston Ballet II (BBII). There was funding from the Metropolitan District
Commission for the event, which took place for many years, but eventually,
as so often happens, funding was withdrawn and the ballet could not foot
the bill for the venue as well as payroll for the staff and dancers. It was such
a shame because for Bostonians it was a lovely way to pass a warm, breezy
summer's night and was a great way to introduce ballet to those who might
not otherwise attend a performance. Later on, as the main company started
to tour during the summer months, it became the ideal venue for BBII to
gain more visibility in the community and for the dancers to have an opportunity to perform leading roles as part of their training.

The following summer we were back at Jacob's Pillow, where our continued progress was noted. "The Boston Ballet returned . . . for the first time
since 1972," Kitty Cunningham reported in the *Berkshire Courier*. "During
the intervening three years they have been sharpening their dancing and
their repertoire." Indeed, the two programs we presented certainly demonstrated the company's versatility. The Pillow's Ted Shawn Theatre isn't the

right space to put on a full ballet such as *Swan Lake*, but we did show off our Balanchine chops with Tony and Anamarie performing *Tarantella* while Augustus (Gus) van Heerden and I took the leads in *Allegro Brillante*. Two of Ron's ballets (*Holberg Suite* and *Rags*) were featured, while the company's ability to tackle dramatic, contemporary material was highlighted in our performances of *The Road of the Phoebe Snow* and *The Abyss*. We'd revived Talley Beatty's *Phoebe Snow* earlier that year—when I got the chance to perform the lead—and had premiered Stuart Hodes's *Abyss* during the Boston season as well.

Based on a Russian tale, Hodes's work was even darker than Beatty's, depicting a young couple that is ambushed by a group of men who drag the woman away and assault her. It's a delicate task to portray such a disturbing incident in a ballet for both choreographers and dancers alike; without words, the necessarily theatrical movements can become laughable melodrama. But Hodes, a former dancer with Martha Graham's company, was well versed in how difficult subjects could be conveyed successfully through the medium of dance. The piece was originally made for the Joffrey Ballet, where Tony had played one of the assailants; we danced the lead couple both in Boston and at the Pillow. Tony and I were commended for our performances, which I attribute to our private emotional connection that helped us delve deeper into this wrenching story.

Of the company's visit to the Pillow, Valerie Restivo wrote in the Albany-based *Times-Union*, "The Boston Ballet Company is fast proving how wrong we are to call non–New York ballet 'regional' and imply that it belongs in a lower category of the art.... When I first saw the Boston Ballet five years ago it was in its sixth year and still showing both the shakiness and the flush of youth. It has lost both the flush of innocence and the shakiness."

As we were busily growing up, so too it seems was "regional ballet." Writing earlier that year in the *Saturday Review* about the evolution of ballet in America, Walter Terry counted Boston Ballet on a short list (four) of "major non–New York professional ballet companies." By Terry's estimation, Pennsylvania was at the top: "The Boston Ballet Company has less money and is not quite so strong in all performing areas as the Pennsylvania Ballet, but under E. Virginia Williams it has grown into a major company with a splendid repertory of classics ... Balanchine ballets ... and first-rate modern works." Meanwhile, Terry noted that the "regional ballet movement, which got under way in 1956, has presided over the evolution of more than 200 ballet companies in our land." It was a bit strange to realize it, but we were now the elders to those younger companies, groups such as the ones we "starred" with on some of our guest-artist gigs. Like us not so many years ago, they were just starting out.

———

ALTHOUGH TERRY, mentioning Tony and me by name in that *Saturday Review* article, applauded Virginia's "sharpness in recognizing new talent," I was now in my late twenties, not a spring chicken in the ballet world. But if one's body is healthy, it's often the beginning of a dancer's richest time as an artist. At least, that was my experience and my good fortune. Oh, there were still aches and pains, surgeries, and yes, hairline fractures ahead but nothing that stopped me prematurely. And, like Cinderella, in 1975 I even discovered my own "magic slippers," which gave my dancing a new kind of life. After all of those years, I switched pointe shoe brands, which, to a ballet dancer, is almost like changing out of one's skin. My very first pair of pointe shoes was what pretty much every other first-year pointe student wore back then: Selva's with a "duro-toe," a suede-like tip. After that I'd only worn Capezio's, but lately I was having a particularly hard time with them. A wonderful fact about our field is that pointe shoes are made by hand, so dancers enter into a kind of intense but anonymous relationship with their pointe shoemakers. In a company such as Boston Ballet, it's typical to go through several pairs of pointe shoes in a week, and it's crucial that each pair fits as perfectly as possible for each dancer. Within each pointe shoe brand—such as Capezio, Freed of London, or Bloch—there were a handful of styles, each with differences such as length and shape of the box, hardness of the shank (the shoe's inner sole), and the fit of the heel, and from there, dancers can request even more exacting specifications from their makers. As you can imagine, it's of the utmost importance that the shoes fit like proverbial gloves. For whatever reason, I'd been getting a shoe here and there that had a lump on the platform, and one day, someone came in with a pair of Schachtner's, a brand I'd never tried. They were practically weightless, as if you had a tissue on your foot. Well, between that and the fact that there was never a "lump" in them, I decided to change my pointe shoes for the second and what ended up being the last time.

It's fun to think that maybe my new "magic slippers" had something to do with what was for me a somewhat charmed fall and winter season that year. Though I wasn't in any of the company premieres such as Lorenzo's *Carmina Burana*, I received notice for my dancing in some of our old stand-bys. Of our performance in Michel Fokine's *Les Sylphides*, Gerald Fitzgerald wrote in the *Patriot Ledger* that my partner James Dunne—a friend and former Joffrey dancer who'd followed us to Boston—and I offered "new aspects of a familiar work." Meanwhile, with so many performances by so many companies over so many years, it's easy for people in "the biz"—dancers and critics alike—to get a little weary of the whole *Nutcracker* thing. But that year, veteran Elliot Norton wrote in the Sunday *Boston Herald*, "Miss Young has been with the company for several seasons and has always seemed attractive and accomplished. But her performance last night was something quite extraordinary."

As I've noted, I got my share of, shall we say, less-than-thrilling reviews over the years. They stung, of course—but reviews such as Norton's never failed to lift me up and are the ones that actually made it into the scrapbooks.

13

La Belle au Bois Dormant

La Belle au Bois Dormant. Origin: French. *The Sleeping Beauty.*

WHEN HE WAS A CHILD, George Balanchine made his debut in *The Sleeping Beauty* as a page. How fitting that the man whom many consider to have been the standard-bearer of ballet choreography in the *twentieth century* should have gotten his start in this masterpiece by the man seen as the king of ballet in the *nineteenth century*, Marius Petipa. The 1890 work was heralded as a triumph not only for its dazzling crystallization of ballet technique but also for its musical achievements. Indeed, this first collaboration between Petipa and Tchaikovsky forever lifted expectations for not only the quality of music used in a ballet but also the ways in which the choreography should be designed to truly connect with that music. Of all the knowledge that Balanchine inherited from his formidable dance ancestry, it is in this area—musicality—that his ballets achieve their ultimate sublimity.

Despite the ballet's exalted status, when Boston Ballet staged its first full-length *Beauty* in 1976, complete productions were rare in the United States. "With this production," Iris Fanger wrote in the *Christian Science Monitor*, "the Boston Ballet becomes the only American company to have the full-length work in its repertoire." It's hard to imagine that today, for the classics are now relatively abundant in the United States. Though American ballet companies' repertoires have become increasingly stocked with contemporary works, it hasn't meant—thankfully—the death of the traditional repertoire. Full-length productions of *The Sleeping Beauty*, along with *Swan Lake*, *Giselle*, *La Sylphide*, *Don Quixote*, *La Bayadère*, and of course *The Nutcracker*, are now more familiar presences. Indeed, they are often more easily "marketable" to some portions of the audience than contemporary repertoire. Nonetheless, it seems that many viewers now understand that the "either/or" stance is unnecessary; a healthy mix of the old and the new is a great way to appreciate and enjoy the evolution of ballet.

Even so, the popularity of the classics in America can't rival Russians' devotion to them. Whereas Boston Ballet today may put on one or two big ballets per season, the repertoires of the Bolshoi Ballet and the Mariinsky Theater include many of the classics year after year. Russian audience members don't have the same "but I saw *Swan Lake* last year" attitude that one hears here, but then again ballet in Russia is practically a national pastime. The Russian companies have much longer seasons than ours can afford, and there are legions of Russian balletomanes who flock to the bounty of performances. We have our fiercely devoted fans too but far, far fewer in number.

These "big" ballets are quite expensive to produce. *Beauty* is certainly one of the most lavish of the lot, which surely puts a curb on many directors' dreams, but as the company headed into its twelfth season, it was on stronger financial ground than it had been for quite a while. What a welcome scenario after so many years of shakiness. Not surprisingly, the stability had come at some cost. In the Boston Ballet Society's (the volunteers' association) March 1976 newsletter, the topic was addressed both transparently and diplomatically. Several key figures who had helped out financially or as members of the board of trustees were lauded, including Bradley Higgins and new chairman Stuart Yoffe. Special mention went to Harry Wilcott, who as former "Chairman of the Board . . . led us into the big leagues." Before proudly citing the company's current fiscal and artistic standing, the article also commended soon-to-be-outgoing general manager Michael Judson, who "proved to be the right man at the right time. Although we went through a painful reorganization period, we were able to adapt to changes and to reach a new plateau."

Of course the between-the-lines reality was that a serious shake-up was occurring behind the scenes. By November, a new general manager, Robert Brickell, was in place. Most of what the public saw during that time, however, was the business-as-usual glamorous facade of ballet companies everywhere. Particularly dazzling was the opulence that emanated from this brand-new *Beauty*. As it happened, some of the elements were hand-me-downs. The National Ballet of Washington, one of the original regional "cousins" that had also sprung up from those first Ford Foundation grants, had recently gone under. That meant we were able to purchase, at a reduced rate, designer Peter Farmer's costumes and scenery from that company's production of *Beauty*. (The good news for the DC area, by the way, is that a new company, the Washington Ballet, was quickly formed. In 2016 it celebrated its fortieth anniversary after beginning as an outgrowth of the venerable teacher Mary Day's long-running Washington School of Ballet.)

For our first *Beauty*, Virginia again tapped into Lorenzo's considerable knowledge of the classics and thus the two of them staged the ballet together. Oh, it's a difficult ballet, one of those in which there's nothing to "hide behind" in terms of technique. As I mentioned earlier, BB's production combined all the technically demanding elements of the Mariinsky—courtesy of Lorenzo Monreal, and Royal Ballet versions—thanks to Virginia's copious notes, which created the most difficult version imaginable. What a challenge! The series of fairy variations in the prologue offer a primer of pointe technique; though short, the women performing them are quite challenged for the minute or so each solo lasts. There are tests for men in the ballet, too—Prince Desiré's solos, of course, but also the Blue-bird's—and like the women's, the virtuosity lies in the performer's ability to merge artistry with precision and stamina. If the ballet itself is often called the "jewel" of classical ballet, then certainly it follows that the big roles are sought after and fought for, and considered to be "jewels" in a dancer's repertoire. In that first series of performances, I shared the lead role of Aurora with Edra Toth (Edie), who had returned after a year away, and the promising young Dierdre (Dede) Myles, whose name by now had a spelling change courtesy of Virginia. I had two princes, Woytek Lowski and Elaine Bauer's husband, David Brown. One of the most fun things about opening night was that Rose appeared as Carabosse, the "evil" fairy, opposite Lefty's Lilac Fairy, the "good" one. The Gumm Sisters unite!

"Boston Ballet's sumptuous production," noted Iris Fanger in the *Christian Science Monitor*, "shows signs of becoming . . . a perennial favorite." And after the overall success of that first run in 1976 we ended up performing *The Sleeping Beauty* four more spring seasons in a row; it was unofficially known as our "Easter *Nutcracker*." One could joke that it gave the company a chance to get its money's worth on those sets and costumes. The first time around, we really didn't have enough stage time prior to opening to get used to all of the elements in this big production. Between the flying scrims, a flying Carabosse, waving wands, and not quite enough dancing space with the enormous sets, it was a serious challenge to put it all together in the time and space allotted. The lack of stage rehearsal time was something that several of the reviews mentioned, if sympathetically. There's a reason most plays and musical theater productions have a series of "previews" before the official opening—there are a lot of kinks to work out. But even the biggest ballet productions rarely have more than a week of "tech" rehearsal in the theater, and most of that time is spent working out production details such as lighting, sound, and fly cues (placement and removal of scenery). But when the curtain goes up on opening night, we must be ready—or at least appear so! Because of this experience, the decision was made that in the future we would do a pre-series in Providence, Rhode Island, for each of our seasons. This would give us an edge before appearing in Boston and expanded our audience to the south.

I did a respectable job in my virgin performances as Aurora, even though I was once again dealing with a bum ankle that required surgery the day after we closed the run. In the meantime, it meant I had to accomplish the treacherous promenades and balances on the "wrong" leg, which was a nightmare. Despite the gracious reviews I received, I knew there was much room for improvement. One can *always* improve of course, but this ballet in particular always kept me on my proverbial toes. Over the years there would be some bobbles and wobbles and then, blissfully, performances with rock-solid balance and calm. It seems, fortunately, that the sum of my overall record was in the plus column. In a review during the fourth consecutive year we'd presented *Beauty*, Christine Temin wrote, "Young's dancing has always been, and still is, the finest thing about this production." Of course, I was but one of so many other wonderful artists. For Elizabeth Varady, Edie's Aurora was pitch perfect in the premiere production. "Edra Toth, who's been on leave . . . gave the kind of magical performance that breathes life into fairy tales." Rose's Carabosse, Varady said, was "vibrant, menacing," while Lefty's Lilac Fairy was "comforting, gentle."

While it was a gift to be able to explore and develop this ballet over time, it's the only one that caused my heart to flutter on the drive to the theater. None of the other ballets I danced ever did that to me, and I confess that when we put *Beauty* to bed for a while, I, for one, didn't mind all that much.

———————

WAS THERE A CORRELATION between the extraordinary Russian dancers now on the Western ballet scene—notably the famous "defectors" Rudolf Nureyev, Natalia Makarova, Alexander Godunov, and most recently, Mikhail Baryshnikov—and the rise in productions of these classics, most of which had been created in St. Petersburg? Although they'd had some exposure to the traditional works, a large part of the American audience's ballet education had been in the post-Romantic- and post-Classical-era ballets and, following the trends of the ongoing ballet "boom," in modern-inflected dances too. And often, even when traditional ballets were presented, they were staged in a kind of hodge-podge way, with scenes and choreography sometimes put together rather haphazardly, depending on who had learned what version. The kind of authenticity that someone such as Hans Brenaa brought when he staged *Napoli* on us was, at the time, a luxury. But now that these native Russians were in the West—with the DNA of Marius Petipa and Lev Ivanov coursing through them, and ready and able to share their precious knowledge—the flood of information was exhilarating. Like students who'd skipped several grades ahead, there were gaps in our schooling, and the golden time for filling them had arrived.

Makarova had recently set the "Kingdom of the Shades" scene on American Ballet Theatre (ABT). This glorious excerpt from Petipa's 1877 ballet *La Bayadère*, which Makarova eventually staged in full for ABT, begins with a large corps de ballet snaking their way onto the stage, either down a ramp upstage left or from the upstage left wing. One by one the "shades"—spirits who appear in the male lead's opium-induced dream—enter and execute a simple pattern consisting of walks, arabesque, and cambré. The cumulative effect of dancers joining the zigzagging line and repeating this little phrase over and over again until the stage is filled with ghostly figures is mesmerizing, and Western viewers were hooked. "This scene . . . really has no story (even though the full-length ballet is complex in its narrative), but the beauty of its choreographic architecture is matchless. It is one of the most exquisite ballets in the world and a terrifying test of dance ensemble," Clive Barnes wrote in the *New York Times* after the premiere, going on to compliment Makarova's part in the occasion. "Miss Makarova has caught the precise and fleeting style of the choreography, as well as the cohesive weight of its masses. . . . This is beautiful."

Just after our *Beauty* premiere, the Boston Ballet Society presented two recent Russian émigrés, Valery Panov and Galina Panova, as part of a big fundraiser for the company. The band of volunteers had grown right along with the rest of the organization. In 1966 it consisted of about three dozen women, and by 1968, it had grown to have a board with enough members to actually staff committees that covered education, subscriptions, membership, and sponsors and patrons. They still stitched costumes, stuffed envelopes, and performed a myriad of tasks, but they had now pulled together into a more official entity and began organizing events such as this "Evening with the Panovs."

The plight of the married couple had drawn negative attention to the Russian government's tight restrictions on its citizens' ability to travel freely. Rather than escape as others had done, they tried to leave legally, but after applying for exit visas they were fired from the Mariinsky (the Kirov Ballet), jailed briefly, and then forbidden to even take company class. After two years, authorities finally bowed to international pressure and granted the Panovs exit visas. The Boston Ballet Society fundraiser, which included a preperformance cocktail reception and a postperformance party on the stage, marked the first time the couple danced in Boston. By now, Virginia and her long list of "faithfuls" had been teaching Boston all about ballet for a decade and a half. While members of this thus-educated city knew that guest artists were no longer needed to "prop up" Boston Ballet artistically, they certainly welcomed the glamorous opportunity to hobnob with these Russian stars. For seventy-five to one thousand dollars per person, they did just that. That the proceeds went to us was icing on the cake.

————

OUR TRIP BACK IN TIME to *The Sleeping Beauty* didn't slow down our continued immersion in more contemporary ballets. For the company's second foray into garnering new works by bringing choreographers to Boston for the Choreographers' Series, Lorenzo's and Ron Cunningham's contributions were supplemented by works by two guest choreographers, both female, who added a strong international flavor to the program. Saeko Ichinohe—whose *Suspicion* had won Boston Ballet's Vestris Competition in 1968—created *Chidori*, based on a Japanese folk tale and set to a Japanese score, while the Israeli choreographer Ze'eva Cohen's *Goat Dance* had Iranian and Greek influences. Along with the movement vocabularies themselves, our field's increasing diversity was demonstrated in the greater use of these ethnic and cultural flavors and female choreographers.

As always, our Balanchine "diet" remained healthy throughout 1976. Company standbys such as *Stars and Stripes* and *Scotch Symphony* were complemented by the return of *Serenade, The Four Temperaments, Tchaikovsky Pas de Deux,* and *The Prodigal Son*. For the latter, Tony was an obvious choice for the title role, both physically—his powerful physique and panther-like jumps were a perfect match for the choreography—and metaphorically, even if it had been three years since we'd returned. He shared the role with Woytek, which showcased each equally but also served to show audiences how different dancers in the same role can bring two very different interpretations to light. Finally, after so much history with *Scotch Symphony*, I got the chance to perform the Sylph with Tony.

The whole company got overall kudos for the lessons we'd learned by dancing so much of Balanchine's repertory for so many years. *The Four Temperaments,* aka *Four Ts,* is one of Balanchine's "leotard ballets," in which the dancers wear simple practice clothes rather than decorative costuming. Not only sartorially stark, the choreography is lean, even austere, with lots of slicing legs punctuated by sharp pelvic thrusts and geometrically angled arms. It's abstract, like most of Balanchine's ballets, but he did use as a base the classical idea that humans possess four temperaments or "humors." The ballet is thus split into sections titled "Melancholic," "Sanguinic," "Phlegmatic," and "Choleric." The score, Paul Hindemith's *Theme with Four*

Variations, was commissioned by Mr. B himself in 1940, so that he could, according to the New York City Ballet website, have "a short work he could play at home with friends during his evening musicales." That tidbit, and the fact that the ballet itself came later, in 1946, is a reminder of the central importance of music in his life. Indeed, when he was young, Balanchine also trained seriously as a musician and might just as easily have gone into a career in music. What a relief he didn't! But one wonders what the music world missed out on.

That year, Ron Cunningham's *Cinderella*, set to Sergei Prokofiev's moody and romantic 1945 score, premiered during the November 1976 series. Although the title heroine and her prince, Edie (Toth) and Gus (van Heerden) received high praise, the ballet itself failed to excite the critics. Perhaps its daunting position in the program, following either *Prodigal Son* or *Scotch Symphony*, was too hard an act to follow. It struck a nerve with some critics who questioned, *where* was Boston Ballet going? And who was our target audience? Some applauded us for our versatility, while others gave us brickbats for not settling down to one style. But the deeper point, it seems, was that if we were going to "do it all" we'd better be sure to do it all quite well. Interestingly, we did bring Ron's *Cinderella* to China in 1980, and it was very well received there.

Wasn't it ironic that now we were finally financially healthy—thanks to the good work and difficult decisions being done and made by our stalwart volunteers and stoic trustees—our artistic stability was being debated? Or maybe it was just another sign of our maturity, that it was time for the organization to look at itself honestly—and forge ahead bravely.

14

Pas de Chat

Pas de chat. Origin: French. Cat's step. In a pas de chat, the dancer springs off one foot and the other quickly follows, so that for a moment, at the height of the jump, both legs are tucked up underneath the dancer in the shape of diamond.

BECAUSE OF THE REHEARSAL, technical, and performance schedules that revolve around *The Nutcracker*, ballet dancers—and everyone else involved in the show of course—rarely join the multitudes who make annual pilgrimages to their family homes for Thanksgiving. For many years, Lefty and her husband David hosted an "orphans' Thanksgiving" at their South End home for those of us who couldn't travel for the holiday as we usually opened the run of *Nutcracker* the very next day. It was always a huge feast and one of the many times that cemented the bond among Lefty, Rose, and me—a bond that had loosened only enough to let our husbands in.

By now Tony and I had moved to Roslindale, a neighborhood of Boston south of the city proper. Tony, whose nickname was Tony the Cat, told one writer that "I like to nest; it is important to me to have a home," and so we were renting a lovely two-bedroom, ground-floor apartment in a two-family house on one of the area's main thoroughfares. Although noisy when the big trucks hit one of the inevitable New England potholes, our kitchen, bedroom, and back porch were on the far side so we were shielded from much of the noise. We had full access to the garden and garage and a full basement. Such luxury we enjoyed after a studio apartment in NYC and a one bedroom in the South End. With a park right across the street, our two dogs were ecstatic.

It's fairly common for romantic relationships to develop within a ballet company, and the topic was frequently irresistible to reporters. Often, when Tony and I guested somewhere, the local newspapers there would make our marriage a highlight of a feature article about the upcoming performance. We'd also had our share of such stories appearing in the Boston-area publications too and had thus developed quite the repertoire of responses—some sweet, some tart, and some matter of fact—to what became familiar questions.

Sometimes the three couples—Tony and me, Lefty and David, and Rose and Al—were all featured in a story together. As the company's production stage manager, Al was the only nondancer, but in one such Sunday *Boston Globe* article Rose explained how they were able to help with each other's work. Al "may not be able to tell me the technical ballet things, but he'll say whether things work on stage," she said, while "we might be reviving a ballet we hadn't done for a while and he'll be going over the lighting cues and he'll ask me what's happening on stage" during a particular cue. One frequent theme in these features was the fact that both partners were working the same unusual hours. Tony once said something along the lines of "how many wives would be willing to make dinner every night at 11:00," which of course sounds dated now, but I was in truth the main chef of the couple. However, "Al does like to cook," Rose told the *Globe*, adding, "He gets carried away with his concoctions." And more often than not, we were the grateful recipients of each other's endeavors in the kitchen.

As to actually dancing with our spouses, David commented on the less-than-romantic aspect of it: "You know each other so well you don't feel you have to be as tactful as with a partner you're not married to." Yes, sometimes the work just needs to get done. But mostly, we all appreciated the main aspect of performing together, the true joy and beauty of dancing with someone you love. When we went to perform in Sarasota in early 1977, Tony told a local journalist, "We have tremendous rapport on stage because we understand each other and our roles." After all, as he said in that *Globe* piece, "we live closer than any two people I know. . . . We have breakfast together, we take class together, we have rehearsals together, we go to [physical] therapy together, we have dinner together."

But as it turned out, Tony and I, *because* of work, were apart for a significant part of 1977. Dennis Wayne, a former colleague of Tony's from his Joffrey Ballet days, had formed a new touring group called "Dancers" and enticed Tony to join. He also persuaded James Dunne and Dede Myles to join his company. James never returned, but Dede did, after joining Houston Ballet for several years. I was happy to be invited to perform with "Dancers" in July, opening the Spoleto Festival in Italy. It was my first taste of dancing abroad, and if it wasn't exactly blissful in terms of what I danced, as I was stepping in as a replacement in only a few of the works, it was a beautiful place to have my own little "European debut."

Tony and Dennis were old pals; they'd grown up together in Brooklyn and had gone to the High School of Performing Arts together. Tony, despite his status and opportunities within Boston Ballet, had off-and-on frustrations with casting. As early as 1974, when we had recently rejoined the company, he told a reporter, "My talents have been mismanaged. . . . They aren't using me to my fullest potential." Virginia rebutted in a way that hinted at a long-standing back-and-forth. "Tony doesn't want 100 percent," she said, "he wants 200. Today he says this and tomorrow all will be forgotten." Tony was rarely shy about saying—sometimes heatedly—what was on his mind. I guess it was just a cultural difference. I remember the first time we went to have dinner with his family in Brooklyn: just asking to have the salt and pepper passed sounded like a fraught discussion. My Yankee upbringing was far quieter. His "fiery" nature sometimes meant that suddenly, in his eyes, I was liable for something I hadn't done but that he perceived I had. We had lots of wonderful times together, but it was hard to deal with that aspect of his personality. Naturally, I was sure that as we grew together, it would change. To Tony, it was just a normal part of a relationship. To his credit, and knowing his own mindset, he once told me, "If you wanted a calm, comfortable life [meaning one with no discord between us], you married the wrong person."

―――――――

ANOTHER TOPIC that occasionally came up in the "dance couple" interviews was children. The question was not usually whether we'd start a family but when. This was more of an assumption back then. Trying to be polite, I'd deflect as best I could. As I told a reporter at the time, it seemed to me that my sister-in-law Phyllis Heath tried to reconcile the roles of mother and dancer and found that mother took precedence. She stopped dancing herself and turned to teaching. I figured I would probably do the same when and if the situation arose. By 1977, my responses must have become even vaguer. "Their heavy schedule of work and travel has also led them to postpone starting a family," Dorothy Stockbridge wrote in the *Sarasota Journal*. Oh, what can I say? It crossed my mind, as I think it does most women's, but something told me it might not be a good idea, and not just because of Tony's restlessness. Today, thanks to both union regulations and evolved thinking on the subject, female dancers who wish to have children have much more job security than in my day. As my responses indicated, it was usually seen as an either/or. Now, women take class up until they have the baby and then get themselves right back in class and back up on that stage.

Later, when my life circumstances were different, I did think more seriously about having children. But even then it was with the fantasy that their father would be tending and playing with them while I hovered in the kitchen, happily cooking dinner. I admit that in general I am not much of a "little kids person." We just don't seem to relate to one another.

On the other hand, I love teenagers, even with all their foibles. Best of all, I love *teaching* teenagers, which I discovered the first time I tried my hand at it. Sydelle Gomberg, the founder of the dance department at the Walnut Hill School of the Performing Arts, invited me to come and offer a "master class" to her group of advanced students in February 1977. Sydelle, who later became director of the Boston Ballet School, is, despite her formidable pedigree, one of the most gracious, modest people you could meet in the field. As a teenager, she had studied at the School of American Ballet in New York City with legendary teachers including Balanchine, Anatole Oboukoff, and Pierre Vladimiroff. She danced with the Metropolitan Opera and Radio

City ballet companies and performed on Broadway before coming back to Massachusetts where she and her new husband Ralph—who went on to become the principal oboist for the Boston Symphony Orchestra—raised four children. Later, she received teacher training at London's Royal Academy of Ballet. There she learned the importance of safety through the use of proper technique, something she quietly but firmly insisted on during her long, much-respected teaching career. Even so, she knew that inviting dancers such as myself—though I had no teaching experience—was a wonderful boost for students every now and again. But I was terrified at the invitation and told her I'd never taught before. With her usual wry wit she asked me, "Well, did you take class this week?" When I said yes, she responded, "Well then, you must know what to do." On that day I learned that I could, in fact, teach and that I even liked it. Perhaps my own memories of what it was like to be at that age, always trying to emulate more advanced dancers and at the same time trying to balance all of the *imbalances* of being a teen, fueled my desire to teach. Giving versus receiving corrections had its own rewards, especially when I saw the light bulb go off above their heads as they realized that what they had just learned could be readily implemented to improve their technique.

I learned a lot about teaching from Sydelle over the years, and thankfully, I managed not to ruin any of her students during my teaching "debut." She wrote me a lovely thank-you note, claiming I was a "perceptive and intuitive teacher." Although it would be years before I taught on a regular basis, I remembered that note and still have it. That in itself is a lesson: one of the best gifts a teacher can give is encouragement.

———————

ONCE TONY EMBARKED UPON his "leave of absence" from Boston Ballet, we both juggled our now-separate schedules, looking for ways to spend time together here and there. Some of those visits were arranged around a guest appearance somewhere, such as the Sarasota visit in January when we performed the pas de deux from *Le Corsaire* and *Stars and Stripes* with the Florida West Coast Symphony. Days later, in Palm Beach, we joined the eminent critic Walter Terry in a lecture/demonstration called "The Development of Dance in America." As far as these "runouts" were concerned,

Florida was a particular magnet for me both because it allowed me to see my parents and because it was exciting to see another part of the country where ballet was increasingly on the map. My parents would take a March trip to Florida each year when I was growing up, and I was blessed to be a part of those trips. It gave me an opportunity to study with many different teachers as we passed through various cities. Among the best was Thomas Armour in Miami, who trained many astute dancers and remembered me from year to year. He was always supportive and complimentary to a young student showing promise.

Regarding the development of ballet in Florida, in less than a decade, Miami City Ballet would appear on the scene. Today it's one of the biggest companies in the United States and highly respected in particular for its performances of the Balanchine repertoire—thanks to cofounder and former City Ballet principal Edward Villella, as well as his successor Lourdes Lopez, also a former NYCB star. Miami City Ballet is another example of the remarkable influence that Balanchine had, whether directly or indirectly, over the growth of ballet in America. Like everyone else, he worked like a dog when the genre was in its infancy here, choreographing everywhere and anywhere. As he and Lincoln Kirstein were building toward what became New York City Ballet, Balanchine also choreographed for the various touring troupes borne of the Ballets Russes enterprises, but he didn't limit his talents to the ballet scene. He made dances for Broadway, Hollywood, and even, famously, for the Ringling Bros. and Barnum & Bailey Circus. (It's always charming to imagine Balanchine putting the elephants through their paces.) Yes, he needed employment just like anyone else, but his incursions into all of those worlds helped to spread the gospel of ballet even before there were many homegrown companies.

Following in the footsteps of Virginia and her peers, who were among the first beneficiaries of Balanchine's inspiration or direct generosity, Villella was one of many NYCB disciples who continued the work of building or reshaping many American ballet companies. They're not NYCB clones. Although their repertoires are well stocked with Balanchine ballets, most have an individuality that reflects the stylistic imprint of that organization's artistic director and sometimes, as in the case of Miami City Ballet, the ethnic and cultural flavors of the company's home city.

There's a lot of geography to cover in a country this large, but ballet companies with ties to Balanchine are indeed widespread. The Dance Theatre of Harlem, however, is also based in New York City, but it was never seen as encroaching upon someone else's territory—indeed, the creation of DTH helped to address a major problem in U.S. ballet companies. Cofounded by former NYCB principal Arthur Mitchell and the ballet teacher Karel Shook, DTH's mission was primarily to provide opportunities for ballet dancers of color. Certainly in 1968, when the group launched, there were very, very few black or brown dancers up on the ballet stages; in 1977, Boston Ballet may have been ahead of most companies with three black dancers — principal dancer Augustus van Heerden and corps members Sheridan Heynes and Darryl Robinson — in its ranks. One would think that the numbers in major American ballet companies would have leapt up since then, but sadly they've only crept up. The numbers of Asian and Latino dancers in ballet companies, however, has increased more sharply. In '77, Stephanie Moy (Asian American) was rising in the company while Nicolas Pacaña (Filipino), a newer addition, would also quickly become a leading dancer. The optimistic view—boosted recently with the enormous attention that's been paid to the issue vis-à-vis the hugely popular American Ballet Theatre ballerina Misty Copeland—is that the ongoing, concerted efforts to right this wrong will ultimately balance the scales, but the progress sure has been slow.

Was Balanchine being purposely provocative when, years earlier in 1957, he cast the black Arthur Mitchell and the white Diana Adams in the central pas de deux of the premiere performance of his masterwork *Agon*? Another of his "leotard ballets," and another of his great collaborations with the composer Igor Stravinsky, *Agon* includes a duet in which the dancers seem to be engaged in a formal battle that tests both their physical strength and their emotional will. It's intensely intimate—the two twine and grapple with one another, though elegantly—and is frankly erotic, even by today's standards. Imagine the shock to some audience members in 1957 to see Mitchell manipulating Adams in one contortion after another, her crotch often directly opposite his face, or one of her legs wrapped around his torso.

Agon is a great ballet, but in all the years I danced with Boston Ballet, we never performed it, although it has since entered BB's repertoire. (However, we did get to see Jerilyn Dana dance it as her "swan song" when we went to

see her in Montreal!) Dance Theatre of Harlem meanwhile, whose founding was largely prompted by Mitchell's anguished frustration at Martin Lu-
ther King Jr.'s assassination, triumphed for decades. While offering dancers
of color the chance to perform the same repertoire that their white counterparts did, it also "proved" they had every right to do so. In recent years,
the company has endured crippling financial problems and has struggled to
survive. Yes, money woes are a familiar story in the ballet world, but given
DTH's historic relevance, it is one that is particularly painful.

———————

LIKE VIRGINIA, Balanchine had important partners who were crucial to
the enduring success of his empire. Perhaps the two most important figures from early on were the wealthy philanthropist/writer Lincoln Kirstein
and the dancer/choreographer Jerome Robbins, both native New Yorkers.
Kirstein and Balanchine met each other in Europe when both were still
young men, soon after Serge Diaghilev's sudden death had abruptly dis-
banded the Ballets Russes. Discovering that Balanchine had no definite
plans, Kirstein convinced him to come to ballet-neophyte America where
he could put his rich ballet heritage to work.

    Robbins, who began studying dance in high school, rose quickly within
the New York City dance scene, performing on Broadway as well as with
American Ballet Theatre. At Ballet Theatre, he created his first work for
a major company, *Fancy Free*, a cheeky yet ingenious frolic depicting three
sailors on shore leave. It became an instant hit and catapulted him; he and
composer Leonard Bernstein were quickly talked into creating an evening-
length Broadway musical out of *Fancy Free*. The result, *On the Town*, was
the first of many iconic musicals that Robbins choreographed; others included *The King and I*, *Fiddler on the Roof*, and perhaps most famously, the
groundbreaking *West Side Story*. Thus, like Balanchine, Robbins worked
in several spheres including Hollywood over his long career, but again, like
Mr. B, it was the ballet world he was most dedicated to. Though he started
out at Ballet Theatre, he laid his deepest roots at New York City Ballet.
Only a year or so after they'd founded New York City Ballet, Kirstein and
Balanchine asked Robbins to come onboard not only as a dancer but also as
associate artistic director. He stayed on, with a few interruptions here and

there, for the bulk of his career, his title eventually, like Balanchine's, simply "ballet master."

Robbins's eclectic training in modern dance and composition as well as in Spanish and Asian dance forms resulted in an overall artistic versatility, a unique choreographic style. In many of his works, dancers transition seamlessly between "formal" dance steps and everyday movements such as strolling and even skipping. Today, such pedestrianism is common in concert dance, but Robbins was noted early on for his successful blending of simplicity and stylization. As with missing out on *Agon*, I'm sorry to say that during my career, Boston Ballet only presented one Robbins ballet that we performed in 1977, but at least it was a hoot! His 1953 *Fanfare*, set to Benjamin Britten's *Young Person's Guide to the Orchestra*, is a giddy party of a dance, in which the performers, in costumes depicting the instrument they portray, represent the orchestra. As Laura Shapiro wrote in the *Boston Globe*, acquiring a Robbins ballet was "a major addition to the company's repertoire," adding, "It's playful and inventive but much more suitable for children than adults." Later, in a 1980 gala in Boston in which we also performed, Mikhail Baryshnikov and Gelsey Kirkland performed excerpts of Robbins's beautiful 1976 ballet *Other Dances*. I guess the next best thing to dancing in this sublime work set to equally sublime music by Frédéric Chopin was to have seen this legendary ballet duo perform it live.

Though we were "Robbins poor," we had amassed enough of a store of Agnes de Mille ballets to warrant an "Agnes de Mille Festival" in May 1977. In addition to *Fall River Legend*, *Rodeo*, and *Summer* (now subtitled *Death and the Maiden*), we performed her rollicking *Logger's Clog*, an abstract piece evoking the long-ago movements of Maine men rolling logs downriver. In his *New York Times* review of our de Mille program, Clive Barnes drew an interesting connection between her and Robbins. "Of all the true red-white-and-blue American choreographers," he wrote, "there are only two in captivity—Jerome Robbins and Agnes de Mille." Their contributions had also been publicly honored earlier with each receiving a *Dance Magazine* award, a prestigious honor that, according to the publication's website, recognizes "the outstanding men and women whose contributions have left a lasting impact on the dance world." The list of recipients over the years is heady, chock-full of great dancers, choreographers, teachers, writers, and directors.

The previous year, Virginia had been added to that illustrious "Who's Who" of the dance world, receiving a *Dance Magazine* award of her own. Even so, it was not a time to rest on laurels; those questions about where we hoped to go—and whether we could realistically get there—didn't go away. Robert Brickell, the general manager, heard the musings loud and clear. He put forward a rather bold five-year plan that included the possibility of a satellite home for the company, more touring, and debut performances in New York City. There was no doubt that the latter would incur financial losses, but no visiting company ever performs in New York with the hopes of making money. Brickell hoped to gain a national reputation by performing in New York, thereby raising awareness of the company with both the media and our Boston audience.

Brickell seemed to face a crossroads. If we stayed as we were, we risked the dancers being continually overworked, as we had developed an expansive repertoire but only had thirty dancers, which was quite modest when presenting full-length classics. Furthermore, our ticket sales were flat and even heading toward a decline. It was yet another nerve-racking time, because if we took the sharp curves that Brickell was steering us toward, we might fly, but we might also crash.

———————

ONE ASPECT OF Brickell's plans was for substantial improvements to our production of *The Nutcracker*. If Boston Ballet—like most companies that perform it—was going to continue to depend so heavily on the financial gains from the holiday ballet's success, Brickell knew it was more than time to polish it up. Although new costumes and sets were further down the road, some of the choreography had been revamped, with Virginia and Ron Cunningham sharing staging credits, and Sydney Leonard and Lorenzo Monreal listed under "additional choreography." Sydney—who had continued to manage her work as ballet mistress with the company, teacher in the school, and her full-time "outside" job with the *Atlantic Monthly*—was for many years responsible for the majority of the children's roles. An enormous task! But she somehow did it, whipping all of those kids into shape so they could hold their own onstage with the adults. I already admired the heck out of Sydney, but eventually, when I staged *The Nutcracker* for Georgia Deane's local company, the Greater Milford Ballet, my respect for her increased even more. I tried to channel at least some of her indomitable energy and organizational skills, and while my staging experience went just fine, I still marvel at how she did it all those years. And Georgia became yet another mentor who helped guide me into my next profession.

By the time *Nutcracker* season rolled around, Tony's name was "officially" back on the roster—no more asterisk next to his name indicating that he was on leave. Even though we were paired only once in that year's run (as Sugar Plum and Cavalier), it was fun to have him back on stage with me. And it was especially nice to have him back home in our Roslindale nest, just in time for Thanksgiving.

15

Tendu

Tendu. Origin: French. Stretched. In battement tendu, the dancer's working foot slides along the floor until it and the leg are fully extended. It's one of the first steps a ballet student learns, and as it is crucial to developing and maintaining the "line" of the legs in nearly everything a dancer executes, it's one of the most frequently repeated steps in daily class.

ART IS SUBJECTIVE," so goes the maxim. I will never figure out how one person could love a certain ballet while someone else could loathe it. And forget about balanced perspective if you are actually *dancing* in that ballet. Indeed, there were very few pieces that I thought were subpar when I was rehearsing and performing them; one is naturally dedicated to the process and thus deeply engaged with the material. Maybe that means that one has temporary blinders on, but I suppose that's a good thing for both the dancer and the audience. Any ballet after all, whether tepid or terrific, is made better when dancers are fully committed to it. But why the pendulum can sometimes swing both ways so dramatically is a mystery to me.

Remember how much I disliked working with Anna Sokolow when she set *Time + 6* on the company? Remember how I wished that Lorenzo's *Carmina Burana* had remained in the repertoire? In both cases audiences and critics felt differently; one writer described *Time* as "remarkable" while another called *Carmina* "vulgar." Polar-opposite opinions were often voiced about many aspects of the ballets. Around this time, for example, one critic said of the corps de ballet that "something has happened to the corps . . . [they] have become a finely honed unit," while another wrote that "many of the corps are still dancing at a student level." I wonder how much attention Virginia paid to the seesawing viewpoints; it couldn't have been easy to have her every move scrutinized, and it must have been particularly annoying to hear grumbling coming from within, as happens in every institution inevitably I suppose. And so another maxim comes to mind: you can't please all of the people all of the time.

Thankfully, many things the company did were widely embraced. Among the programmatic successes in 1978 were two ballets by outside choreographers, *Trio*, by Atlanta Ballet's associate director Tom Pazik, and *Aureole*, by the great modern dance choreographer Paul Taylor. *Trio*, which I performed with Gus van Heerden and Nicolas Pacaña, was a lovely piece set to a J. S. Bach concerto. *Trio* was one of those "dancey" ballets and a pleasure to do, as was *Aureole*, although disappointingly I wasn't cast in it, hard as I tried to be. I learned it along with everyone else and just loved working on it. I took it in stride though, cheerfully calling myself a "modern reject" and again noting that several of the dancers in the company had much more previous modern training than I. The cast—Rose, David Drummond, Larry Robertson, Ilene Strickler, and Leslie Woodies—were marvelous in it and deserved the kudos they received. I also wasn't cast in *Visions of the Dark Night*, the new work Sokolow made for the company that same year—but in that instance, given my earlier history with her, I wasn't disappointed and was relieved that I was needed in *Giselle* instead. Such castings contributed to my later being dubbed "Her Pinkness" by Donn Edwards as a cute way he and others consoled me for not being put in the more modern works. The joke was "oh, that's because they need her in the pink tutu piece."

Even though *Aureole* is a confirmed Taylor masterpiece today, it had its critics when he created it. The number of modern works in ballet companies had continued to increase since 1962, when Taylor made his dance, but in 1978, even a lyrical work such as *Aureole* was still somehow too "modern" for some viewers. Ballet dancers performing with bare (and sometimes flexed) feet was still enough of a novelty to be striking. Today, *Aureole* actually looks quite balletic, the women in feminine white dresses and the men in white tights, dancing in a stately manner to a Handel concerto. It's once again all about perspective, in this case the perspective of time. For the most part, however, the company's performances of *Aureole* were embraced, with one critic writing that she hoped we'd "dance it forever."

I did in fact wear the "pink tutu" quite a lot throughout 1978, though it wasn't usually pink and the length varied depending on what we were doing. ("Romantic" tutus fall all the way down to midcalf, while "Classical" tutus either droop gently down to midthigh or stick straight out from the hips.) Notwithstanding the Choreographers' Series in January, the *Aureole* performances in March, and the Sokolow work in May, it was another tradition-packed year for me and for the company. In addition to *Giselle*, I reprised lead female roles in *Swan Lake* (in a guest performance with the Erie Philharmonic in Pennsylvania), *Coppélia*, *Sleeping Beauty*, and *Les Sylphides*. Woytek Lowski was my partner for most of them, although Tony was Franz to my Swanhilda in one performance of *Coppélia*.

While Woytek and I had a wonderful dance partnership both technically and artistically for many years, it was also always special in a different way when Tony and I got to dance together. In the same way that I was a self-titled "modern reject," Tony was becoming more accepting of what roles he was better suited for and coming to grips with those that he wasn't. Sometimes artistic directors can pigeonhole a dancer as a type, as with Virginia originally thinking I couldn't be more than just a lyrical ballerina. But even the finest dancers are not excellent in everything. So Tony, whose physique and training made him a knockout in many of the more athletic, theatrical, and powerful roles, had to work hard to soften his technique for the classical roles.

Tony once told a reporter that he knew he wasn't "the prince" so it tickled us that in that one *Coppélia* show, we got a lot of attention. Laura Shapiro wrote that "the real substance of the ballet was provided by Laura Young and Tony Catanzaro." The photo ops were abundant—pictures of us as Swanhilda and Franz seemed to be everywhere, including smack in the middle of the montage on the front page of a splashy eight-page, full-color, fifteenth-season advertising insert the company put into some of the local papers. If Tony wasn't the "ideal" classical ballet prince, it was hardly seen as a detriment to most viewers. Comedic timing was paramount to both of us, and Tony had an innate sense for the pauses that amplified the others' reactions. The audience could actually see the thought process leading to the punch line.

Dancing with regular partners is usually a more fulfilling experience because the more two people dance together, the higher the level of nuance and detail is attained, and the freer you both feel during a performance. But it can also be hugely exciting and satisfying to dance with a new person, particularly if that person is of the quality of John Meehan, who guested with us in our 1978 revival of *Giselle*, while Woytek was on leave. Meehan, though a principal dancer with American Ballet Theatre, had not yet performed the role of Albrecht. It was thus my great honor to dance opposite him in his debut. He was spectacular as a partner, a true gentleman, caring. It sounds like a silly thing, but during one performance, I had forgotten to take a clip out of my hair, in advance preparation for my upcoming "mad scene." (Ballerinas performing as Giselle have to slip off stage prior to the mad scene and rearrange/loosen their hair so that it comes undone fairly easily during the mad scene.) So, during the act 1 waltz, John noticed what many others wouldn't have, caressed my cheek, put his hand around my head, and surreptitiously took the clip out. I was so grateful because I've seen performances when the dancer hadn't loosened her hair sufficiently—watching Giselle or her stage mother yanking at her hair definitely ruins the drama!

With Woytek as my Prince again, in November 1978 I made my own debut, this time in Ron Cunningham's production of *Cinderella*. And in December, of course, we danced lots and lots of *Nutcrackers* together in Boston. We even appeared in excerpts of the ballet on TV, in "Backstage at the *Nutcracker*," a behind-the-scenes special filmed by a local television station and narrated by Joan Kennedy, who had previously "guest starred" with us when she narrated Sam Kurkjian's *Peter and the Wolf*. It wasn't my first TV appearance; a few years back, Woytek and I had danced the *Nutcracker* pas for a New Year's Eve telecast at Symphony Hall with the ever-popular Arthur Fiedler and the Boston Pops.

Although we had had our own music director, Michel Sasson, for nearly a decade, Fiedler was such an ingrained part of this growing Boston tradition—Boston Ballet's *Nutcracker*—that he had continued to conduct some of the performances, and almost always on opening night. What a personality—I guess you could say he was lovably cranky. The hugely popular *Nutcracker* was such a perfect vehicle for him to fuel his burning passion to bring classical music to the general public and to make it "accessible" to all. Each year, on his special day, we celebrated his birthday at the end of the performance with a cake onstage, and audience members and dancers singing "Happy Birthday" to this Boston icon. His sense of humor was evident in many performances. While dancing Dew Drop in the "Waltz of the Flowers," I once looked down to see him conducting with a whisk broom. Susan Ring, our intrepid stage manager, finally discovered why the walnuts for the act 1 party scene kept mysteriously disappearing. They were actually being pilfered by Maestro as they were his favorites! Thereafter, walnuts were glued into the prop basket, while Sue made sure Fiedler had his own bag of walnuts on his dressing table at each performance. Problem solved—thanks Sue! Ever the sleuth and problem solver, we depended on Sue to keep things running smoothly both at home and on the many future tours here and abroad. We all came running when Sue would call, "Bus is ready." We knew we only had minutes to board. She always ran a tight ship—and had an admirably staunch sense of humor. She'd go around to the dressing rooms and collect our valuables to be put in the safe before she called us to the stage for "places." One night during a *Nutcracker* run some of the men in the corps de ballet left some festive but X-rated "gifts" for Sue to find in their dressing room. I will say no more, but suffice it to say that if any of those men are reading this, they're probably enjoying a hearty laugh at that memory. I know Sue will get a good chuckle too.

Our 1978 *Nutcracker* had much to celebrate—Robert Brickell's promise of new sets was fulfilled that year—but something to mourn as well. Maestro Fiedler's health had begun to fail that winter, and he was thus unable to help us kick off the season as usual; he died in July 1979. Fiedler's absence warranted comment from no less than Mayor Kevin White, speaking from onstage before the opening-night curtain.

Though the twenty-two mostly sold-out performances proved the ballet's popularity, for performers and everyone involved in the production, the inevitable tedium of repetition fostered good-natured grumblings. It was impossible to imagine that someday the schedule would hover around fifty shows per season. Even though it has one of the most beautiful scores in ballet, I was known to stop Christmas shopping and flee whenever "Waltz of the Flowers" blared over any department store's sound system. The critics—who only *had* to see it once—often began their *Nutcracker* reviews with their own mild expressions of boredom. Ah, human nature, but the good news is that the better part of those natures always triumphed: as corny as it sounds, once we got on stage, we were as swept up as anyone else in the "magic" of it all. And the critics? They often owned up to their own defenses melting away, to varying degrees of course, but most of them confessed to moments of pleasure.

But what a shot in the arm the new sets proved to be. There were few, if any, dissenting opinions about the sets: everyone seemed thrilled. "Magnificent," "splendid," and "spectacular" were among the critics' compliments about the predominantly blue-hued backdrops and sets (Virginia's favorite color was blue). Created by the highly respected design team of Helen Pond and Herbert Senn, the sets were not only visually stunning but also dependable. Whenever the Christmas tree in the old set had to "grow," it groaned and swayed and got caught on itself, only to drop precipitously as it untangled. It made people both on and off the stage genuinely nervous. Pond and Senn, who for many years worked closely with Sarah Caldwell, designing dozens of sets for her Opera Company of Boston, were particular about what they'd work on. Boston Ballet was the only ballet company they'd agreed to work for when they created sets for our premiere of *Giselle* a decade earlier.

An important aspect of Pond's and Senn's design was that the set would not only last—the $150,000 price tag was a hefty investment for the company in 1978—but also still work if, and when, the Music Hall stage was renovated. After struggling to find and keep a proper and affordable performance venue in our early years, the Music Hall, where we'd been performing since 1970, was not perfect but at least provided us with a stable base. Originally called the Metropolitan Theatre, the Music Hall was in a decent location in the theater district and therefore a fairly short distance from our South End studios. For a ballet company though, it had some drawbacks. There was a sixty-foot proscenium arch and a very shallow depth, and the house was sometimes wiltingly described as "barn-like." The 4,200 seats were twice, maybe even thrice, too many to fill for most of our productions aside from *Nutcracker*.

The biggest negative was the stage, which was much too small for the scale of the company, particularly when we were presenting large productions. In countless articles, writers commented morosely or sarcastically on this obvious handicap. In her review of *Coppélia*, Laura Shapiro, referring to the large sets and voluminous costumes of that ballet and others like it, wrote, "Whenever the Boston Ballet turns to the nineteenth century, we learn anew that not very many peasants can dance on the head of a pin, which is about the size of the Music Hall stage once it's been hung about with cottage fronts and taverns and clusters of merry townsfolk." In addition, there was an old trap door a foot square, smack dab on center, that contained many depressions. Although rarely used, there it was. In executing traveling fouettés, we had to jump over it, halfway down the diagonal! Keeping the trap door in your peripheral vision was key to pulling it off.

Tackling the size issue was yet another of the big plans on Brickell's recent "must-do" list, although it would be two years before we were able to really stretch our wings fully, to soar and fly across our home stage freely.

THAT *NUTCRACKER* SEASON was not a happy one for Tony. Because the Choreographers' Series was right around the corner, we were in rehearsals for that during the holiday run. The series had become a much bigger deal, with choreographers from around the world vying for a spot on the program. Tom Pazik had double-cast two couples for his new ballet *Tzigane*—Tony with Rose and Larry Robertson with me. There was a good deal of tricky partnering; our entrance alone involved the male running all the way in from the wings to center stage, while carrying the female up on one uplifted hand, her legs reaching in two directions.

One day when Larry was performing elsewhere, Virginia asked me to rehearse with Tony instead, which was fine with us. We really should have marked out some of the really elaborate lifts beforehand, but I leapt toward him in a grand jeté that turned into a partnered cartwheel, and as we went into the lift, I jumped with too much vigor and he propelled me upward to the point that I completely left his grip and was sailing behind him. Good partner that he was, he twisted to catch me and bring me back down safely. If he hadn't done that, I may well have broken my neck. We didn't know it immediately, but soon after learned that that catch had caused a couple of discs in his back to shatter. So he returned to New York—but this time for surgery—and he was out for the *Nutcracker* run as well as the spring season.

Apparently, this incident convinced Virginia and others that it was time for Boston Ballet to partner with the sports-medicine unit at Boston Children's Hospital. Over time, this developed into what is now a very important relationship. The company has in-house physical therapists from the Children's staff who work with company dancers in everything from day-to-day aches and minor injuries to emergencies and postinjury or postsurgery recovery. They are simply wonderful, caring and knowledgeable. Under Dr. Lyle Micheli's direction, dance medicine at Boston Children's Hospital has become world class. Micheli himself is seen as a minor God in the Boston dance community; though there are now several trustworthy surgeons with whom dancers will trust their joints and tendons, he was the original "dance injury whisperer."

———

SO, WHICH CAME FIRST in America, the popularity of *The Nutcracker* or the popularity of ballet in general? In some ways, because the dance or ballet boom of the late 1960s through the 1970s ran parallel to the middle of my own career, it's hard for me to have the clearest perspective. I certainly could see how we'd grown from a ragtag bunch of teenagers—racing from school to get to class and rehearsals, and performing in runouts in countless nondance venues all across New England—into a professional ballet company full of fine, mature dancers. The runouts we did now and again were nothing compared to the traveling of the generations of dancers that came before us, who were constantly on the road because permanent ballet companies were virtually nonexistent.

Now, in addition to the big companies in New York and San Francisco, as well as the companies in Boston, Pennsylvania, and Houston, there were a growing number of small- to midsized companies. These were the new generation of "regional" companies, but that term no longer meant quite what it had. With more companies spread all around, the necessity for travel had greatly diminished for dancers and audiences alike. Most of those companies, regardless of their size or artistic level, learned not only that could they present their own *Nutcrackers* but also that they should. The ballet's popularity had exploded in the decades since San Francisco presented the first full-length version in 1944, so much so that it is often referred to as a company's "bread and butter," as it ensures ticket sales that constitute a large portion of an organization's annual income.

Then again, when London's Sadler's Wells Ballet came to New York City in 1949, the performances of Margot Fonteyn generated wild excitement with the kind of star-struck wonder usually reserved for movie stars. The adulation was about the heightened prowess of these individual artists, no doubt, but interest in ballet itself had also begun to increase. On TV, ballet had been one of the "acts" that Ed Sullivan occasionally featured on his popular show, and in the mid-1970s, the new PBS series *Dance in America* began airing performances of top-notch ballet and modern companies and dancers.

Meanwhile, two major films about ballet came out in 1977: *The Turning Point* and *The Children of Theatre Street*. The first, a story about a young ballet dancer who makes it big in a fictionalized company, was based fairly obviously on American Ballet Theatre. It starred Mikhail Baryshnikov and Leslie Browne, who, just like her character, was at the time a relative unknown and went on to become a principal with ABT. The film was directed by choreographer Herbert Ross, who was married to former ABT and NYCB ballerina Nora Kaye. Though sometimes campy and rife with stereotypes about "temperamental divas," *The Turning Point* got some of the most important things right. The majority of the roles were cast with professional dancers, many of them among the biggest stars of the day; thus the class, rehearsal, and performance clips were glorious. My only quibble was that, while decidedly a comic sequence, no self-respecting mentor would push a clearly drunk corps de ballet member out onto a stage. Better to have a hole in the formation than the total chaos that would assuredly ensue.

While most of the footage in the documentary *The Children of Theatre Street* involved children, they were students of St. Petersburg's venerated Kirov School, which had trained so many of the great Russian dancers, and thus this film also showed exceptional dancing. Naturally, we were impressed by the rigor of the training, but there were some scenes that made us glad we hadn't been born in Russia; director Robert Dornhelm didn't shy away from some of the harsher—especially to American sensibilities—

aspects of the school. A group of girls, maybe nine years old, who were filmed while auditioning for one of the precious few spots, were naked except for briefs. Their bodies were pulled and prodded into various stretches and positions so that the panel of judges (male and female) sitting at a table could see if they looked pliable enough. Still, being able to see "inside" the legendary academy where Baryshnikov, Natalia Makarova, and Rudolf Nureyev came from, and then being able to see the legends themselves performing live, was a unique, even mind-blowing, new experience for audiences.

All of this meant that more people, newly curious about ballet, were going to see ballet, and it also meant more children studying ballet, hoping to become the next Fonteyn or Nureyev. So, the perfect storm that is *The Nutcracker* gained force. With so many children in the schools, companies could cast large numbers of them in such a ballet. In turn—as savvy directors and general managers know—more children on stage means more ticket sales beyond those sold to ballet fans among the general public. The mothers, fathers, siblings, aunts, uncles, and grandparents of those performing children were certainly going to want to see them up on stage every time they were scheduled to perform. Within this bottom-line reality is probably where the seed of a lot of the *Nutcracker* grousing lies. Performing the same ballet over and over, year after year, can result in some ho-hum moments. But the very ubiquitousness of the ballet, with another version of it being advertised around every corner, has also led to what many call the "commercialization" of it. And when a production crosses the line from sweet to syrupy, there go the rolled eyes, mine included. It's a shame though, because it is simply a lovely ballet, and indeed, many productions continue to be just that. So I'd like to think that the majority of the American obsession of *The Nutcracker*—like the whole dance boom—all starts with the art form itself, the dancers, and their glorious dancing.

After all, the American modern dance scene was "booming" too, and *it* didn't have a *Nutcracker*—nor, at the time, scores of children chomping at the bit to study modern dance. Today there are some modern dance *Nutcracker* spoofs or spinoffs, naturally, but even something such as Mark Morris's funny *The Hard Nut* is finally a celebration of the ballet rather than a condemnation of it. Locally, modern choreographers and dance companies were gaining ground. In the late 1970s, choreographers such as Martha

Armstrong Gray, Dawn Kramer, Susan Rose, Marcus Schulkind, Beth Soll, and Deborah Wolf were among those at the forefront. They were presenting their works in solo concerts or in newly formed companies, mostly in Boston and Cambridge, its sister city across the Charles River. And like Sam Kurkjian's Boston Repertory Ballet, several chamber-size ballet companies also began to emerge in the area around this time; most of the founders had had some connection to Boston Ballet. Clearly, the local dance audience was growing too.

IN TERMS OF "bread and butter" though, not even *The Nutcracker* can keep a company budget fully funded. Fundraising by the board of directors and the Boston Ballet Society continued as always. There were opening-night galas, champagne receptions, and all kinds of events designed to entice donors to write checks. The society even managed to secure Princess Grace of Monaco—who was in town in part to promote the local premiere of *The Children of Theatre Street*, which she had narrated—to attend one such fundraiser. We dancers were often invited, particularly to the postperformance parties, because naturally many ballet patrons wanted the chance to meet and hobnob with their favorite dancers. We often called it the "fourth act" because we knew we still had to be "on" in a certain sense. In some ways, it was glamorous and fun and, of course, exhilarating, to get such wonderful feedback immediately following a show, before the reviews came out. And dancers are always starving after a performance, so even those like me who were a little socially shy were perfectly happy to feast on the fancy food being offered. Fairly quickly, though, exhaustion would overcome our elation. No matter what character we had portrayed on stage that evening, by then we were back to being mere mortals. Our feet hurt!

16

Tour en l'Air

Tour en l'air. Origin: French. Turn in the air. In a tour en l'air the dancer pushes off from a stationary position and executes one or more revolutions with the legs lengthened and pressed together. In the traditional repertoire, this step is almost always performed by men.

ONE OF MY FAVORITE pastimes over the years, and especially once I had a little backyard, has been gardening. And one of the most important things I've learned from gardening is that plants will grow according to the space given them. In 1979, Boston Ballet took the bold step of spreading its roots onto the international stage. In July, the company would embark on the first of what would become several tours abroad—but before that, we brought the world to Boston.

Now that the annual Choreographers' "Showcase/Series" had become a "Competition" with a top prize of five thousand dollars, Boston Ballet received a lot of attention from the press and also from the dance world. Ballet competitions had been gaining in popularity in the prior fifteen years, but these were mostly geared toward individual performance. Not surprisingly, Russian dancers dominated many of the early events, such as the first one held in Varna, Bulgaria, in 1964. That International Ballet Competition is considered to be one of the most prestigious to this day. Many of us were ambivalent about participating; for one thing, the cost was prohibitive unless one had a sponsor, as most, if not all of the competitions, were abroad. Secondly, it begs the question, can dance be judged? Should it be? Fortunately, I was of the generation who didn't "have to" compete in that arena as we were already deemed professionals. Over time however, competitions have grown to be seen by many as important for a ballet dancer's résumé, and indeed, the ballet competition industry has grown enormously, with many highly publicized events held around the world.

But it was not typical for competitions to be centered on choreography then, so the applications poured in from near and far. Virginia and the artistic staff had more than 250 videotape entries to sort through, finally winnowing the finalists down to seven who were each brought in for several weeks to set a new work for the company. However, like the competitions for ballet dancers themselves, the same question arises: can and should one ballet be judged against another? Boston Ballet's experiment proved to be a fairly friendly experience for the visitors. Tom Pazik, the only choreographer who'd previously created works on the company, told the *Wall Street Journal*'s Peter J. Rosenwald, "We all reached a point quite early on when we realized that we weren't competing against each other but only against ourselves," while Bruce Wells, a former dancer with NYCB, put it more bluntly: "Ballets can't compete with each other like teams in a football league."

While none of the finalists were female, the three judges were all women: dance critic P. W. Manchester; Royal Danish Ballet associate director Kirsten Ralov; and choreographer Anna Sokolow, who of course was already familiar with the company from her previous residencies. We'd also briefly worked with Ralov the previous summer to begin preliminary preparations for the company's premiere of August Bournonville's *Wednesday's Class*, which was scheduled to premiere later that year.

That January was particularly intense as we dove into rehearsals with the visiting choreographers, right on the heels of a *Nutcracker*-filled December. There were a few injuries, resulting in last-minute cast changes and, as needed, choreographic changes. I was in two ballets, Wells's *Violin Concerto*, a lyrical, abstract work set to the first movement of Tchaikovsky's famous concerto, and Stuart Sebastian's *Accident*, in which I played a woman who quarrels with her lover right before the lover dies unexpectedly—due to an inadvertent push from me! Wells's piece, with its Balanchine-inflected ballet vocabulary, was more universally well received than Sebastian's, which drew mixed responses. Some viewers appreciated *The Accident*'s drama while others found it melodramatic.

At a glamorous after-party on opening night, critic Walter Terry announced the panel's choice, presenting the award to Constantin Patsalas, a young Greek dancer and choreographer with the National Ballet of Canada. His *Piano Concerto*, titled after Alberto Ginastera's composition, was abstract and marked by a more contemporary vocabulary. Elaine, her husband David, Gus, and Carinne Binda garnered acclaim for their leading roles in that piece. When he accepted the award, Patsalas singled out Elaine, calling her an inspiration.

Nicolas Pacaña also earned kudos for his work throughout the program. Together we received praise for our partnership in Wells's *Violin Concerto*; Nicolas became one of my most frequent partners during this time, as a serious hip injury began sidelining Woytek. By the end of 1979, Woytek retired from the stage and left the company to become ballet master with ABT and, later, the English National Ballet. He was an extraordinary coach and teacher, from whom I learned a great deal. Thank you, Woytek.

Although the company, as expected, lost money on the endeavor and though few of the critics raved about any of the ballets themselves, the overall consensus was that Boston Ballet had taken both a big risk and a big step forward by showing it could hold up just fine to the widespread scrutiny the competition drew.

But to my mind, the best thing we got out of that competition was Bruce Wells. By the beginning of the next season he was on the company roster in two capacities, as a principal dancer and as a resident choreographer alongside Ron Cunningham. Bruce's performing career was nearly over, but Virginia wisely guessed that his choreographic gifts could serve the company well, and this proved to be so for years to come. Working with Bruce was always a pleasure, and I learned very quickly to keep my mind focused during rehearsals. The better choreographers will always take information from the dancers in the creative process, whether it's ultimately utilized or not. Bruce would often say something like, "Oh, I like that!" or "That's really nice! Keep that in!" during a rehearsal, and I'd gulp and hope I remembered what I'd just done. But it was part of the fun, to be challenged to figure out how to actually re-create something you'd just kind of tossed off. In later years, Bruce served as interim artistic director and then associate artistic director during Bruce Marks's directorship. Best of all was the lifelong friendship that Bruce and I began developing then and continue to enjoy today.

————————

OUR SEASON FOLLOWING the Choreographers' Competition was richer with Balanchine ballets than it had been in the past few years, so preparations for our upcoming European debut were intense because we were due to perform an all-Balanchine program. Aside from *The Sleeping Beauty* (marking the fourth consecutive year we presented it), the Boston series was composed of repertory programs, each anchored by one or two Balanchine ballets. None were company premieres, but they were all amongst Mr. B's finest: *The Four Temperaments*, *Serenade*, and *Symphony in C*. The company also performed a revival of Léonide Massine's colorful romp *Gaîté Parisienne*, Tom Pazik's *Trio*, Ron's new ballet *Cuibono?*, and Bournonville's *Wednesday's Class*. The last three, along with *Serenade*, made up the program we brought to the Ocean State Performing Arts Center, in Providence, Rhode Island, in May. This was the first phase of the ambitious plan to create a second "home" for the company. In addition to the idea that each Boston series would first be presented in Providence as a way for us to better prepare for our home performances, we'd also be developing a larger audience base. Almost immediately, however, the low viewer turnout put a damper on the idea, and although we went back once or twice per year for the next couple of years, it never took hold as hoped. For me, that very first visit to Providence was not a happy one: *Wednesday's Class* almost became my swan song with Boston Ballet.

While companies around the world perform the masterworks of choreographers such as Balanchine, Petipa, and Bournonville, they rarely perform them with the same stylistic specificity of the original cast. Nor are they expected to. One cannot absorb, for example, all of the nuances of a Balanchine-trained dancer in just a few weeks of rehearsal. The spirit of the choreography will be well presented of course, but it won't always be, in a word, "pure." This is why it's crucial that experts are engaged to come and stage certain ballets and then coach the dancers further. Good stagers ensure that a certain amount of the desired style is imprinted on each group of dancers they work with. After the wonderful experience we'd had years earlier when the Royal Danish Ballet's Hans Brenaa came to work with us on Bournonville's *Napoli*, we were in for a rude awakening when it came to rehearsing *Wednesday's Class*.

In order to preserve the specifics of the Bournonville style, his successors developed a Monday–Saturday series of classes. The classes were designed not only to teach students in the Royal Danish Ballet (RDB) academy but also to keep the company dancers properly conditioned and always ready to perform the Bournonville repertoire with authority. The title *Wednesday's Class* simply refers to the midweek class that RDB's Kirsten Ralov mined to create a condensed version as a performance piece. Ralov, who had served as one of the judges for the Choreographers' Competition, and her husband Fredbjørn Bjørnsson staged it on us, and we were the first American company to perform it.

But we weren't given that all-important coaching; we'd come for our daily technique class in the morning but were instead given the "Wednesday" Bournonville class. No insights were offered on how to accomplish the niceties or devilish intricacies in the technique; we just did the class, over and over again. I found myself struggling with quite a bit of the technical particulars but was left more or less on my own, to sink or swim. The longer I went without instructive corrections, the worse I got, the more demoralized I became, and the more my blood boiled.

Some people believe in the stereotype that ballet dancers are temperamental divas. In all of my years in the business, I can honestly say that the majority of people I worked with were absolute professionals. Of course one is sensitive about the work, and it can be frustrating, even upsetting, to struggle with a particular step or phrase or even a whole ballet. After all, your body is the instrument; your very being must interpret and project the artistry within the dance—thus, if something isn't working, it's personal. However, most of us know how to balance the personal with the professional. But we are human, and well, you know what they say about pride and falls. In the weeks leading up to the premiere, I wobbled and teetered my way through *Wednesday's Class* and continued to do so right up until our dress rehearsal in Providence. There I was, struggling like mad, and though I kept trying, I kept falling out of one thing and then another. From the back of the theater, I heard Virginia yell, "Laurie, pull yourself together!" Reverting to my thirteen-year-old name certainly tweaked a nerve, and her tone just did it for me. I stopped, looked out into the house, and said, "Virginia, I *am* trying." After a pause and a deep breath, I blurted, "As a matter of fact, I'm *done* trying," and I walked off. Back in the dressing room, I packed up, got in the car, and went home, not caring if it meant I was fired.

Sure, that could sound like a "diva" reaction, but I was not going to go out in front of an audience and make a fool of myself. Tony, whom I called as soon as I got home, saved me from that embarrassing fate—as well as the much worse one of losing my job. When he picked up the phone, I said, "Tony, I just a pulled a 'Tony.'" He was still in New York, rehabilitating from his disc surgery, but he knew this was serious. This was so unlike me that he called Virginia and then drove up and worked with me the next day. He had a very good eye and was a very good coach; the fact that he was a modern-turned-ballet dancer gave him keen insights into what was needed, and he was able to get it across to me so I could accomplish the choreography. As they say, the show must go on, and it did, including me on opening night in Providence without any wobbling. Thanks, Tony.

———————

WITHIN TWO MONTHS we were across the ocean, outside of Genoa, Italy, opening the Nervi Festival. That *Wednesday's Class* experience, which at the time had felt like a real career crisis, melted away, replaced by a truly poetic career-affirming moment. We danced on an outdoor stage surrounded by pine trees, and as our performances coincided with the full moon, *Scotch Symphony* looked particularly romantic. To top it off, we could hear the gentle swish of the ocean behind us in the background. However, it was a wee bit treacherous—those enormous pine trees dropped their long needles all over the stage. Women would come out with their broomsticks in between every ballet and sweep the needles off the stage, and a whole new set would fall during the next ballet, so that by the end of each one, it was as if we were doing an impromptu loggers' jig! But it was simply gorgeous, and we were blown away to be dancing in such a venue.

Even while we were preparing for this exciting first for the company, there were whispers about bigger doings: the possibility of a tour to China, as well as some kind of change or addition to the top artistic level. There was speculation that perhaps, for the first time in the company's history, Virginia would "officially" share the artistic leadership. There was naturally much talk—some rumors and some facts—about who was being considered. Peter Martins, the Danish-born New York City Ballet star who had guested at Boston Ballet with Suzanne Farrell a decade ago, was one of the early possibilities. That didn't pan out, but within two years Martins was given the first of his leadership roles within City Ballet, and he's been the sole artistic leader of that company since 1990.

Soon though it seemed clear that Violette Verdy, another NYCB-related dancer who had also guested with us many times, was at the top of the list of candidates. In 1977 the elegant French ballerina retired from Mr. B's company to take on the directorship of the renowned Paris Opera Ballet, the first female to do so in its centuries-old history. Early on, however, difficulties between Verdy and the famously political opera began to materialize. Boston Ballet's board and administration were serious about pushing the company to a higher level and were only too happy to cast a line and try to lure Violette to Boston. Among the administrative leaders now were Michael Judson, as general manager and president, and Maryellen Cabot, the chairwoman of the board. A month after we returned from Italy, they had their catch: the *New York Times* reported that Verdy had "been named associate artistic director of the Boston Ballet" and would join the company the following year.

It was a big announcement, but we had little time to digest it. After barreling through another busy fall and *Nutcracker* season, we rounded the corner into 1980, which began "as usual" before becoming one of the company's most extraordinary years ever and since.

———

AMIDST THAT YEAR'S Choreographers' Competition and seasons in Providence and Boston, the company began preparing for its second international tour, which had blossomed into a major undertaking. The rumors from last year were true: we were going to China, the first American ballet company to perform there, post-Cultural Revolution. With stops in Peking

(Beijing), Shanghai, and Canton (Guangzhou), the tour would also include Hong Kong, Israel, Italy, and France. In contrast, our one-stop European debut the previous year was like dipping a toe into the touring experience. Now we were leaping into the deep end.

Ma and Dad decided to jump in the pool too and traveled with us to China, where Dad jumped, quite literally. He had had a partial knee replacement in 1979 and was very leery of any twisting motions. Walking past the koi pond in the Beijing Hotel, he lost his balance and instead of twisting to gain his footing, he did a dancer-like move, allowing himself to drop and roll—unfortunately, right into the koi pond. It was a most embarrassing moment for him but a cause for much affectionate mirth within the company; some of the younger men had come to calling him "Dad," and he responded to their jokes with reciprocal humor to his "sons."

Ma had always been very interested in China, and when they got married, Dad told her that one day he'd take her there. He'd always wondered if it had been an empty promise, but when the tour was announced he asked if I'd mind and did I think the ballet would approve of them following us around the world. The Boston Ballet Board approved heartily, so they went to China with us, where they celebrated their fortieth wedding anniversary. Their presence made this incredible experience even more special; it was lovely to have my parents there. Although Tony had recently returned to performing following his back surgery, there was a sense that it might be too risky for him to be so far from his doctors for so long. So we'd be separated again for nearly three months, and this time I was the one leaving the nest. "How do I feel about it?" I responded to Gwen Ifill—the now deceased cohost of the PBS *NewsHour* show—"Not terrific."

Our personal disappointment was not the only cloud on the horizon. For all the excitement the tour generated, there was a good deal of grumbling along the lines of why one of the more prominent American companies—ABT, NYCB, or Joffrey—weren't chosen to go on this prominent trip. Among the local critics, Christine Temin's long *Boston Globe* article titled "The Road to China"—in which she enumerated many reasons she thought Boston Ballet was ill suited for the upcoming tour—was seen as shockingly hostile. In another article, Elizabeth Varady summed up the main complaints, writing that "in the past few weeks" since the announcement, "feathers have been ruffled . . . and the troupe's reputation within the dance community has been bruised."

Naturally the hurt feelings went both ways; although in time the negativity was smoothed over, Boston critics were noticeably absent on the tour. Clive Barnes ended up "embedding" with us; in one of his *New York Post* dispatches he wrote of our opening performances that he had "never seen [the company] look so proud, so confident and so willing," further declaring that "the Boston Ballet is the right company at the right time" to appear in China.

Along with the doubters' questions of whether we were up to the task were concerns about how the funds were to be raised. It was estimated that the tour would cost $350,000. Because the China trip was not organized through the Chinese government or through our own State Department, the company was on the hook for the majority of the hefty costs. The invitation had come about largely via board chairwoman Maryellen Cabot's private connections, and there was a dedicated core determined to see this through. Among our staunch supporters were Tom and Anneliese Henderson, a couple whose indefatigable love for Boston Ballet lasted for decades and decades; they served in many capacities over the years, often as supernumeraries in *Don Q* or *Sleeping Beauty*. At the time, Anneliese was a trustee as well as the president of the Ballet Society, the all-important group of volunteers who worked tirelessly not only to raise money but also to educate audiences about the company and about ballet in general. Over time, the society's newsletters and Performance Preview publications became top notch, both well researched and well written. One of the society's China-tour fundraisers was a swanky and fun "dance-a-thon" held at the Park Plaza Hotel in March, made even swankier by the appearance of the dancer and film star Cyd Charisse.

Well, by hook or by crook, we made it to China and happily rose above our detractors' skepticism: I am proud to say that we triumphed, both on and off the stage. The repertory, apparently chosen to please the Communist government, was simple, "safe": two comic fairy tales, Ron Cunningham's *Cinderella* and Bruce Wells's *La Fille Mal Gardée*, coupled with Paul Taylor's *Aureole*. In Peking, on the tour's opening night, June 3, 1980, Gus and I were the leads in *Cinderella*. We'd all been "warned" that the

Chinese audiences didn't usually applaud, and at first it was rather quiet in the pauses; depending on one's perspective, you could either hear a pin or your own heart drop with the silence. But gradually the audience began clapping, and it caught on. At the end of the performance we received a standing ovation, which was a highly unusual occurrence.

Two nights later, Durine Alinova and David Brown danced the leads in a televised performance on Chinese national television, seen by millions of viewers. We were treated like stars both in the theater and out. On the street, people excitedly recognized us from the advertisements and rushed to greet us. On the evening of our dress rehearsal, we were feted afterward at the famous Great Hall of the People in Tiananmen Square, and like the subsequent opening-night receptions in Shanghai and Beijing, it was a huge event. There were over twenty courses served, and with someone from the Ministry of Culture always seated at each table, it felt essential to international relations that we sample everything! Lo and behold, although I hadn't really liked the cuisine before, I became a fan of Chinese food, finally getting the chance to eat authentic, rather than "American-style," dishes. But occasionally spiciness trumped deliciousness. The Hendersons had—but of course—come on the tour, and Tom was quickly found out to be the "food thermometer" of the group. You could see him turning red with his eyes watering and barely able to speak, when he'd sputter out a strangled whisper, "Don't eat that black pepper."

On my own I figured out what I couldn't—or shouldn't—drink. In Beijing we were given some innocent plum wine for a toast at the beginning of the reception, but then they served us Mao Tai, which may as well have been Chinese gasoline as far as I was concerned. At the time, drinking white wine and hard alcohol affected my joints, so I usually avoided those spirits. But it felt impolite to refuse a toast, so, good ambassadress that I was, I gulped down the first one and, for a second or two, thought I was going to die. Thus, each time my glass was refilled, I yelled "gan bei!" with everyone else, then flipped the contents of my glass into a conveniently placed potted plant behind me and, as was the custom to prove that one had indeed downed its contents, turned the glass upside down on the table. Although I made it through the evening unscathed, I'm pretty sure that plant didn't!

The culinary adventures were dwarfed by the enormity of the larger experience. Along with the undeniable thrill of walking and, of course, leaping, along the Great Wall were quieter but equally memorable moments. The first morning, after awaking at the ungodly hour of 4:00 a.m. due to jet lag, I found myself doing Tai Chi right there in Tiananmen Square, alongside countless strangers, who had hung their birdcages in trees next to them for morning exercises. Those beautiful aspects of the culture offset the sobering ones that were constant reminders of the Communist regime. Although we were thoughtful about what we wore, avoiding bright colors, we couldn't help but stick out in that sea of blue "Mao" suits. And while we were also conscious of our behavior, making sure not to take photographs of anything "sensitive," we had chaperones almost everywhere we went.

It was so humid when we arrived in Canton that the walls in the theater we were performing in were literally dripping. Naturally, we figured the best way to deal with the heat and humidity was to rehearse in shorts, tube tops, and just a little pair of socks in our pointe shoes, instead of tights. That worked until halfway through our warm-up class when the air conditioners kicked on. Within fifteen minutes the sweating walls were dry and we were covered with every piece of wool clothing we had with us! Later on, during the tour in France, we dealt once again with temperature extremes; when performing on an outdoor stage in Arles one night, it was cold enough that we had to wear leg warmers during the performance. Even so, both of my calves seized during the first act; it was a struggle to get up on pointe and then I couldn't get down either! Up until then, our union contracts did not have any language about weather conditions, but after that tour, you bet we had a minimum/maximum temperature clause put in place.

We'd flown from one location to the next within the People's Republic of China, but we took a train from Canton into Kowloon/Hong Kong, several hours' journey. After traveling through some obviously impoverished regions, we rounded a bend and came upon the sudden cosmopolitanism of Hong Kong; talk about culture shock! It was like going to Las Vegas after being on a farm. In order to exit the PRC, one had to be physically able to walk across the border. Many in the company were now starting to come down with a debilitating virus, probably something like Norovirus. Mr. Wells, seemingly at death's door for much of the train ride, needed some assistance to actually be able to cross into Hong Kong. Fellow dancer

Pam Royal and I, pretending to be partying with Bruce, gamely crossed as a ménage à trois, me on demi-pointe under his armpit, and Pam, who was five to six inches taller than I was, propping him up on her side. Together, we improvised a choreographic turn and settled Bruce into the nearest chair.

Yes, along with the wonderful life experiences you gather while on tour are the practical ones, such as never send your laundry out while on tour. We learned that lesson while in Israel, our next stop after Hong Kong. After weeks of doing our laundry in the shower, we were told to let the hotel in Tel Aviv take care of our laundry. We happily handed it over, and when it came back, it was all blue—our tights, our underwear, everything—blue. And that "service" had cost us each a week's pay. Getting to Tel Aviv was quite a circuitous path due to the hostage crisis in Tehran, since we could not fly through Iran and could not enter Israel from Abu Dhabi, where we had to go to refuel from Singapore. Athens was the only way for us to get there, so we had the silver lining of a day and a half to visit the antiquities there. Were we rested enough to do that? Definitely not, I'm afraid, but we did it anyway.

On the day of opening night in Tel Aviv, when I went in to rehearse, I was appalled to find company member Nancy Parsons sitting on a bench, white as a sheet and sick as a dog. I knew that I was going to need a rehearsal to go into her place in the *Swan Lake* corps, since I was the last one standing who wasn't already dancing. I had not danced in the corps for almost twenty years, but most of the choreography was unchanged. Needless to say, with only a one-hour rehearsal, I was occasionally a little lost. The steps came back as the music played. The only difference was the arms in one section we called the "wash." They had only been slightly changed, but of course, that old muscle memory took over and the arms of one member of the corps (mine) shot up while everyone else's stayed low. At one point during the pas de deux, I was down on the floor folded over in one of the "swan positions," and with my head on my wrist, I realized, "Damn! I don't know when to get up." But I realized we were in two diagonals, and as I could see the others behind me, I figured that when I saw them move, I'd follow. Suddenly I heard Linda Bass behind me hiss, "Psst. Get up!" What I hadn't known was that I was supposed to stand two counts before everyone moved. Thankful that at least I was on center, I stood up as gracefully and hopefully as unobtrusively as I could and walked to the next tableau, ending up, hilariously, opposite five-foot-eight Pamela Royal. We made the quick, mute decision to make this formation—in which we were all supposed to stand and pose on one leg, our standing foot flat—as visually appealing as possible. Pam thus posed in demi-plié, while I stood my five-foot-two frame on demi-pointe, both of us maintaining placid faces, as if nothing was amiss.

The last six weeks of the tour after Israel we mainly traveled by bus and truck. As you can imagine, traveling for any length of time this way is not the most comfortable, but it did allow us to see our ever-changing surroundings. And as you are in such close and constant interaction with others, it's often a powerful bonding experience. This was certainly true with our group, which already was a pretty close-knit family. Our deepened ties surely helped keep us together as we traveled along Boston Ballet's own ever-changing territory.

17

Rudi, Rudi, Rudi

N O TIME TO REST for the weary—that became our mantra when we returned from our tour, triumphant but tired. Soon after stepping foot back in Boston, it was time to turn our focus toward a new adventure: New York City. For visiting companies, performing at this mecca of the dance world is daunting, especially the first time. Whether real or imagined, there is a belief that the Big Apple critics and audiences are the toughest in the world. A poor reception in New York City more than stings: such a public thrashing can negatively affect future funding, and it can even affect how one's hometown sees you afterward. But a kind of catch-22 exists, and the artistic and executive staffs at Boston Ballet knew it: at this point, *not* going to New York was not an option. It was, after all, one of Robert Brickell's major "to-dos" on that bold five-year plan he'd made a couple of years ago. All things considered, the company had already made serious progress on some of his big-picture initiatives, including the "second home" idea.

Would Providence have eventually succeeded as our sister city if we'd been able to devote more time to establishing our roots there? I don't know, but it was still an accomplishment to have at least tried the Rhode Island experiment. As it turned out, we'd soon be fighting to keep our own home city's loyalty. Meanwhile, Brickell's promise of a refurbished *Nutcracker* had come through (a bit here, a bit there, but it was done), and the sorely needed renovations to the Music Hall were finally nearing completion.

Now we were on our way to New York City, but this item on the check-list hadn't come about as originally planned. As it turned out, we ended up making our debut with no less than the great Rudolf Nureyev. In the whirlwind that surrounded our return from the world tour, several things happened, including the official announcement of Violette Verdy's appointment as associate artistic director. But my understanding was that she'd already been working behind the scenes on negotiations with Nureyev, with whom she'd been friends for years.

Nearly two decades had passed since he had defected from Russia. In addition to his globe-trotting guest appearances with a myriad of ballet companies, his projects turned to staging ballets and then appearing in them with smaller companies. Naturally, his name appeared at the top of the marquee. Without his own full-time company, he depended upon pickup groups composed of individuals hired to perform in a series of "Nureyev and Friends" tours. For those it was more efficient to maintain a repertory of small-scale works, but when he decided he wanted to offer full-scale story ballets, he needed a full-scale company. Violette, who joined us toward the end of our China tour, had arranged for the Paris Opera ballerina Ghislaine Thesmar and Alexander Godunov (the most recent of the famous Russian defectors) to guest with us in France. Violette would soon have access to such a ready-made company—us—and she could also offer Thesmar, a favorite partner of Nureyev's, for his next venture.

Boston Ballet's first date with Nureyev—performances of Pierre Lacotte's version of the Romantic-era ballet *La Sylphide* at New York City's Uris Theatre—was, as the rest of our complicated affair with Rudi would prove to be, intense. Originally performed in Paris in 1832 with choreography by Filippo Taglioni, this first version had been considered "lost." Even today, most ballet companies perform August Bournonville's 1836 version, but recently Lacotte, a French teacher and choreographer, had staged his "reconstruction" of the original Taglioni on the Paris Opera. Productions such as the Lacotte *Sylphide* are often controversial in the dance world. While no one thinks that, for example, "authentic" productions of *Swan Lake* today contain each and every step Marius Petipa and Lev Ivanov included in their 1895 production, there is a level of certainty that the majority of the original is represented. Naturally, in an art form in which information is mainly handed down from generation to generation, with one human teaching other humans what he or she in turn learned from another human—details and nuances are bound to shift and change, or sometimes be forgotten as time goes on. But this method is nonetheless the respected and preferred way to go, even now, when video recording has become an invaluable tool in documenting and preserving choreography. The current danger is that any mistakes made in performance could become either an accepted or disputed part of the choreography in the future.

The particular hiccup with Lacotte's *Sylphide* was that Taglioni's version had fallen out of the Paris repertoire early on; it wasn't one of those ballets passed down from generation to generation. Thus, Lacotte had to rely heavily on notes, drawings, and descriptions. His research was undoubtedly extensive, but in no way could it be proven to be faithful to the original. And there was a much bigger controversy: Lacotte had decided that in order to be faithful to Taglioni's production, his cast also had to look "historically correct." To Lacotte this meant that BB's African American, South African, and Asian American dancers were out. The rest of us were appalled but had no say in the matter. In our little bubble we were proud, given Boston's history of race struggles, of our *relative* diversity, how we welcomed everyone with open arms—but we kept it mostly to ourselves. Again, ballet dancers were often referred to as "boys and girls," and we sometimes bought into the categorization ourselves and felt unable to speak up. But the race issue was a wretched situation; the following year, Gus van Heerden quit Boston Ballet, citing this incident as part of a pattern of what he saw as discriminatory casting within the company.

I was distracted at the time by other things going on for me personally, both at work and at home. To begin with, it seemed that Lacotte was none too pleased about the fact that I had gained some weight while on tour. Had he ever considered me to dance the Sylph opposite Nureyev, the extra weight most certainly changed his mind. At the moment I wasn't quite sylph-like enough. I was disappointed to not be considered, but I was happy for Elaine Bauer to get such a well-deserved opportunity to alternate the lead female role with Thesmar. And she was simply exquisite as the Sylph. "To anyone familiar with Bauer," wrote Christine Temin, "the Sylphide part will seem a natural for her . . . she has always been at her best in romantic . . . ballets. . . . In this performance, she scored a personal success."

On the playbill, predictably, "Nureyev" was printed in the biggest type-face that could fit, with "and The Boston Ballet" below it. Actually, though our name was smaller, the font size was respectable—as was our reception. Clive Barnes wrote, "The Boston Ballet made a handsomely well-appointed New York debut."

As it happened, I was ultimately grateful to be more on the sidelines for this first experience with Nureyev, whose reputation for being occasionally disrespectful (even cruel) to other dancers was well known. Although I've said that most dancers I've worked with were not overly temperamental, Nureyev was one of the few infamous exceptions to that, and I say that with all due respect. Yes, he was a great dancer, but boy he could be mean. We'd heard all kinds of stories about him and his bouts of anger, so I already had the sense that one might not want to cross him. As the rehearsal period for the upcoming New York performances went on, he indeed took a dislike to one of the Boston dancers and criticized her to the point at which she couldn't dance in front of him anymore. He reduced her to a puddle, and I vowed then and there that I wasn't going to let him do that to me. Since I was just cast in a divertissement pas de deux in the first act—and second cast, at that!—my reduced involvement allowed me to keep my distance for now and file away what I'd observed for future reference.

Meanwhile, my landing back in the Roslindale "nest" had its own share of turbulence. While the rest of us were on tour, Virginia had put Tony in charge of the Summer Dance Program and Boston Ballet Ensemble, the ju-nior company. The new apprentices arrived in Boston after we'd left for the tour. When we returned home, I remember going into the studio, throwing my arms around Tony, and crying, "Oh, I'm so glad to be home!" while at the same moment I saw, over his shoulder, a young dancer glaring at us. In the moment I thought it was strange, but I thought, Okay, it's just some kid. But a couple of days later, Ruth Harrington—who, bless her heart, was still the executive secretary of the school after all of these years—called me, her voice a bit slurred. She asked me if I was okay, and while it took me a day or two to put it all together, she knew what others knew: Tony and the young woman were having an affair. During the next year he went back and forth between the two of us, and although we tried to work through it, this was the beginning of the end of our marriage. The following summer, after enduring more than a year of Tony's public dallying, I had a little fling of my own. It was a loving and fun two weeks with a sweet man. When Tony found out about *my* infidelity, he asked *me* for a divorce just as we opened an oddly arranged season: one week of *Giselle* and one week of mixed rep—including my *Rodeo* debut—followed by another week of *Giselle*. We signed our divorce papers during a break in rehearsals at the local Brigham's Ice Cream Shop, and in that last week's run of *Giselle*, the mad scene was especially poignant for me because the man I'd had my fling with was portraying Albrecht, while Tony was portraying Hilarion. Method acting, anyone? Diane, my best friend from high school and apartment mate, knew firsthand that a no-fault divorce could be gotten quickly in the Dominican Republic and helped me make arrangements. It's amazing, actually: you arrive in Santo Domingo late in the evening, you go to bed, a court envoy escorts you to the courthouse at 7:00 a.m., and by 8:00 a.m. you're divorced, sitting poolside with a piña colada in hand.

———

IF I HADN'T MADE a huge splash in the company's New York debut, I sure got a lot of attention from our hometown in the fall of 1980. Virginia and I were among 350 Bostonians selected to be feted at a major gala celebrating the city's 350th birthday. Held outside in Boston's Copley Square Plaza, the black-tie evening included dancing to live orchestras and short ceremonies honoring those of us who had offered, according to the congratulatory letter from Mayor Kevin White's office, "unique contribution[s] to the quality of life in the City of Boston."

This, and other cheerful situations that fall helped me to keep my spirits up during my private "trouble in paradise" state of affairs. In early December, Elaine, Bruce Wells, and I led the company in *Nutcracker* excerpts as part of another big gala, this one celebrating the reopening of the Music Hall. Our once-cramped, moldering ruin of a performance space had been massively overhauled and returned to its former glory, and with the reopening, the theater was given back its old name. Called the Metropolitan Center once more, it was quickly nicknamed, with a wink and a nod to the Big Apple, the Met. The clean, safe dressing rooms—no more overflowing toilets or critters scampering under our makeup tables—were much appreciated, but what was most appreciated was the size of the stage, which had been expanded from the absurdly tiny depth of twenty-eight feet to seventy feet. In addition to the increased depth, now both stage left and stage right could handle massive set pieces for quick scene changes. Before the renovation, stage left had been the home of the huge lighting board dimmer banks, which were a nice place for the dancers to warm up but unforgiving should one need to exit the stage with haste. The Met would now be able to host big visiting dance, opera, and theater groups properly, and the evening's guest performers underscored that: Mikhail Baryshnikov and Gelsey Kirkland performed excerpts from Jerome Robbins's *Other Dances* at this gala. Stars of other media appeared too, including the television host/comedian Dick Cavett, actor/dancer Ray Bolger, pop singer Melba Moore, and opera "diva" Anna Moffo.

Of course we, the home team, were ecstatic. Not only would we have adequate room to move with the kind of breadth that makes dance morph from something merely pretty to something thrilling, but also the company could dream bigger in terms of production elements. Dancers and opulent sets could now coexist without being a danger to one another! The sets that Helen Pond and Herbert Senn had created for our *Nutcracker* were finally fully utilized when Boston Ballet "officially" opened the Met to the public a week later with the company's annual *Nutcracker* run. And in a few months, Virginia's Beantown ballet troupe would at last put on its first full-length *Swan Lake*, with sets designed for the Met's new vastness and choreography by Violette Verdy and Bruce Wells. This production of the beloved Petipa/Ivanov/Tchaikovsky masterpiece would enable us to soar higher in Boston, but it would also help us continue to claim our stake on the world's stage.

But before we dove into that big pond and Violette's first Boston season, 1980–81 started with a full Balanchine program, performed first in Providence and then at the Met. Violette, who had danced for Mr. B at NYCB for many years, was a wonderful teacher and an incredible coach. She had great insights into most everything we were doing. She was a certified ballerina who had danced it all herself and had a lovely way of communicating what she'd learned. Gus and I performed the leads in Balanchine's *Allegro Brillante*, while *Serenade*, *The Four Temperaments*, and—surprise, surprise!—*Scotch Symphony* were also on the Providence/Boston programs. A dancer Violette had brought with her from Paris, the striking and technically refined Marie-Christine Mouis, created an immediate impression. She "made a strong debut in the lead in 'Serenade,'" wrote Temin. "In the final section she created several memorable and passionate images."

Immediately upon joining the company the previous year, Bruce Wells, who'd made such a positive connection with us in the 1979 Choreographers' Competition, had gotten to work in his dual capacity as dancer and resident choreographer. Indeed, it was his version of *La Fille Mal Gardée* that we had brought to China, along with Ron Cunningham's *Cinderella*. Originally choreographed in 1789, *Fille* tells the story of Lise, a farmer's daughter who is in love with another farmer, Colas. Mother Simone—in most versions, as in Bruce's, played *en travesti*—wishes Lise to marry "up." The lengths that Lise and Colas go through in order to avoid Alain (Mother Simone's choice of a husband for Lise) and hide from Mother Simone herself lend the comic ballet its all's-well-that-ends-well hilarity. Elizabeth Varady wrote that Bruce's version was "a charming rendition," and Temin commented that as the two young lovers, "Laura Young and Nicolas Pacaña are sweetly sympathetic, providing the ballet's finest dancing."

To me, the most precious praise came from Bruce. "Dearest La," he wrote in an opening-night card to me, "Who would have ever thought I'd be lucky enough to have you (a year and a half later!) spinning my choreography to gold? Your friendship and support thru out the year will never be forgotten. I love you, and that special quality you bring to 'Lise.' She's irresistible." He signed it with the traditional good-luck phrase used by most dancers—*merde*. Yes, it means shit in French, but it's a term of affection among dancers. "Break a leg," if you think about it, is hardly an appropriate thing to wish a dancer. The feeling was mutual, and that card speaks volumes about how quickly we'd found an artistic match in one another. I loved dancing with him, and I loved dancing in his ballets.

Now, he and Violette had been tapped to co-choreograph the new *Swan Lake*, drawing upon some of the traditional choreography as well as creating new material. This process is fairly typical when mounting these old ballets, which, again, are likely missing some of the original steps as they've been handed down through the generations. The task always is to avoid a mismatch with the mix-and-match. Although they only had a short time to put it all together, Violette and Bruce pulled it off beautifully. "There is no use demanding an 'authentic' version of 'Swan Lake': there never was one," wrote Gerald Fitzgerald. "Verdy and Wells have organized the tradition into a consistent crescendo: each act builds from start to finish so that at no point does the sequence break into a series of disconnected 'quotes.'" Those Met-worthy sets, designed by the British artist Julia Trevelyan Oman, were likewise lauded. As with *The Sleeping Beauty*, it was still rare to see a full-length *Swan Lake* in the United States at that time; thus, like our premiere of *Beauty* a handful of years earlier, this production attracted notice beyond Boston.

Elaine, fresh from her success dancing with Nureyev in New York City, performed Odette/Odile on Boston's official opening night, alternating with Marie-Christine and me. The Boston run opened on March 11, but as Iris Fanger later wrote, the press had been "pointedly told not to come on Wednesday so the company could in effect have an extra dress rehearsal." Gus was Prince Siegfried to my Odette/Odile, and Donn Edwards, a recent addition to the male principal roster, partnered both Elaine and Marie-Christine (MC). We three women found favor, though in different ways, amongst the critics, while Donn received universally high praise. Temin wrote that she wished Donn and I could have been paired, not having yet heard that a week earlier in Providence he and I had, in fact, gotten that chance, albeit under emergency circumstances when MC injured herself midperformance. That under-the-radar "quickie," unbeknownst to us at the time, was the first seed of what became a mutually beautiful and significant dance partnership. Not having any time to get nervous, I performed my first "Black Swan" that afternoon with a partner I'd never danced with!

How strange and funny life is; nearly three months to the day later, I was in London performing Odette/Odile, opposite Nureyev. Less than a year after our New York City debut, we found ourselves tackling another world capital once again in our new production of *Swan Lake*. Now I was ready for prime time, and alternating with MC, I danced with Nureyev. My very first rehearsal with Rudolf was the London dress, and although I remember my knees knocking and a knot forming in the pit of my stomach, that rehearsal was probably the best performance of my life. Leading up to the London shows, he'd been working with Marie-Christine solely as they were dancing opening night, and—she being on the taller side—they wanted to make sure they'd worked everything out. Finally I was told that I was doing the dress rehearsal that afternoon; I gulped and then asked Rudolf if we could work out a couple of details before we just jumped into it. In particular, I wanted to make sure that my foot and leg would not unceremoniously hit him in a very sensitive area as we performed a pirouette into a partnered arabesque turn. After trying that out, off we went to the stage, and after many stops and starts during act 2, we sailed through act 3 on, with no stops and no glitches. The company—my peers—stopped the act 3 rehearsal by applauding. No one was as surprised as I was that we had gotten all the way through it. But it was so satisfying; there had really been no preparation, I was dancing with a legend, and my peers thought it was good. The London press, however, was mixed, although I got a nice mention in the *Observer*. "On Thursday, the Boston-born Laura Young took over and gave a charmingly sure and lyrical performance which also brought out the drama."

One evening, when I had just finished the act 3 Black Swan pas de deux and gone to my dressing room to change back into Odette for act 4, I asked my dresser if she would get me a Coca-Cola from the canteen, but when she came back and said there wasn't any, I suggested apple cider. She came back with a pint of apple cider, and I drank some of it, noting how strange it was that apple cider was carbonated in England, before chugging the rest of it down. At some point in the fourth act, as I was balanced on one knee with my other leg behind me, in a backbend, I saw that the strip lights overhead seemed to be waving back and forth. I thought, Oh, God, I've got to get out of this position; it's making me feel sick! So I flung myself all the way forward, smashing my head on the deck in the process, perfectly in time with the music—at which point I started laughing. The swan corps—who at that moment in the choreography were running in a circle around me—were all looking down, wondering why my back was heaving so dramatically. I found out the next day that I had been drunk as a skunk and that my laughing had been misread as woeful sobbing. The "carbonated" beverage was, of course, *hard* cider. The funniest thing about it all is that I don't think Rudolf noticed, and my dresser thought I was one strong woman!

———————

RETURNING HOME after the big deal of performing in London could have been a letdown, but as it turned out, there was never a dull moment that fall. It was at least interesting, shall we say, to be cast to dance again with Tony in New Mexico. Dierdre Myles, who had yet to return to the company, had staged *Les Sylphides* for the Southwest Ballet, and Tony and I appeared as guest artists on the program, performing *Tarantella* and the *Le Corsaire* pas de deux. In Boston, our excitement about the new "Met" was put on hold by the fact that we couldn't perform in it during the first two series of our eighteenth season: the improvements to our home theater meant that it was now an attractive venue to visiting companies. Temporarily squeezed out, we performed in the beautiful, but smaller, Opera House. This huge frustration aside, I had several wonderful moments to celebrate in those series, including dancing in *Giselle* opposite Donn, as well as my debut—finally!— as the Cowgirl in de Mille's *Rodeo*.

We were back in the Met for our *Nutcracker* season, but days before the following year's *Nutcracker* opening, the Met's roof would cave in—an unthinkable disaster that now seems like a metaphor for the turmoil that Boston Ballet would experience in the months leading up to it.

18

Manèges

Manèges. Origin: French. Steps performed in a circle are referred to as traveling en manège.

NATURALLY, PERFORMING with Rudolf Nureyev in general was daunting, particularly in places like New York City and London. But our biggest test came when we finally danced with him at home for our local audience, many of whom were longtime followers and had seen our ups and downs throughout the years.

It still thrills me, after all these years, to say that we aced that test. We did ourselves proud—and, by extension, our Boston audience—when in March 1982 we performed at Boston's Metropolitan Center with Rudolf in the company's first full-length production of *Don Quixote*. The staging was Rudolf's own; his well-received version managed to honor Marius Petipa's original 1869 creation while also seeming fresh and funny to late-twentieth-century viewers. Once again, like *The Sleeping Beauty* and *Swan Lake*, at that time only excerpts of *Don Quixote* were commonly performed in the United States. The grand pas de deux from the third act was most familiar, as it was often inserted into mixed repertory or gala programs. Balanchine had staged his own full rendering of the comic ballet, but it was only performed by his company and only in New York City. Virginia had taken me to New York to see the 1965 premiere of Mr. B's *Don Q*, with Balanchine himself as the Don, and Suzanne Farrell as Dulcinea. How wonderful to be able to go to the premiere, but I was afraid we wouldn't make it there. Our flight to New York was my first—and worst—flight ever, and I've traveled around the world since then, so I know what to compare it to. I remember holding Virginia's hand as the plane dropped, lifted, and slipped sideways through an electrical storm. It was a white-knuckled flight all the way.

After our Boston performances, the plan was to go back on tour and take *Don Quixote*—with Nureyev at the center of it all of course—to the southern United States and Mexico. Plans were also being worked out for another tour in the fall, with stops including major American cities such as Los Angeles and eventually back to New York.

In most versions, the title character is almost incidental and is usually played for laughs: an old man who mistakes Kitri, a beautiful young woman, for his long-ago love Dulcinea. With his sidekick Sancho Panza, Don Quixote follows Kitri and her lover, Basilio, as they briefly run away from home—and from Kitri's father, who is determined to marry her to the wealthy but unappealing Gamache. The slight (and admittedly clichéd) story line is compensated for by the plethora of spirited dancing with a "Spanish" flair. Petipa's technically difficult passages—particularly in some of the women's roles—were still there, while Rudolf took the liberty of beefing up some of the men's sections. When the ballet was first choreographed, after all, the emphasis was still largely on the ballerina; the few male dancers were primarily there to display her, not to showcase their own talents. Rudolf was not one to stand around like wallpaper. His version therefore, like most updated models, provided challenges for the men too, particularly for Basilio. But since Rudolf performed Basilio the entire run, the company's male principals had to mostly sit by the sidelines during these Nureyev vehicles. Eventually, the ever-diplomatic Donn Edwards admitted that, as a principal dancer in the prime of his career, the large swaths of that period were indeed challenging. "I want to dance, I'm a dancer," he told a reporter. "So I have to put all the touring with Nureyev into perspective and try to feel positive. . . . I've had to maintain blind faith that being in the presence of Rudi day after day . . . is eventually going to pay off." Donn had been cast as Don Quixote, which required little dancing during these long tours, but his prodigious acting skills and maturity were very much needed to be convincing in the part.

By now Nureyev's bravura capabilities were noticeably on the wane, though evidence of his former prowess still emanated from him. His charisma, however, would never dissipate. The physical decline was only somewhat explicable: he was nearing his midforties, and years of the kind of punishing schedule he'd endured as he traveled all around the world dancing here and there would take its toll on anyone. What most of us didn't know at the time was that he was struggling with the early stages of AIDS. The terrible virus would soon loom darkly everywhere and would sweep through the dance world with particular devastation. The Boston Ballet family wasn't spared: we lost many dear men to this horrific disease.

Rudolf was still a huge draw though; any technical weaknesses were counterbalanced with his overall performance—he was legendary for a reason. And he could be, as it turned out, quite a comedian: he and his *Don Quixote* were robustly humorous. The production was also gorgeous, with flamboyant yet handsome costumes and lively sets by the London-based designer Nicholas Georgiadis. And it was expensive, at a quarter of a million dollars, but the company was only paying for half of it. The other half was picked up by the U.S. tour presenter Mel Howard, who was in charge of promoting the tour, which was to begin a mere two weeks after the Boston run had ended.

We had no time to waste and worked like crazy because we knew we had to be ready for this next phase of our Nureyev adventure. Richard Novotny—Rudolf's assistant and a former dancer himself—worked with us during the rehearsals; once again, we climbed to a new level and met the challenge. Ironically, our greater strength as a company helped soften the undeniable fact of Rudolf's diminishing technical abilities. Yes, his name on the marquee was key to attracting thousands of audience members wherever we went, and certainly we were deeply inspired by his great artistry; a lot of our growth was due to his example and his coaching and presence. But once those viewers were in their seats, there was no doubt that we Bostonians had a lot to do with the ballet's overall success.

"Is it *really* the Boston Ballet? . . . The Ballet has never had a production which makes it look as attractive as does this updating of Marius Petipa's jolly, pseudo-Spanish ballet," Christine Temin wrote in one of several pieces she filed during our Met Center series. She admitted "the company's announcement that it would produce Nureyev's version of the ballet was met with skepticism in this corner and elsewhere. Would the troupe be reduced to so much living scenery while Nureyev . . . did most of the dancing? . . . The production turned out to be a welcome challenge; the Ballet has learned much about the art of performing from the stage-wise Nureyev. His own skills have faded." The spate of reviews we received during our Boston season echoed Temin's assessment; praise for Rudolf's formidable artistry was tempered with respectful recognition of his current physical state while the generous kudos for Boston Ballet was largely without reservation. "Meanwhile, and here's the true joy of it, the company has never danced better," wrote Gerald Fitzgerald.

Marie-Christine and I were initially scheduled to share the lead role of Kitri/Dulcinea, and when we weren't performing that, we were to alternate as the Queen of the Dryads in the ballet's gauzy dream sequence. The two of us, along with Elaine—who alternated with Stephanie Moy in the role of Amor in that scene—apparently created a balletomane's version of a dream team. "Imagine Laura Young, Elaine Bauer and Marie-Christine Mouis, all dancing together," Fitzgerald wrote, "each spurring on the others' bravura specialties, each revealing in the contrast the special qualities of her body and personality." Especially lovely were the ways in which Marie-Christine's Kitri and mine were described; neither was said to be "better," but each of us was seen to bring out different qualities in the character. I was thus able to enjoy the praise I received from Temin in the *Globe*: "Last night was also a great personal triumph for company principal Laura Young. How wonderful it was to see this Boston-bred ballerina, a charter member of the company, partnered by one of the world's great stars on her home stage—and dancing brilliantly."

But alas, for Marie-Christine, during the second week of the Boston run, she dislocated her shoulder during act 1. Due to Marie-Christine's height, some of the partnering was more difficult for them to accomplish, especially in the twice-repeated choreographic moment in which a nicknamed "typewriter" turn was required. As anachronistic as it sounds today, the overhead arm that controls the promenade in écarté is quickly whipped to the side and then pushed to initiate a turn, mimicking a typewriter carriage return. As Rudolf and Marie-Christine completed the first sequence, I heard an audible wince and went to look. Everything seemed okay, as MC was already preparing for the second go-round. As they went into the next pirouette, she yelped, collapsing in pain, and Rudolf carried her into the wings. By this time, I had run to the other side to see if I needed to replace her, which was indeed the case.

I had been backstage, warming up to go on in the next act as Queen of the Dryads but flew down the stairs to change into my Kitri costume—the only thing I didn't have time to slap on was the wig. This happened in about three minutes, including getting into pointe shoes! Elaine, meanwhile, who was scheduled to dance Amor that evening, rapidly transformed herself into the Dryad Queen and speedily reviewed the steps she had only learned as the understudy to the role. Stephanie was thus summoned to go in as Amor. That reshuffling was, as always, frenzied only backstage; once on stage, we were cool as cucumbers.

In any event, Marie-Christine was not able to dance Kitri during the run but was able to perform limitedly as the Dryad Queen. It was likely that she wouldn't be able to resume alternating the lead right away so it became increasingly clear that I had quite a haul ahead of me. The tour was about to be cancelled when they could not retain another Kitri for the beginning of the tour. Marie-Christine was supposed to be cleared to dance one week into it. So, as Virginia and the board met in her office, I boldly knocked on the door to let them know I could handle the first weekend's performances in Atlanta (one Friday night, two on Saturday, and two on Sunday), and potentially the rest of the next week. I had already done five *Sleeping Beauties* in a weekend in Providence and didn't die, so I felt I could do the same with *Don Q* and thus save the tour. Kitri/Dulcinea is an extremely physically demanding role, and in addition to the remaining Boston shows, we were scheduled to dance in eight cities in the course of a month. But just like our midperformance emergency switcheroo, there was really no time to think, only to dance.

And what was it like to dance with Nureyev? First of all, the roles of Kitri and Basilio provide many opportunities to ad lib comedically; Nureyev would do this in such a way that allowed me to have fun reacting in different ways on different nights, which kept the action fresh. His partnering was both assured and complementary, and his determination to dance every show rubbed off on all of us. His energy was contagious, and we all became a team.

AFTER APPEARING IN Atlanta, San Antonio, St. Louis, and New Orleans, we had crossed the border and were now performing in Guanajuato, Mexico, in that city's Cervantes Festival. At 6,500 or so feet above sea level, there were usually Mexican EMTs backstage, prepared with oxygen tanks and ready to assist, if necessary, for visiting performers such as ourselves who weren't used to the altitude. I had made it to the end of the ballet, and when the curtain came down I sat backstage and put my head down between my knees, breathing and breathing, trying to recover enough for the bows. I started to rise, but before I knew it, an EMT pushed me back in the chair and put a mask on my face. It was probably a funny but confusing scene, as I pushed him away and he pushed me back, and so on, until finally, he held me down and forced the mask on me. Luigi, Nureyev's personal assistant, came to get me, saying, "It's time for the bows," and so the EMT finally let me go. I stood up and promptly passed out. Rudolf was happy to take a solo bow and gave me a moment to come to before I joined the company at the end.

I had already been campaigning for some relief, as Marie-Christine's shoulder was not quite ready for those "typewriter" turns. Fortunately, the great Japanese ballerina Yoko Morishita was scheduled to step in to dance with Rudolf in our Miami performances. Management petitioned her to join us early to relieve me in Mexico City, our next stop after Guanajuato. At this point, Rudolf—also beat after so many consecutive performances—didn't want to put in an extra rehearsal, even though he'd be dancing with a different partner. I was so thrilled to get a break from dancing Kitri that I said, "Yoko, come on, I know what he does, I'll partner you!" So we rehearsed together, with me standing in as Rudolf. Yoko is even tinier than I am, so it wasn't impossible. In fact, we did so well that her agent came up afterward and joked that we should take our "act" on the road. As it happened, opening night in Mexico City was my unlucky thirteenth performance. When coming out of one of Kitri's explosive grand jetés in the first act, I felt some muscles in my instep "pop" and was hard put to finish the act. Our stage manager, Sue Ring, sent a message to Yoko, who was in the audience, to let her know that she was needed to complete acts 2 and 3.

Marie-Christine was finally able to take on Kitri at the very end of that tour, and I was more than ready to hand it over. Touring can be as glamorous as it sounds but is also quite taxing. The audiences, of course, don't know whether you've been dealing with an injury or are on the brink of collapse from exhaustion. They've paid for their tickets and are there to have a good time and expect to see a great performance. I know the feeling when you witness a disappointing or lackluster performance—I've seen my share of such shows. Early in that tour, when I did five performances as Kitri in one weekend, apparently not every one of those five was top notch—well, I am only human. I got trashed in one review but acquired a new nickname through my efforts in another—"Durably Divine Dulcinea" one writer dubbed me. The whole company proved its durability though.

We had barely returned home when it was time to take off for an overseas leg of the tour—something not on the original itinerary. Presumably Howard, the tour manager, noting the largely successful reception the production was enjoying, scrambled to capitalize on and add to the healthy box office receipts. In August we would tour Italy and France, and in September we'd return to the States to perform in Los Angeles and Detroit. Following that, we would return to the Uris Theater in New York City in January and February, to perform *Don Quixote*. The upshot was that, with the additional touring, our fall '82 and early winter '83 Boston series were scrapped. We dancers weren't involved in that decision, so I can't say whether there was a discussion about possible repercussions as a result of the cancelled home seasons, but the company would indeed get some cold shoulders from disgruntled audience members who felt alienated by our long absence. I think the Boston Ballet management was stunned, and it ended up taking a long time to fully rebuild the audience base.

If we were in for a chilly reception at home later on, the European tour was, metaphorically, on the other end of the thermometer: a warm-up for what was to come. We coined it—and not affectionately—the "tour from hell." Oh, there were the usual comic incidents—I almost knocked myself out when I ran straight into a strut support in one of the outdoor theaters—as well as the usual headaches of other varieties. After our last performance in Naples at the San Carlo Opera House, a restaurant was kept open late for us so we could eat before continuing toward our next destination, Taormina, Sicily, which we got to by ferry after first traveling by train to Catania. In the restaurant, there were also about twenty American sailors; there was a lot of drinking and folderol, but we thought we'd pulled ourselves sufficiently together before we boarded the train. We knew we couldn't leave our suitcases anywhere unattended and even made a plan in which the women stood on the platform in a tight circle with the luggage, while the men stood in another circle around them. We did all this, but one of the dancer's wallets was lifted before she even made it into the circle. We were susceptible to the same petty crime that regular tourists were, I guess. Despite that, and the fact that it was about a hundred degrees on that train, we continued the celebration that we'd begun in the restaurant. It was August 4—our company manager Sandy Robinson's birthday and the day before mine—so we had a cake on the train as the party rolled on. (As we were taking our bows the next night, the audience lit candles, in the traditional way of showing how much they liked the performance; someone in line behind me whispered, "Quite the birthday cake, La!")

When we finally called it a night on that train ride and climbed into our berths, most of us naked or close to it because of the extreme heat, we figured the gentle rocking of the train would bring blissful sleep, only to be jerked awake twenty minutes later. At first, we panicked, but then we pulled out of the station again, only to have the same thing happen twenty minutes later. This happened all night long: it turned out we were on the milk train! When we arrived in Catania, having barely slept, they put us on the ferry and, after that, a bus. We finally arrived at the theater a half hour before that evening's performance—barely enough time to pull ourselves together, let alone get in a proper warm-up. Well, we couldn't get our sleep back, but we could—thanks to union rules—put in for overtime to compensate for the lack of proper time off between travel and performance.

But it turned out that I, as Rudolf's Kitri, was in for what our hosts thought to be star treatment. I was taken to a "special dressing room," which was gotten to by going around a corner (past rooms formerly occupied by gladiators, where the rest of the company and Rudolf were quartered), up a stone staircase and into a cavernous room with a dirt floor and a single light bulb hanging by its cord. By this time I was already beside myself, wondering how I'd get myself ready in time. I burst into tears and begged to be put with the corps de ballet—there was no way I could make all of my quick changes and get back on stage in reasonable time from this room that felt as if it was miles away. Well, we all got ourselves ready and were making our way through the ballet when, in the tavern scene, Rudolf used his prop mug to try to knock my mug off the quickly passed tray of libations and then proceeded to curse me and the company with the bluest words he could find. Yes, sometimes dancers talk on stage, but it's not often that they carry on in this way. It's a good thing that audiences rarely pick up on such discord—it would surely spoil the often "other-worldly" mood of a ballet performance.

I couldn't imagine why he was mad at me, but by now I knew that he would often take his anger out on whoever happened to be there at the time. We still had the grand pas de deux to do so I tried not to worry about it, but after the performance I went to his dressing room to ask what had happened. He wasn't upset with me, he said, but with the company for the overtime we'd put in for that would come out of his proceeds. I lost no time in explaining that we'd had a nearly sleepless journey, and it was fortunate we'd even made it through the performance. His comment? "Oh." But that was the end of it; he never again questioned the extra money going to the dancers.

I don't think Rudi was purposely looking to make us uncomfortable. It was the tour presenter for this leg (whom Rudi called "Poopsie") who handled all of these arrangements, but he certainly maintained his ignorance by turning a blind eye to the situation. The conditions were even worse for the musicians, a Czechoslovakian orchestra, who traveled on buses almost the entire time. They weren't put up in hotels, and for meals, they were mostly provided with canned food. Rudolf, meanwhile, was never put on a bus; he was driven by limousine. We were amused to read in a 1983 article preceding yet another tour the company undertook with Rudolf his "compliment" regarding our ability to make do on the road. "They understand better the hardships of traveling," he said. "Make less complaining."

But the "tour from hell" would not stop. It had all started in Pisa where we found that the theater had been blown away by a tornado and had to rearrange the tour on the spot. "An Act of God a Day" became the refrain. Even though we were struggling through a myriad of adversities, the box office was doing so well that Poopsie and Rudi thought we should stay and do another week of performances, ending in Milan. A vote was taken amongst the dancers, and the consensus was that we were ready to go home and there-fore would not agree to the extension. Management came back to us to plead their case for continuing, citing the benefit of nurturing our relationship with Mr. Nureyev. We relented—except for a few who had previous engage-ments back home—and stayed on. In Milan, they prepared a huge going-away meal for us under a big tent after the last performance. I was never sure what precipitated the ensuing food fight, except that Rudi was upset about *something*, and as he was getting up to exit the tent, he slapped a dancer hard on his back (one who was already having back problems). Violette was beside herself, asking him why he wanted to hurt another dancer like that. Rudolf and his entourage exited down the center aisle, giving each row of dancers the "devil's horns" gesture, over and over again. I was relieved that he pulled that incantation back when he got to Donn and me, but I don't know why we were spared. As they continued out, verbal exchanges still flying, one dancer had had enough of the harangue and tossed his beer in Rudi's direction. Rudi's assistant began pummeling the dancer—and then the food really started flying. Needless to say, we were glad to be done and heading home.

————

BUT THERE WAS GRUMBLING aplenty as the tours with Nureyev con-tinued elsewhere while our performances in Boston had become infrequent. Most of the dancers, of course, never stopped working. After the August/ September tour, Donn and I danced in Canada as part of another "Stars of" tour, this one with the Canadian ballerina Karen Kain and danseur Frank Augustyn. We performed the pas de deux from Bruce Wells's *La Fille Mal Gardée* and Balanchine's *La Sonnambula*. Back in Boston, I performed as a guest with David Drummond's chamber-size company, Copley Square Ballet, a side project that he founded while he was still dancing with the company.

We were all looking forward to finally performing in Boston again, when unfortunately the Met Center's roof caved in, just days before *Nutcracker* opened. Elaine's husband David, who had retired from dancing after the world tour in 1980 and was now the company's general manager, hustled to secure the Hynes Auditorium for the holiday performances. Essentially a big, unglamorous convention hall, the Hynes was hardly ideal, but it was a way to salvage what could have been a complete disaster. As it was, it was estimated that Boston Ballet had lost at least one-third of its subscription audience while we were touring.

Although it was clear that the company had a good deal of repair work ahead, as soon as *Nutcracker* was over, we were back on the *Don Quixote* treadmill with Rudolf. Thankfully, we were well received in our New York City performances and, thus bolstered, ready to try to win our hometown's heart back during the spring 1983 season, which was comprised of two mixed programs bookending a run of *Swan Lake*. If we relaxed a bit after the first series—which included *Fille*, Ron Cunningham's *Jeu de Cartes*, and Balanchine's *Symphony in C*—the relief evaporated when Virginia dropped the bombshell that she'd be stepping down as co-artistic director. Violette would be the sole director while Virginia would be called founder and artistic advisor.

After a relatively calm *Swan Lake* season, another dark cloud appeared amidst our third series, which opened on April 27 and included Bruce's *Preludes*, Violette's *Album* (both world premieres), and Balanchine's *Concerto Barocco*. On the morning of April 30, 1983, George Balanchine died. The loss to the worldwide ballet community was enormous, and to we longtime Boston Ballet dancers, it was a particularly painful postscript to Virginia's announcement. The end of an era seemed upon us.

We knew that one day Virginia would hand over the reins, but some of us thought it wouldn't be for quite a while. I guess I'd always assumed she'd be there at least as long as I was still dancing with the company. Rumors fueled the disappointment: Had she been asked to step aside? Or was the relationship with Violette too tricky to navigate? Even before Violette had arrived, there had been talk about whether the arrangement had been forced on Virginia. While both women behaved professionally, maintaining a diplomatic front when asked about the situation, speculation about whether Violette and Boston Ballet was a happy marriage had been nonetheless nearly constant since her arrival. By now, I too had learned the art of circumspection and kept my more provocative opinions to myself, while simply acknowledging my sorrow over Virginia's announcement. "Of course, 20 years from now would have been too soon," I told Temin. "She is my mentor: I've worked with her for 23 years. I owe her my career."

Some of the newer dancers within the company, however, weren't so guarded about the various crises plaguing the company. I can understand that; when I was younger, I had been known to occasionally express my passionate ideas publicly. Though I scratched my head or clenched my jaw in certain situations, now that I'd been around as long as I had, I could sometimes take the longer view. But for the next generation, the post they'd just hitched themselves to was looking rather unstable.

Thus, as the Boston Ballet rounded the corner into its twentieth birthday, it was in serious trouble. After years of working hard to rise from amateur to professional status, and from being a regional entity to being nationally—and even internationally—recognized, it was a particularly shocking situation in which to find ourselves. Led by the company's new president Joel Garrick we pressed forward. A new slogan seemed to speak to those audience members irritated by our long absences as well as serve as a reminder that we needed them: "It's your Ballet, Boston." If our hometown felt betrayed by our affair with Nureyev, the hope was that sharing him again would go a long way toward reconciliation. And so, after a final European tour with Nureyev in the summer of 1983, we came full circle and offered another *Don Quixote* season in Boston, where that particular journey had begun. And it was clear that the company's renewed vows to Boston weren't empty promises; off on a new adventure of his own, Rudolf was about to take over the artistic directorship of Paris Opera Ballet, the post that Violette had left in order to come here. This time, when Rudolf left, we weren't going with him.

I did not do the last European tour as I had fractured a metatarsal, and I was unsure that I had recovered sufficiently to dance Kitri once more in Boston in the fall. However, the night before we opened, Rudolf tore a calf muscle during the preview performance, and the entire run was cancelled before it even officially began. I was saved from possibly making a fool of myself on stage or, worse, reinjuring myself in the process. Our Boston audience, naturally, was profoundly disappointed.

19

Temps de l'Ange

Temps de l'ange. Origin: French. Angel's step. A jump in which the dancer's head and upper body are arched while the legs are together in the air
and thrown back with the knees slightly bent.

WHILE BOSTON BALLET was busy rebuilding its relationship
with Boston, my personal connections with friends and colleagues old and new continued to be sources of joy and inspiration. In particular, my onstage partnership with Donn Edwards grew. In
addition to being a beautiful classical dancer, tall and handsome, he was
impeccably trained, with long legs and gorgeous feet. And he was a strong
and considerate partner. There is a myriad of physical and artistic details
that good partners discover and develop together, but Donn's attention to
detail was exceptional. During a dress rehearsal for one of our first performances together, we struck a pose in which he was behind me, both of us
looking up on a high diagonal. He asked, "Where are you looking?" and I
fumblingly tried to explain which little blue strip on which band up there
in the flies I was eyeballing; he said, "Okay, fine," and accordingly adjusted
his gaze toward the next little blue strip, so that our profiles matched exactly.
And indeed, such specificity is what creates those harmonious lines in ballet.

We were good friends too; like Lefty and Rose, he was someone I could
laugh, grumble, or sigh with. Even though, like Boston Ballet, I was marking my twentieth year as a professional, I could still suffer great moments

of doubt. So, although I increasingly found myself in the role of "wise mentor" to the younger dancers, I too occasionally needed reassurance. After
one heartfelt conversation in which I shared some of my fears with Donn,
he wrote me a long note—on paper towels, yet—which still moves me to
this day when I read it. "For so many of us the dignity and honesty with
which your aura of beauty is created—both on and offstage—are a constant
inspiration."

Similarly, my friendship with Bruce Wells was augmented by our artistic
work together. Like many professional dancers, I was fortunate to get the
opportunity to perform the works of many great choreographers of the past
and present as well as possible stars of tomorrow. What is rarer is the chance
to have one choreographer create several original works on you, but Bruce
did just that during his years as one of the company's resident choreographers. I'm flattered to have been one of his "muses." In addition to *Violin
Concerto* (his entry for the 1979 International Choreographers' Competition) and his staging of *La Fille Mal Gardée*, I performed in the premieres
of his 1982 *Mendelssohn: Violin Concerto* (with Donn as my partner) and
Preludes, which Bruce choreographed in 1983 for Anamarie, Elaine, and me.
It was extra special because it was rare for the three of us to dance in such an
intimate situation. Usually when we were on stage at the same time it was
amidst the relative hubbub of one of the big story ballets. But in *Preludes*,
we "Gumm Sisters" portrayed the title group of Anton Chekhov's play "The
Three Sisters," on which the ballet was based.

I loved dancing all of Bruce's ballets, and they were also well received by
critics. *Madrilene Pas de Deux*, which he made in 1983, was equally successful but was a departure from Bruce's usual lyricism. Choreographed on the
heels of our Nureyev adventures, the duet—created for Donn and me—was
a cheeky send-up of big, flashy ballets such as *Don Quixote*. Donn and I were
given intentionally ostentatious bravura steps, all accented with over-the-top
faux-"Spanish" flourishes, *and* we were given license to ham it up—albeit
artfully. Bruce knew that subtle satire would work better than slapstick.
Oh, what fun we three had with that ballet. When we danced it during
the company's April 1984 "Gala Week" program, Sharon Basco wrote that
the ballet "was given pseudo-serious performances by two of the company's

finest dancers, and certainly its best comedians, Laura Young and Donn Edwards."

That gala program, one of the few moments that actually felt like a celebration in what was supposed to have been a joyous anniversary year, was stuffed with eleven pieces. Many were only excerpts from longer works, but even so, the show was bursting at the seams. It began with a joyous "defilade"; this traditional entrance of students was choreographed by none other than the indefatigable Sydney Leonard, who had continued to be a main figure in the school all these years and would remain so for two more decades. It ended with Bruce's *Waldmeister Overture*, an effervescent tour de force for us grown-ups.

While it's intensely satisfying to have the opportunity to develop over time the kind of dancer/choreographer relationship that Bruce and I had, sometimes a guest choreographer can also tap into a dancer's particular strengths and special beauty immediately. That was certainly the case in 1980, the first time Choo San Goh, the young resident choreographer at the Washington Ballet, was commissioned to create a piece for Boston Ballet. The result, *Leitmotiv*, was made with Elaine in the central role, and she was born to dance it. Overall, Choo San and the company were a good fit, and he was brought back the next year to choreograph yet another ballet on the company, *Due Pezzi Sacri*. Then came the biggest commission of all: a production of *Romeo and Juliet*, which the company had never done before, even though Virginia had long hoped to stage the full-length version of it. She knew that I too yearned for the chance to take on the iconic, dramatic role of Juliet, and when she saw the rapport that Donn and I had established, she was determined to see us in the lead roles. Of course, Virginia couldn't dictate casting, especially now that she wasn't at the helm, but fortunately Donn and I were among the four couples Choo San chose to portray the star-crossed lovers.

In many ways Choo San's production followed other traditional settings of the ballet—the striking, deeply hued sets by Alain Vaës (Marie-Christine's then husband) conjured the Renaissance, for example, and Choo San used the familiar score by Sergei Prokofiev—but there were some excitingly unique touches. The movement vocabulary was rooted in classical ballet but with a somewhat quirky approach, particularly the way Choo San designed port de bras. He was very specific about what he wanted to see from us, but he would show the movements on his own wiry frame so quickly that we had to watch him really, really closely to mimic the way he'd moved his arms. We four Juliets would get together and compare notes and try to figure out the details. Sometimes we didn't quite get it right, but he knew exactly what needed to be corrected and eventually got us all on the same page.

One of Choo San's most interesting constructs was the way he conveyed the specter of inevitable doom that permeates Shakespeare's tale, via an invented character whom he simply called "Fate." Marie-Christine, Elaine, and Loretta Dodd, a stately and up-and-coming corps de ballet member, alternated in the role. Clad only in a silver-gray unitard and gray headdress, the ballerina dancing the role was a chilling presence, skimming here and there with swift, whisper-soft bourrées. One striking motif was the way Choo San sometimes had Juliet dance the same movements as Fate but a count or two later, underscoring the idea that Juliet's actions were beyond her control. At one point, Fate ran thrillingly across the stage as a huge piece of black silk trailed behind her from the fly space like a giant forbidding storm cloud. It was meant to land swirling around Juliet's feet, but on occasion we found ourselves engulfed in its folds. Blessedly, this moment was followed by a blackout.

In retrospect it's hard not to see that theatrical gloom as an omen of the real-life darkness that descended upon us on May 8, nine days before the premiere of Choo San's *Romeo and Juliet*. I still vividly recall how we were working in an upstairs studio when corps member Victor LaCasse ran in and told us that Virginia had died.

———————

VIRGINIA'S DEATH was desperately shocking, not simply because it was inconceivable to think of Boston Ballet without her, but also because she was only seventy and hadn't been noticeably ailing. We knew that she was going into the hospital for a scheduled procedure to address her circulation—nothing that we understood to be dire. In fact, true to form, Virginia was in the middle of orchestrating the Malden recital from her hospital bed. Unfortunately, days after the surgery, she developed a blood clot that killed her. It's one of those things she probably would have survived had it happened today.

Oh, Virginia! How much I owe her, how much we all owe her! No, she didn't do it by herself, and I in no way forget or discount all the others who worked alongside her. I didn't set out to write a juicy tell-all—in case you hadn't noticed—nor did I think that in this single account I could write about all of the people who were important to the company and who were important to me. But of all the visionaries who dreamed of serious ballet in Boston, it was Virginia at the forefront, Virginia who pushed us the most into the professional realm. I'm just glad to know that Virginia was alive to see the high praise she received in a lovely twentieth-anniversary commemorative booklet issued a few months before her unexpected death. "She has built The Boston Ballet into a Company of international promise," the main essay read. "In the process, she has become recognized as one of the true pioneers of American dance." Also in the booklet, underneath a full-page portrait of Virginia, critic and longtime Boston Ballet observer Elliot Norton wrote, "My respect for the achievements of E. Virginia Williams is virtually unlimited. Against almost impossible odds, she created a ballet company which does Boston credit. She has enriched our lives."

I have never, ever forgotten what E. Virginia Williams did for all of us, and I am eternally moved and grateful for everything she did for me personally.

———————

NATURALLY, as it proverbially "must," the show went on. *Romeo and Juliet* opened on May 17, nine days after Virginia's death, many of us still raw with emotion. Performers often find that such intense feelings of grief can provide an outlet when channeled judiciously through a character. While Choo San's choreography was tightly constructed it still allowed us to bring our own interpretations from our own backgrounds and experiences to the ballet. And I indeed rode the waves of my deep sadness about Virginia's death, grateful that my art could provide something of a cathartic outlet; I was taken by surprise, however, to find myself, as I recounted in this book's prologue, literally weeping as I lay on Juliet's bier at the end of the ballet.

Usually, one's real-life emotions are kept in check by the engrained habits of professionalism.

In any event, performing offered a way to *escape* that grief too, even if only briefly. I just loved Choo San's third-act bedroom pas de deux; Juliet is trying to get Romeo to stay, and all the partnering was choreographed to be off balance. When Romeo finally turned around and fled, it felt real to me, very dramatic and passionate. Choo San's balcony scene felt wonderfully expansive; some people criticized it, complaining that there was too much running, but to me it felt like the rush of young love. As it happened, the opening-night cast was particularly youthful; although it's not a set rule, the tradition in many ballet companies is for lead roles to go to principal dancers. Choo San went against that convention by giving first-cast honors to Dierdre Myles, who had by now returned to the company, and Devon Carney, a relatively new member of the male corps. Marie-Christine and Jean-Philippe Halnaut were the second cast; Donn and I, the third, while Elaine and a new principal, Christopher Aponte, were fourth. Oh, of course it was disappointing not to perform on opening night as I was accustomed to, but then we all had our turns. Nonetheless, it was as rewarding to dance Juliet as I'd imagined it would be. "The moving performance of Young," wrote Christine Temin, "suggests the truth of the old saying that the best Juliets—great ballerinas like Fonteyn and Ulanova—are two or three times the age of Shakespeare's adolescent."

Choo San was only in his midthirties when he created *Romeo and Juliet* and was one of those potential choreographic "stars of tomorrow." But sadly, three years later, he became yet another of the many victims of AIDS, passing away at only thirty-nine.

———

AS IT TURNED OUT, the offstage drama at Boston Ballet immediately following Virginia's death ratcheted up even more with the development of a new twist. Before the *Romeo and Juliet* run had ended, it was reported that Violette had told people she was resigning, but then, after meeting with board chairman John Humphrey, she agreed to stay on. That discussion happened in the morning, and that night after the performance a company meeting was called in the theater; Humphrey and former board chair

Giselle, act 2, with Donn Edwards, 1984.
Photo © Bernie Gardella.

With Donn Edwards in *Romeo and Juliet*.
Photograph by Jaye R. Phillips.

As Juliet, 1985.
Photo © 2016 Jack Mitchell.

White Swan from *Swan Lake*, act 2, with Donn Edwards, 1985.
Photo © Bernie Gardella.

Black Swan from *Swan Lake*, act 3, with Donn Edwards, 1985.
Photo © Bernie Gardella.

Above
With Devon Carney in Bruce
Marks's *Pipe Dreams*, 1986.
Photograph by Jaye R. Phillips.

Left
Rehearsing *Coppélia* with
choreographer Hans Brenaa
(*middle*) and Dierdre Myles
(*behind*), 1986. Photograph by
Jaye R. Phillips.

With William Pizzuto in *Coppélia*, 1986.
Photograph by Jaye R. Phillips.

In the Fiandaca silver gown worn at my twenty-fifth anniversary gala with my soon-to-be husband, Chris Mehl, 1986. Author's collection.

With Sydney Leonard (*left*) and Ruth Harrington (*middle*), gala night, 1986. Author's collection.

With Jack Mitchell, his photo of me in *Rodeo*, and my silvered pointe shoe. Author's collection.

"Quand Voulent les Étincelles." A black-and-white photo of me on pointe on the train rail and then painted by an artist to add color and make sparks fly. Created for the fund-raiser "Significant People," 1986. Peter Urban, photographer, and Gordon Fiedor, artist.

Paper Ballerina in *The Steadfast Tin Soldier* with William Pizzuto, 1986.
Photograph by Jaye R. Phillips.

Photo shoot for *Boston Woman Magazine*, 1986.
Photograph by John Burke.

Raymonda with Fernando Bujones, 1988. Photograph by Jaye R. Phillips.

With Fernando Bujones in *Esmeralda*, 1988.
Photo © Bernie Gardella.

Twenty-Fifth Anniversary Gala Rose Adagio with my four retired Princes, *right to left*: Bruce Wells, Donn Edwards, James Capp, and David Brown. Photo © Bernie Gardella.

Left to right: La, Rose, and Lefty, the "Gumm Sisters." Twenty-Fifth Gala, 1989. Author's collection.

Don Quixote, my final bow with Devon Carney, 1989.
Photo © Jerry Berndt, courtesy of Boston Ballet.

With Chris while on vacation, 2016. Author's collection.

Maryellen Cabot explained that Violette would stay but that president Joel Garrick would leave. That agreement lasted a very brief time; the next few months were tumultuous. Like a bad divorce, what started out as private business soon escalated into a public squabble. It became clear that Violette had struggled with some of the administration from the beginning of her tenure at Boston Ballet and initially cited Garrick as the major source of tension. It was suggested that the straw that broke the camel's back came when Garrick weighed in on programming, an area usually left to the discretion of the artistic staff. There was much back-and-forth in the newspapers, but in the end, Violette was wooed back to New York City Ballet to teach and coach. By the end of June, she had resigned (again), this time for good, and now she held forth openly to the press.

This was hardly the end of the turmoil within Boston Ballet. There was a sort of coup attempt by a portion of the board that tried to reinstate Cabot as chair, but when that failed, Cabot resigned from her trustees post in protest, as had vice chair Sunny Dupree. Cabot told Temin, "The Ballet has become too concerned with the wishes of an inner circle of the board and not concerned with artistic excellence." Close to five hundred thousand dollars in the red, the company's questionable stability put its eligibility for several annual grants into jeopardy; one from the Massachusetts Council on the Arts and Humanities and one from the National Arts Stabilization Fund were together worth several hundred thousand dollars.

For me, and many of the dancers, the only brightness during this time came when Bruce Wells was named as interim director for the next year while a search for a new artistic director was undertaken. Along with Bruce, Choo San was mentioned as a possible permanent director, as was former company resident choreographer Sam Kurkjian. In the meantime, if anyone could try to steer us back to some normalcy, Bruce could. I was more than happy to publicly voice my support for him, which I did in board meetings and even on the NPR radio show *On Point*, which was locally produced. A few dancers in the end did leave, although not quite the droves that had been darkly predicted. Soloists Jean-Philippe Halnaut and Katya Kolodzie and corps member Alexandre Proia left as a result of the turmoil; Marie-Christine had toyed with the idea but in the end stayed on; and Ron Cunningham, who had served as co-resident choreographer with

Bruce Wells—and for several years before Bruce had joined—also soon left to head the Sacramento Ballet. Another prominent departure was that of David Commanday, who had only recently taken on the role of the company's music director. Did I think of leaving too? No. It was a terrible, terrible time, and it felt especially terrible, happening on the heels of Virginia's death. But that in itself felt like a pretty good reason to stay. She had put everything into this company. And so had I.

———

THANKFULLY, the usual distractions and never-ending work of class, rehearsal, and performing took most of our attention. That summer I performed the "Black Swan" pas de deux from *Swan Lake* at the Hatch Shell with Devon Carney. Those free concerts on the Esplanade were just beginning to be performed by members of the junior troupe, the Boston Ballet Ensemble, rather than the main company, a practice that continued for many years. Devon and I thus appeared as guests alongside this increasingly capable group of young hopefuls. Devon, who like Dede (Myles) had been promoted to soloist after *Romeo and Juliet*, eventually gained principal status. Dede, who probably should have been given the same nod, added many more leading roles to her roster, including, in Boston Ballet's November "Balanchine Celebration," the main ballerina part in the company premiere of Mr. B's *Capriccio for Piano and Orchestra,* better known as the "Rubies" section from *Jewels*. For myself, I got to perform my old friend *Scotch Symphony* with my new friend Donn.

Even this, the all-Balanchine program, which also included *Prodigal Son* and *Tchaikovsky Pas de Deux*, was initially dogged by a potential crisis. Boston Ballet's "rights" to perform the works was now called into question by Barbara Horgan, the executor of Balanchine's estate. Horgan was eventually one of the founding trustees of the George Balanchine Trust, the entity that was set up in 1987 to ensure that Balanchine's ballets were staged and performed to his standards. She was in theory just doing her job, but after Boston Ballet's long history of performing these ballets, and the early mentorship of Mr. B himself—once an official artistic advisor to the company—it was a tough pill to swallow. In the end, we were allowed to perform the Balanchine program, but I have no idea how that actually transpired.

The familiarity of *Nutcracker* season was broken up for me that year with my staging of the holiday ballet for the Greater Milford Ballet Association, led by the charming and hardworking teacher Georgia Deane, whose students and their parents made up the bulk of the cast. Georgia and I had met years earlier when she asked me to teach for the Dance Masters seminar in Boston, and subsequently for her school in Mendon. The previous year I had staged *Les Sylphides* for Georgia's sister Helen, for her group on the North Shore, the Salem Ballet. In this, only the second year of what became a longstanding tradition for Georgia and me, the production was given a major boost with the score being played live by the Greater Marlborough Symphony Orchestra. The art of staging ballets is a specific but extremely useful skill to develop. Teaching the choreography is only one part of staging a ballet and in some ways is the easier part. Helping all of the dancers look their best is one of the challenges I find most compelling, particularly when working with nonprofessionals. My goal is to achieve something everyone can be proud of. The headline on one local review read, "'Nutcracker' Was a Miracle of Professionalism for Area," so I guess we succeeded. The most important thing, though, was seeing the joy and pride on the kids' faces. I could remember what that felt like when I was their age.

Another potential postdancing career skill I began to dabble in was choreography, although I'll say right away, it wasn't one that ultimately grabbed me. I did have fun, though, creating a work for David Drummond's Copley Square Ballet, the company that I'd guested with previously. My ballet, *Occasional Waltzes*, was an abstract work for seven dancers, with music by six different composers. It was both playful and romantic; fortunately, despite my recent professional and personal hardships, I hadn't lost my belief in fun or love.

20

En Avant

En avant. Origin: French. Forward. When a dancer moves en avant, he or she is traveling downstage, toward the audience.

I T WASN'T technically a vacation, but no one had to twist my arm to join the group of company members that traveled down to Bermuda in January 1985. Billed as "The Boston Ballet Chamber Company," we performed as part of the tenth-anniversary season of the Bermuda Festival. Although my sections on the mixed program we presented were physically taxing, I was determined to sneak in plenty of beach time. Between getting away from Boston in the heart of winter and the recent turmoil, the trip promised to be something of a respite for me. Alas, it was January in Bermuda and cold and windy, so no sun bathing for me.

Well, you know what they say about best-laid plans. As it turned out, before we left I came down with a nasty case of the flu and had to get a shot of B12 to get out of bed and onto the plane to Bermuda. What had sounded like a working holiday was now becoming a slog. My weakness from being sick was compounded by the fact that the stage we danced on was concrete. And as luck would have it, *Madrilene* and *Preludes,* the two ballets I performed, were full of jumps. Professional stages and studios are almost always equipped with "sprung" floors that are built with a small amount of give so dancers have a bit of cushioning designed to protect their joints, which is particularly important in the landings and rebounds of allegro work. After being sick in bed for about two weeks, my musculature felt nonexistent;

my brain got me into the air, but then there wasn't much left to control my descent onto the unforgiving concrete floor. After a couple of performances I had what I thought was a pulled hamstring muscle and thus treated it that way, but it didn't seem to get any better. It was in this miserable condition, by the way, that Bruce Marks—one of the short-listed candidates for Boston Ballet's next artistic director—first saw me dance. So, it was in my best professional interest to dance through the injury and as full out as I could, which ended up being a big mistake.

Back in Boston, after a series that included excerpts of *The Sleeping Beauty*, Arleen Walaszek, the company's physical therapist, was working arduously on that leg one day until she finally said, "You know, La, I can't get rid of this tight band of muscle, and it's all around your thigh. I think you need to have a bone scan." Off I went to Dr. Lyle Micheli who diagnosed it as a stress fracture; it had started at the back and gone completely around my femur. He told me that I had to get off that leg immediately or the bone would break completely—and then I'd be out for months. So I took what I thought was enough time off, skipping the March series of performances.

I knew I wanted to be back by April, in time to dance my last *Swan Lake* run with Donn, who had announced that he was leaving at the end of the season. Everything felt fine until the dress rehearsal, when I felt what I now recognized as bone pain. I'd indeed refractured the femur, but—and here's the part I'm sorry to have any students read—I did most of the *Swan Lake* performances anyway, grinding through the thirty-two fouettés on that leg night after night. I bowed out of the very last show, not because I had finally wised up, but so that I could get through another tour. Principal dancer Christopher Aponte had arranged a series of performances in Taiwan, and naturally I was loath to pass on the opportunity to perform in Asia again. In Taiwan I performed a variety of pas de deux on the mixed bill, several with Donn, and *Le Corsaire* with Aponte.

In the end my body eventually gave out, as was inevitable; one night in Taiwan my quadriceps simply seized as if to say, "That's it, you are not doing anything more." This was one time that I was determined to make lemonade out of life's lemons. We had open-ended plane tickets and two weeks before we were due back in Boston, so a couple of us had made arrangements to go to Hawaii. If I hadn't gotten my beach holiday in Bermuda, you bet I was

going to have one in Maui! Leslie Jonas and I flew in from Taiwan; Bruce
Wells, from Washington, D.C.; and my high school girlfriend Diane, from
Boston. Diane was the first to arrive, so she had picked up the rental car and
found the way to the condo before heading to the airport to welcome us
with mai tais so that our party could begin immediately. She chauffeured
us to the condo on the beach we had rented for the next two weeks, and
what a fun, lovely time it was. We went parasailing, which didn't require
me to put pressure on my leg, but did give me the unforgettable experience
of essentially swimming with the dolphins. And every morning, now on a
cane, I would just walk and walk along the beach, slowly and methodically.

I paid for gambling with my leg, though, and was altogether on that cane
for nearly six months. Coincidentally, my absence from the stage overlapped
somewhat with Rose's, but her brief incapacitation was for the happiest of
reasons: in December she and Aloysius Petruccelli (Al) became the proud
parents of a baby girl, Jessica Monique. Together, Rose and I resumed dancing with the company by the beginning of the fall 1985 season. Al was no
longer the company's stage manager; that position had been taken over by
Phil Jordan, although with the growth of the company, the job was now
split. As director of production, Phil proved to be a worthy successor to Al,
as did his wife Susan Ring, who took on the title of stage manager. Phil and
Sue also became cherished friends and remain so to this day.

———

WHEN IT CAME DOWN TO the final selection for the permanent artistic
director, I was asked to serve with the board of trustees as a dancer represen-
tative. It's good practice to include dancers on the board, both for the sake of
transparency and of course because the artists' voices are crucial to the conversation. As you might imagine, however, there is often a bit of trepidation
on the dancer's part: will airing their opinions in such a setting possibly put
one's career in jeopardy? It may seem paranoid, but the fears aren't exactly
improbable. In any event, it meant I was thus part of the search process,
which included interviewing the candidates and then having dinner with
each, usually at one of the board member's homes. I feared that a newcomer
might come in and say, "Okay, here I am. I'm going to wrench things around
and see where we wind up." It is an artistic director's prerogative to shake

things up as much as he or she wants to, certainly, but I didn't think that more shaking up was what the company needed after several years of rocky terrain. To me, Bruce Wells represented excellence combined with an understanding of Boston Ballet—and the promise of a smoother transition emotionally for the dancers. We knew what to expect from him. But in the end, Bruce Marks was offered the position and in fact was very successful during his twelve-year tenure at the helm. Before coming to us, Marks had been the artistic director at Ballet West, based in Utah. Though that company was smaller and less well known than Boston Ballet, under Marks's direction it had grown considerably and was respected within the dance community. His business acumen was often touted as a prominent feature in his leadership roles; quite the charismatic charmer, Marks was an effective fundraiser. By the end of his second year in Boston, not only was the crushing debt that had grown to over a million dollars erased, but also there was now even some reserve money in the kitty.

A former dancer with American Ballet Theatre and the Royal Danish Ballet, Marks also had significant pedigree as a performer, and immediately set about getting his artistic staff in place. The disappointment that some had about Bruce W. being passed over for the top job was somewhat mitigated when Marks named him associate artistic director. Two Bruces were certainly better than none! I was also delighted to learn that he'd appointed Sydelle Gomberg as the director of the school. I considered Sydelle, the former dean of the arts at Walnut Hill School of the Performing Arts, and the chair of its dance department, to be a mentor when it came to teaching. As you may recall, with her special blend of warmth, wit, and wisdom, she helped me survive my first foray into teaching a class, and I would look to her—and of course to Sydney—for guidance in that area for years to come.

As is often the case with someone coming in from the outside, Marks brought in some new faces. In her role as ballet mistress, former ballerina Anna-Marie Holmes became one of the company teachers and coaches, working alongside our beloved longtime regisseur and ballet master, James Capp. By now, after a year of guest conductors, permanent positions were filled with Ottavio de Rosa named as music director and Myron Romanul as principal conductor. At the administrative level, in the end Elaine's husband David retained his title of general manager.

With Donn's imminent departure I was about to lose a fabulous partner, but soon enough two new leading men came into in my life. One, William Pizzuto (Billy), was an accomplished dancer who had worked for Marks at Ballet West and came aboard as a principal when Marks took over. Another male principal who danced with the company during that time was the refined dancer Frank Augustyn. On loan from his permanent company, the National Ballet of Canada, he appeared frequently as a guest over the course of several years. Marie-Christine and Frank proved to be a particularly lovely match—as Bruce W. had known they would be when he contracted Frank. Both tall and stately with model-worthy looks, they were an elegantly glamorous pair on stage.

Although Frank and I danced Balanchine's *Tchaikovsky Pas de Deux*, we weren't as physically compatible, but Billy—a dashing and playful partner —and I were and hit it off right away. Billy and I opened Boston Ballet's twenty-second season—and the first with Marks as artistic director— as Basilio and Kitri in the company's restaging of Nureyev's *Don Quixote*. What a bold, perhaps curious move to begin with the production that had been first a boon and then baggage for the company. I'm sure that even the confident Marks breathed a sigh of relief when thankfully, this time around, no one was injured and the production went seamlessly. Following *Don Q*, we dove into preparations for the *Nutcracker* season, which was cochoreographed by the two Bruces. Toward the end of the run, two nights before Christmas, as I came off stage—huffing, puffing, and sweating—I met Christopher Mehl, the guy who was to become my *other* leading man but as an offstage, rather than onstage, partner. A friend of corps de ballet member Christopher Adams, Chris M. was watching from backstage because Adams hadn't been able to get him a ticket for that show. In the moment, we said a brief hello. After the performance, however, Adams brought him downstairs and asked if his friend could smoke a cigarette in my dressing room. Back then you could still smoke indoors but not just anywhere as in the past. It was known which dressing rooms were "smoking" and which were "non." As Chris recounted later, when he walked in the doorway and saw me with an unlit cigarette in one hand and a Beck's Dark beer in the other (my postperformance carb-loading of choice in those days and the "carrot" on the end of the stick calling to me to get through yet another set of fouettés), he thought, Now that's the woman for me. I was likewise immediately attracted; he was quite handsome but also funny, sweet, and smart.

About a week later I decided to throw a New Year's Eve party and make sure he was invited. We talked more that evening, the chemistry between us just bubbling to the surface. Chris was endlessly fascinating to me, sensitive, goofy, and dependable all at once. A true man of many talents, he is an excellent musician, filmmaker, cook, gardener, hair stylist, and foot masseur extraordinaire. He came to a performance a month later when he was doing his thesis project for Emerson College, focusing on a new research program directed by Ellen J. Wallach that was called "Life after Performing: Career Transitions for Dancers." After the performance he asked me if he could interview me for his thesis; I was thirty-eight years old at the time and figured I would be facing retirement myself in the not-too-distant future. So I agreed, suggesting that he come over to my house after he was done with school Tuesday night, a night I wasn't performing. That Tuesday also happened to be Valentine's Day, so he showed up with a bottle of wine. And the rest, as they say, is history.

Our romance blossomed right away, and it was the most natural thing in the world to us; we were so compatible, like the proverbial peas in a pod. Chris turned out to be the gem I knew he was. About eighteen months later, on August 23, 1987, we married. We've been in love, and laughing a lot, the whole time, for thirty years and counting. Tony was the great love of my youth; Chris is the great love of my life.

———————

CHRIS'S REQUEST to interview me for his thesis project—and my acceptance—wasn't just a red herring, an excuse to get together. I really did know that "career transitions" loomed ahead for me. Indeed, the previous summer, while I was still recuperating from my broken femur, I was cast in an entirely new role when Marks named me assistant artistic director of Boston Ballet II. Led by soloist Richard Dickinson, the company's junior ensemble was composed of dancers who had been recruited from the school's big Summer Dance Program, an intensive workshop that attracted students from all over. These programs are now ubiquitous, serving both as financial resources for ballet companies and as a way to seek out potential young talent. Today, Boston Ballet's Summer Dance Program is five weeks long, but in the heyday of the "ballet boom" years, ours and other schools ran the sessions for up to eight weeks, and students clamored to score a coveted spot, happily giving up their entire summers. Summer students who were offered contracts in Boston Ballet II continued training throughout the year and sometimes appeared in ensemble sections with the main company in larger productions. They also performed in lecture/demonstrations or mini-performances throughout Massachusetts, often at schools or nursing homes. The young dancers' biggest moment to shine came every summer when the group performed outdoors at the Hatch Shell.

As Richard's assistant, I shared both teaching and "schlepping" duties. While packing up costumes and dancers and trucking off somewhere could be tiring—after all, I was still dancing full time—it brought up fond memories of my early days with Virginia and Sydney, when we toured as the humble little New England Civic Ballet. "Guerilla ballet" lived on. When I took over as director the following year, after Richard left for the Ohio Ballet, I remembered how Virginia seemed like the mother hen to us chicks. I found myself feeling the same way about these young dancers, so fresh-faced, eager, scared, and hopeful all at once.

My history with the company was also on Marks's mind. One day he asked me just how long I'd been there, and he came up with the idea of throwing a gala celebration for me, to celebrate my twenty-five years of dancing for Boston audiences. At first, I was reluctant, both because it was uncomfortable to be the only one so honored and because I was admittedly suspicious that this was maybe more about creating a fundraising opportunity for the company. Understanding that it was first and foremost a great honor, I graciously and gratefully accepted. The math did require a lot of explaining, however, since Boston Ballet itself was only twenty-three years old. So my gala ended up being a good opportunity to remind, or even inform, many people about the company's early history, about New England Civic Ballet, and about Virginia's professional ballet studios. My reluctance about the whole thing aside, I was proud of my part in that history.

And so on November 6, 1986, after a performance of our new production of *Coppélia*, I was feted in quite a grand manner. First, immediately after curtain, an onstage tribute to me unfolded; it included slides of me and of Virginia too. William Como, then *Dance Magazine*'s editor in chief, read a complimentary address, while I madly changed from Swanhilda into "me." As a gift to me, the designer Alfred Fiandaca created a gorgeous but body-hugging silver gown that also had an overpanel of ruffles that made it reminiscent of art deco. Sheridan Heynes—a former dancer turned wardrobe master—waited just offstage in the quick-change dressing room with towels powdered with cornstarch to dry me off, so that I could get my sweaty body into that slinky gown. When the tribute and slides were done, the upstage curtain opened at center back, revealing me in all my twenty-fifth silver glory. Students from the school laid blankets of flowers at my feet, silver mylar confetti fell from the fly space, and scores of my dear colleagues, present and past, hugged and kissed me. It was, as you can imagine, extraordinarily moving, made even more so because of the presence of my parents, my brother, my newfound beau Chris—and of course because of the absence of Virginia.

After this, we were driven to the Ritz-Carlton Hotel, a posh Boston landmark, for an equally lavish dinner. It was wonderful to celebrate with so many of my true friends, who had been right there with me during the highlights of my career and had also supported and encouraged me in the low moments. Donn was there too; he'd returned to the company but was now serving in an administrative position. In his new role as development officer, he'd done a lot of the work putting my gala together and had one of my pointe shoes "silvered" for the occasion. Proceeds from the event went into a scholarship fund in my name. For years it gave me great pleasure to select, from the many hardworking and talented young dancers coming up in the school, one special student to receive the scholarship.

———

WHAT A CHANGE Marks's first two years in charge proved for all of us. One of the first things he did was lop off "The" from our title, and refine and modernize the company logo, signifying a new era. After the whiplash-like couple of years we'd had, the atmosphere was finally relatively calm. Buoyed by this and the overall positive reception of Marks, there was a renewed sense of excitement that extended beyond us to the public and the critics, who seemed to have faith in the company again. Marks, Wells, and the growing organization buckled down and got to work refurbishing the many good things we already had, while revitalizing and expanding upon the qualities that made Boston Ballet special. Virginia's work went forward. Marks's programming for the 1986 season reflected the kind of repertoire she'd developed over the years. A handful of "classic" story ballets were grounded by dramatic one-acts and purely abstract ballets and then spiked with a bold new contemporary work. The last was provided by the modern choreographer Mark Morris, whose somber, mysterious *Mort Subite* depicted an anonymous, agitated ensemble; it was a bit of a departure for Morris, whose previous works had often been lighter in mood. Thirty years later, Morris is one of the leading figures in modern dance—his keenly musical dances have led to favorable comparisons to Balanchine—but when Marks commissioned him in 1986, he was just beginning to make a name for himself. As a younger dancer, Marks himself had been lauded for his adroitness with modern choreography, and as a director, he would prove to have a strong interest in bringing full-fledged "moderns" to set works on the company. Occasionally one of these walks on the wilder side fizzled (*Bee Hive* comes to mind), but Marks's experimental streak showed gumption.

Along with *The Nutcracker*, that year's story ballets included a revival of Choo San's *Romeo and Juliet*, an old-but-new-to-us production of *Coppélia*, and Bruce Wells's brand-new *A Midsummer Night's Dream*. Though based on Arthur Saint-Léon's original version, this *Coppélia* was more rooted in character dance than other versions. With staging and additional choreography by the Royal Danish Ballet's Hans Brenaa and Hans Beck, it was more suitable to the nonflashy style of the Danish company. In any event, it was a delight to work with Brenaa again, who came back, after all of these years, to stage the ballet and coach us. Additionally, we had the enriching and exhilarating experience of working alongside the incomparable Danish dancer/mime Niels Bjørn Larsen, who appeared as a guest artist in the role of Dr. Coppélius.

And oh, Bruce Wells's *Midsummer*, in which I danced Titania, queen of the fairies, was just the loveliest ballet you could imagine, full of magic and mischief. Bruce is a master at telling the story through the movements rather than through copious amounts of dry mime. There were beautiful children flitting about the stage like fireflies, gauzy fairies, electric sprites, and even good doses of slapstick humor. It was all ingeniously woven together, like gossamer, into a fine work of art. It could be a symbol of that moment in Boston Ballet's history: as if, after being entangled in a spider's web of confusion, we'd been sprinkled with fairy dust and freed, sometimes even finding ourselves floating just above the surface.

21

Changement

Changement. Origin: French. Change. Changements are simple small jumps in which the dancer jumps straight up and switches legs midair so that the other foot lands in front.

MOST DANCERS, at one time or another, have been asked the same question: what is your favorite dance/role? I'm sure that often the answers are the same: whatever one I'm dancing at the time. That maxim was usually true for me too, but of course there are standouts, roles that particularly resonated at the time and that remain powerfully in my mind's eye now—and some even linger in my muscle memory. The special ones are like gifts to a dancer, and we know we have to make the most of them in the moment because there's no way of knowing if you'll ever get the chance to perform them again.

Fortunately, I did get to perform one of my all-time favorites, Agnes de Mille's *Rodeo*, several times over the years. I've told the story of how Billy Pizzuto and I had the privilege of going to New York City for private coaching by de Mille herself. Having this happen so late in my career made this particular "gift" even more precious to me. Some people are surprised to hear that dancers take class every day, but aside from the fact that it's the only way to maintain strength, flexibility, and overall technique, the truth is that you never stop learning. If that weren't so, I would have been bored. Gleaning much from my time with de Mille, and adding that fresh knowledge to my more mature perspective, it was deeply satisfying to get the chance to take on her Cowgirl again. We performed *Rodeo* a few times during the company's twenty-third season, including at Boston's Faneuil Hall Marketplace. Located between the city's waterfront and Government Center districts, the hall itself is one of Boston's most historic sites, built in 1742 and used throughout history as both a market and a meeting hall. "Quincy Market," the adjacent shopping area that had been recently rehabilitated, is now a famous tourist destination. But it was already considered a local landmark, so the fact that we were invited to perform during the market's tenth-anniversary celebration was a sign that the company was back in Boston's good graces. Riffing on an all-American theme, the program included, in addition to *Rodeo*, Balanchine's *Stars and Stripes* pas de deux. The two Bruces also collaborated to offer a special, Boston-centric pièce d'occasion, which they co-choreographed to a series of songs by the popular Boston-based rock band the Cars. The youthful and carefree ballet, *Shake It Up*, delighted the audience, and they *ate* it up.

But yes, of course I had my favorites. In the company's striking 1986 brochure, principal dancers were each given a two-page spread that included, along with our bios, two photographs taken by the famous dance photographer Jack Mitchell. In my pictures I was costumed as two of those favorites, Juliet and the Cowgirl. My "desert island" short list of roles also includes Giselle, Odette/Odile from *Swan Lake*, and Kitri from *Don Quixote*—oh, and *anything* by Balanchine. It's nice to realize that I didn't typecast myself. There are some similarities, I suppose—three tragic figures and three "spunky" figures—but the movement quality for each is quite different. In the case of *Swan Lake*, you get both types for the price of one, making for the greatest challenge to change personas midperformance not once but twice! In any event, each certainly felt like an entirely different character, and I thoroughly enjoyed plumbing the depths of them all.

A follow-up to the universal question about favorite roles is, what do I wish I had been able to dance but hadn't the opportunity? Do I have any regrets? As the song goes, I've had a few but only a few. I have always rued the fact that I missed out on performing the lead female in the late John Cranko's hilarious *Taming of the Shrew*; I think Kate and I would have gotten on tremendously. But alas, that ballet came into Boston Ballet's repertory shortly after I retired. Mostly though, I really count myself as fortunate; Boston

Ballet's repertoire was eclectic and challenging enough to usually keep me on my metaphoric toes.

I was also fortunate in that when I wasn't cast in something, the feeling was mutual, if you know what I mean. I knew I wouldn't be right for the part, either artistically or technically. But it wasn't easy to turn down the chance to perform in Balanchine's *Theme and Variations* when the company danced it for the first time in 1987. Originally created for Ballet Theatre in 1947, it's one of Balanchine's most classical ballets, an unabashed homage to both Petipa and Tchaikovsky (it's set to the final movement of the composer's Suite No. 3 for Orchestra). Romantic, powerful, technically difficult, and very, very fast, the piece has ballerinas wearing classical tutus while the men wear white tights; there is little to hide behind. Marks asked me if I'd like to do the lead female role. I think if he hadn't asked me, if he'd just put me in it, I would have just done it. But he did ask me, and I declined, telling him I thought it was too fast for me at that point. I was rounding the corner to forty, and I felt I wouldn't be up to par. While I knew it wouldn't have been good for me, nor the company, I do wonder if it made Marks see me differently, as less of an asset.

The tables were turned the following year, however, when Marks brought Birgit Cullberg's *Miss Julie* to the company. Based on August Strindberg's play, the 1950 ballet and the title role were highly dramatic. But for that program, I was cast instead in Bournonville's *Napoli*, a ballet I'd already done many times over the years, and with all of the jumping, I always seemed to have a flare-up of Achilles tendonitis afterward. In other words, it *wasn't* a ballet I cared to revisit, but *Miss Julie* was another story. I more or less begged him to cast me, but he said he needed to be able to have something for the soloists to do; I asked one more time—for just one performance—and he said no. It was the first and last time I'd ever asked for a role.

———————

IN MAY 1987, Rose became the first of us three "Gumm Sisters" to hang up her shoes, retiring at the close of the twenty-third season, after the last performance of the *Tales of Hans Christian Andersen* program. Like *Shake It Up*, this was a collaborative effort between Bruce Marks and Bruce Wells, although much more ambitious, as the evening was composed of three individual ballets. I performed as the Paper Ballerina, Billy's fated love in *The Steadfast Tin Soldier* section. Rose performed two very different variations on the "mother" theme: in *The Ice Maiden*, she was an innocent who falls victim to the title's chilly meanie; while in *The Wild Swans* she took on the role of the Evil Stepmother who places a curse on her eleven stepsons. Of course, for *that* role, Rose had to rely on acting chops. In real life she was a doting mother to Jessica Monique, who by now—where did the time go?—was two years old and able to totter across the stage after the last performance. Holding Marks's hand, Jessica made her way into her mother's arms while Rose got her turn at being celebrated by her adoring fans—and by us, her adoring colleagues. None of us wanted to see Rose leave the company, especially Elaine and me. Rose had been an inspiration to us all with her intense personal beauty, her extraordinary acting skills, and her unofficial title as the most powerful woman in the company. This was evidenced when Dr. Micheli and the sports medicine team had us dancers do a stress test in order to compare us to "normal" people. We all did pretty well on it, but Rose was the star.

Tales of Hans Christian Andersen and the following year's program called *The Scandinavians* (the one that included *Miss Julie* and *Napoli*) were in a way Marks's love letters to Denmark and the surrounding region. He considered Denmark his adopted country for, after dancing with American Ballet Theatre (ABT), he became the first American principal dancer to join the Royal Danish Ballet (RDB). There, he met Birgit Cullberg, whose works appealed strongly to him, and Harald Lander, the former RDB director who choreographed the immensely popular *Études*, which was the third piece on *The Scandinavians* program. *Études* is a stylized depiction of how classwork progresses, from pliés and tendus to pirouettes and allegro; it builds up quite thrillingly, so that by the end, the audience is usually cheering along while the dancers are sailing through huge jumps and electrifying turning sequences. It's the closest dancers come to being hailed like sports stars in an arena. The formidable skill of the dancers in accomplishing the over-the-top bravura displays makes it great fun for the performers and audience alike. Marks's strongest connection to the Danes, however, was Toni Lander. Toni was a famous Danish ballerina in her own right, and Harald Lander's former wife. She also danced at times with ABT, where she met Marks. They were married in 1966 and had three sons. Though they were no longer together by the time Marks got to Boston Ballet, her untimely death in 1985 was clearly a deep sorrow to him. Imagine being the artistic director of a ballet company and raising three sons on your own. Bravo, Bruce!

Thus Marks brought *Études* to Boston by way of not only Copenhagen but also New York City via ABT, where it, and of course *Theme and Variations*, were familiar to audiences. That company also yielded up new additions to our roster. Carla Stallings, who'd been a soloist with ABT, joined us as a principal at the beginning of our twenty-fourth season: Leslie Jonas had been promoted recently, so even though Rose had retired, there were now so many strong leading ladies that in the season-opening *Giselle* series, five different women performed the title role. As the newest member, Carla got one show, while soloist Lori Nowak received an unexpected—but well deserved—boost when she got two of those coveted performances, one of which was opening night, with Billy Pizzuto as her Albrecht. I was originally scheduled to perform that opening with Billy, my now-regular partner, but some last-minute shuffling occurred when Elaine was sidelined with ongoing back issues. As a result, I had my own surprising career stimulus when the casting musical chairs meant that I was paired with Elaine's Albrecht, Fernando Bujones.

At the time Bujones joined Boston Ballet as a "permanent guest artist," he was a star dancer with ABT and is now recognized as one of the greatest male dancers of his generation. Although he was born in Miami, his mother was Cuban, and he received some of his early training in Havana at Alicia Alonso's Vaganova-based school, which continues to produce some of the finest classical dancers in the world today. But he received the majority of his training at the School of American Ballet, and so, when he won the gold medal at the 1972 International Ballet Competition, he was the first American male to do so. He was invited to join New York City Ballet (NYCB), but the long, elegant, powerful Bujones, the epitome of the classical "prince," instead joined American Ballet Theatre and its repertoire laden with such roles. As I was delighted to discover, Bujones was the quintessential prince offstage too: a thoughtful colleague, sweet yet thoroughly professional, and very accommodating. Good thing too because we met for the first time at our dress rehearsal. I saw him standing over by our stage manager Sue Ring's call box, so I gathered up my courage, walked across the stage, stuck out my hand, and said, "Hi Fernando. I hope we know the same version!"

As it happened, the production we were performing was itself new, at least to our company. Staged by the company's ballet mistress Anna-Marie Holmes, this was the Kirov Ballet's version, with choreography by Leonid Lavrovsky based on the original by Jean Coralli and Jules Perrot. Anna-Marie had a strong connection with the esteemed Leningrad troupe. While still performing, she and her former husband David Holmes had had the honor of being the only North American dancers allowed to appear with the company. In Russia, Holmes had even been allowed to perform the title role in Lavrovsky's *Giselle*, which was noted for its emphasis on realism-based characterizations à la Stanislavski. Holmes arranged for one of her mentors, the former Kirov ballerina Natalia Dudinskaya and her husband, Konstantin Sergeyev, who was also a former dancer and a former director of the Kirov Ballet, to come and coach us. They had a wealth of artistic information to impart. Anna-Marie herself was hugely influenced and inspired by her time in Russia. Soon, under her supervision, the curriculum of the Boston Ballet School would be overhauled and its teachers would undergo extensive training in order to adopt the Vaganova syllabus.

These days, with former NYCB principal dancer Margaret Tracey directing the school, the syllabus has morphed again, with an emphasis on the brisk, clean, and light quality associated with Balanchine. Thus, a full circle of sorts has been drawn, all the way back to the company's early days when Virginia trucked down to New York to watch Mr. B teach when he was a mentor to her and an official adviser to Boston Ballet.

But most memorable and important to me about that production of *Giselle* was the remarkable experience of dancing with Fernando, one that I was to repeat again the following year when Elaine's back injury flared up. Then, the ballet was *La Sylphide*. I'd never gotten the chance to perform the lead role of the Sylph; the last time the company performed it was many years ago, in New York City with Nureyev—when, if you recall, I'd been deemed insufficiently weightless. Now, all of these years later, although there were no concerns in *that* department, I still wasn't cast in the lead. But I was still in the habit of following one of Virginia's hard and fast rules: if there is something you want to dance, get your butt in the studio and learn it.

It's both humbling and smart to put yourself in the back of the room and pick up what you can while others are in the front getting the lion's share of attention. This lesson from our earliest years indeed paid off in so many ways, even when I didn't get to perform something I'd understudied. Of course, in theory, union rules don't "allow" you to spend extra time doing something like that—learning and rehearsing something you're not scheduled to dance. But I didn't care about that; I wanted the information. It made me a better dancer. In this instance, Elaine's disappointment aside, the extracurricular work paid off: I had the double pleasure of dancing a role I'd otherwise perhaps not have performed and another opportunity to work alongside the great Bujones.

———

MEANWHILE, I had married my real-life prince, Chris, at the end of a very busy summer, the first in which I was fully in charge of directing both the summer program and Boston Ballet II. For the junior ensemble's August series of outdoor performances at the Hatch Shell, I choreographed *Champ Dances*, set to music composed by Chris and his friend Chet Cahill. Chet and his wife Billie became my great friends too, and the four of us quickly became like family. *Champ Dances* was my second piece for BBII (the previous year I'd choreographed *Albinoni Suite* for the young dancers), and although I enjoyed collaborating with Chris and Chet, with both dances I sweated through the choreographic process. While my earlier experience with David Drummond's Copley Square Ballet had been fun, choreographing wasn't something that I had a driving desire to do. I was known to say that choreography for me is perspiration, not inspiration. But since Marks had encouraged me to create something for BBII, I was willing to at least be game and give it another try. I like to joke that I was glad he coerced me into choreographing so I could find out that it wasn't something I really wanted to do.

What I really did enjoy, however, was working with the young dancers in the junior company, something I continued to do for another ten years or so. I began to discover that for me, teaching was as rewarding as performing. I simply love it. In a way, it's as big a performing art as being on stage. It's thrilling when you see the kids "get it," when you see the light bulb moment;

when you offer just the right slant on what they've got to do to achieve, say, a double pirouette and then they *do* a double pirouette, they're stunned, elated. But I was just beginning to learn how to teach, so when I received an award from the Dance Teachers' Club of Boston in 1987, it wasn't because I'd somehow managed to become a brilliant teacher in such a short time. Sweetly, this organization, which had honored Virginia years earlier for her contributions to the dance world, recognized me for my "devotion to the art of dance and for the joy and beauty you have given to Boston."

In terms of choreography, I'm a much better "janitor"; I like to clean up other people's works, help the movement and patterns, and make the dancers look their best, so the choreographer's vision is honored and allowed to shine. Thus, directing BBII while I was still dancing allowed me to realize that through teaching, rehearsing, and coaching, I had something else I could offer Boston Ballet in addition to dancing. And for me, the work was both comfortable and enriching.

Here's another little funny thing I discovered about myself: as director of BBII, I had to welcome the thousands of audience members who sat out there each evening under the stars and tell them a bit about the dancers and about the evening's program. It turns out that after nearly three decades of using only my body to speak to a crowd, I was quite comfortable using my voice. I chalk it up to Dad, who was a ham radio operator and who, when I was fairly young, taught me how to be one too by speaking clearly into a microphone. In addition to my increasing ballet studies and entry into high school, I studied and earned my novice license in Morse code. In case ballet didn't work out, maybe I could go into broadcasting! Public speaking— who knew?

The first night I introduced BBII I remember being surprised for a brief moment when I heard my voice bounce back to me in that vast open space along the Charles River. At first it rattled me. Due to the great distance from the stage to the Arthur Fiedler Bridge, there was a ten-second delay in my voice reaching back to me on stage. Hearing the words I was speaking in my head and then my voice from ten seconds ago was initially confusing. When I realized I mustn't listen to my echo, things moved along well, and ultimately I found I was pretty good at it.

The day after BBII's last summer performance that year, Chris and I got married in the backyard of the house we'd bought in a neighborhood on the southernmost edge of Boston. As our collaborative effort on *Champ Dances* was a major event for us, and our parents had not yet met, the "rehearsal dinner" was a picnic on the Esplanade. For the wedding, Chris's friends Bob and Roz Koff provided violin and keyboard music; his former professor Micki Dickoff made a video; Bruce Wells made the cake (chocolate, my favorite); dear friend Henry Wong made my dress, and Sheridan Heynes made the headpiece. All of our closest and dearest family and friends were there to celebrate. We still live in that lovely, peaceful house surrounded by trees and gardens that we've created and nurtured along the way.

––––––––––

WHILE I WAS LEARNING how to juggle this sudden confluence of many roles—dancer, director, teacher, and, not least of all, wife again—the company, under the two Bruces' leadership, had finally regained its balance, and then some. The artistic situation had stabilized to the point that the company felt secure enough to push forward with some much-needed and long-delayed improvements. In 1987 a $7.6 million capital campaign was undertaken, with two main goals: financial security and the major rehabilitation of our crumbling studios and offices on Clarendon Street. The neighborhood where we were headquartered had been steadily improving around us: in place of the one greasy-spoon choice we'd had for many of our early years in the South End there were now nice bakeries, decent places to get lunch, and even a fancy dinner now and then. But as often happens in similar urban situations, with the improvements came higher rents, and a lot of people were priced out of the neighborhood. This gentrification thus created an imbalance of another kind in our midst.

To the wonder of many of us who'd been there from the company's penny-pinching, hardscrabble early days, Boston Ballet was apparently joining the middle class too. Architect Graham Gund's designs looked as if we'd skipped ahead into royalty: the old Pennock building was getting more than a makeover—it was being made into a palace. We'd now have seven studios —seven!—with one, the "Grand Studio," running the length of the building, so the full company could rehearse ballets with the same amount of space as that of the stage at the Wang Center for Performing Arts (the new name for our old performance home, the Metropolitan Center). Not only would the dancers fit in there, but also the orchestra could rehearse with the dancers. There'd also be a state-of-the-art physical therapy room and exercise equipment, nice locker rooms, and lounge areas. After morning company class, smaller groups could be scheduled more easily throughout the day in the other six studios as needed. Afternoon school classes would occupy several studios, but with efficient planning, there was now ample room for everyone. And along with being outfitted with properly sprung floors surfaced with new marley, the studios themselves were simply beautiful, most of them with big windows overlooking the South End's handsome brownstones and relatively quiet side streets.

As the company began to surge forward again, Marks reached back and reinstated something that had been near and dear to Virginia's heart. In 1988, the Boston International Choreographers' Competition returned, and once again, the event drew lots of press and attention from within the dance world, and just as in the "old days," over two hundred videos were sent in for consideration. *Unlike* the old days though, four of the five finalists were women, although the "gold medalist," Ralph Lemon, was male. But the fact that Lemon was an African American and a modern dancer/choreographer was a reminder of the ways in which the relatively conservative ballet world was continually diversifying. Because the competition performances were held in February, Elaine and I were precluded from dancing in them. Throughout that month she and I were on a fourteen-city summer program audition tour, she as director of the Children's Summer Workshop and I as director of the Summer Dance Program.

The two of us did the audition tour together for many years, often right before returning to dance in the February seasons. I would teach the barre to auditionees while Elaine would do it with them, and then she taught center so she could give all her recruits the eagle eye. By reversing the process for the older group, we both managed to stay in shape enough to be able to go right back into rehearsals upon our return. But the schedule was punishing. In order for us to dance as well as scout for these programs, auditions in fourteen cities had to be crammed into seventeen days. At the end of each day we treated ourselves to a delicious meal, a bottle of wine, and some crème brûlée. Of course, with such a tight schedule and with the travel agent trying to save the company money, snafus were inevitable.

On occasion we had been booked into what ended up being a less-than-respectable hotel when all others were booked due to conventions, and we'd have to think on our feet to find another place. We definitely did not want to stay in a place where we weren't safe. One weekend, we were carrying a briefcase full of cash—audition fee proceeds from five cities—and were dismayed to find ourselves in a Miami motel without a safety deposit box. We were told that there weren't any because they had all been drilled open. Hmm. So now they knew we had something valuable with nowhere to store it. Thus, we two diminutive ladies in our black trench coats went walking down the South Dixie Highway with a briefcase full of money, desperately seeking food—since, of course, this low-end motel didn't have a restaurant. Needless to say, we were very nervous and never got our crème brûlée.

————

IN MAY 1988, we had the bittersweet joy of closing the company's twenty-fourth season with Bruce Wells's *A Midsummer Night's Dream*. I loved performing this ballet again, but I knew that soon after the *Midsummer* run, Bruce would be leaving the company. I was so grateful for all Bruce had done for me—personally, as my friend, and professionally, as the creator of many ballets that were so wonderful to dance—and for the company. I'm glad he wasn't "thrown under the bus" during the challenging years of Violette Verdy's tenure and that he was given an important role even after Marks came in. And so, we held another celebration to honor yet another person moving on from Virginia's cradle. It happens; I know that. It doesn't make it less difficult to see your dearest colleagues take their final bows on the stage they've graced for so long.

And I'm human. It crossed my mind more than once that before long it would be my turn to take that bow.

22

Révérence

Révérence. Origin: French. Reverence. Ballet classes traditionally end
with révérence, typically a short and simple exercise composed of port
de bras and curtsies or bows intended to thank the accompanist and
teacher. The bows and curtsies at the end of performances are essentially
révérences too, the dancers thanking the audience for their presence and
attention.

IN 1989, TWO YEARS AFTER I celebrated my twenty-fifth year as a
Boston ballerina, it was Boston Ballet's turn to mark its own silver anniversary. There was indeed much to revel about, and accordingly, a fancy
gala evening was presented for the next-to-last performance of the March
program to commemorate some of the company's proud history. Virginia
Williams and Sydney Leonard, the two women who'd probably contributed the most in terms of sweat equity, were represented in the performance
lineup. Virginia's lovely duet *Sea Alliance*, which had been a touring staple
in the early years, was reworked for the event for Dede Myles and Shawn
Mahoney, a new member of the corps de ballet who'd recently come up
through BBII. Sydney restaged her *Defilade* that she'd created for the
twentieth-anniversary gala program; this exhilarating processional was as
joyous as it had been five years earlier, showcasing students of the school as
well as my BBII charges and, finally, company members.

Boston Ballet's long-standing tradition of cultivating a repertoire that
encompassed the past, the present, and the future was evident in this gala
program. "Warhorses" such as the Black Swan pas de deux from *Swan Lake*

and the wedding pas from *Don Quixote* mingled with Bruce Marks's contemporary duet *Inscape*, set to music by Béla Bartók, and a solo from Maurice Béjart's *Seven Greek Dances*. Modern choreographer Monica Levy's *Ghosts* provided a reminder that Marks had recently reinstated the Choreographers' Competition; Levy's piece had won second-place honors the previous year. In keeping with the occasion's overall grandeur, the "grand polonaise" from Balanchine's *Theme and Variations* opened the evening. Fernando Bujones, who performed the Béjart solo, also appeared in his own staging of the act 3 divertissements from Petipa's majestic *Raymonda*. The company's best and brightest were everywhere on this sparkling program: veterans, up-and-comers, and even a young future star or two.

Of the latter, the seventeen-year-old wunderkind Jennifer Gelfand, along with her equally precocious partner Daniel Meja, whipped the crowd into something of a frenzy with their on-the-edge-of-your-seat performance of the *Don Q* pas. From an early age, Jennifer had exhibited a rare, prodigy-like talent. While a young student in the school, Jennifer had danced the lead child's role of Clara in *Nutcracker*; I remember it well because I was her Sugar Plum Fairy! In recent years, she'd been traveling to New York City to study with David Howard, seen by many as a kind of guru ballet teacher to the stars. When in NYC, I too had studied with him at the Harkness House as often as finances would allow. His classes were ever challenging, musical, inspiring, and full of insights and wisdom. Though Jennifer was still a teenager, her enormous talent was evident to everyone, and indeed, after appearing as a guest soloist in the May 1989 full-length production of *Don Q*, she joined the company officially the following season, jumping over the ranks right to principal dancer status.

There were many other new faces in addition to Jennifer and Daniel; in particular, it seemed that we were suddenly teeming with men. Indeed, there were more male principals than females, with Simon Dow, Michael Job, and Serge Lavoie joining Fernando, Devon Carney, and Billy Pizzuto at the top.

Naturally, in this gala program I held court in the "veteran" category, and such a court it was! Marks had the cheeky idea of having me dance the Rose Adagio from *The Sleeping Beauty* with four of the company's now-retired leading men, colleagues who had given me so much support—both physical and moral—at different stages of my career. While I'd been proud of the work I'd done developing my "Aurora" over the years, because of the ballet's exceptional technical difficulty, you may recall that I was relieved when it had been put to bed after several seasons. But this time around, with Elaine's husband David Brown, Jimmy Capp, Donn Edwards, and Bruce Wells as my Cavaliers, the usually nail-biting, endurance-testing, and composure-challenging Rose Adagio was just a joy to perform—despite the fact that I'd strained a groin muscle a few days before the opening. As always, once on stage and with some minor choreographic adjustments, any discomfort seemed to magically evaporate, particularly during this "family reunion." It seems that I was seen giggling once or twice; I could hardly help myself.

Elaine herself was always in the wings during that Rose Adagio party, there to offer her own support of course but also because she performed directly after us on this program. Somehow, despite the serious and often debilitating problems she was now frequently experiencing with her back, she performed Fokine's iconic *Dying Swan* solo, her rippling port de bras and extravagant arches belying any pain. She was—as she'd always been—breathtakingly beautiful, the epitome of ethereal grace. I stayed to watch every performance I could. This moving portrayal of a swan's last flight was, in fact, her own swan song. She retired from dancing after these performances, so now I was the last Gumm Sister still traversing the boards.

———

THE PUBLIC EXTRAVAGANCE of the big twenty-fifth-anniversary celebrations aside, our daily company life was spent laboring in our decidedly *unstylish* temporary home in the nearby suburb of Newton, Massachusetts. There were four "studios" made from a medium-sized classroom, the cafeteria, and the gymnasium. The gym of the former Bigelow School was retrofitted to serve as two big studios separated by a not-so-soundproof wall, in which the company could have class and rehearse, while other classrooms now housed administrative offices. When rehearsals were going on in both of the gym studios, we likened it to "dueling Steinways." At times, it could be thoroughly confusing, since many of us were in every ballet, and the conflicting music would cause attention spans to drift. Nonetheless, though it was a far cry from the sophisticated space we would move into once our Clarendon Street building was renovated, Newton ultimately served us well.

In this new environment, and with a great deal of business and marketing savvy, the school began to rapidly grow. By the time the South End studios were ready for our return, there were enough students to warrant opening a satellite school right there in Newton. Today, under the direction of former company member Tamara King, it has the largest enrollment of Boston Ballet School's three campuses; in addition to Boston and Newton, there is also a branch in the North Shore town of Marblehead.

Our ad hoc work atmosphere was a funny contrast to the chic aura that often surrounded the company in that glittering anniversary year. Like Cinderella, during the day we sweated and toiled in the humble quarters of our temporary home, while at night we were magically transformed into one glamorous creature or persona after another. In addition to seeking perhaps lesser-known choreographic talent through the Choreographers' Competition, Marks made a point of spicing up the repertoire with contemporary ballet works from the current generation of "hot" international choreographers, many of them based outside the United States. In the "Iconoclasts" program, the company premiere of William Forsythe's *Love Songs* was paired with Jiři Kylián's *Symphony in D* and James Kudelka's *Alliances*.

Although Forsythe was American born, he would become famous for the works that he created overseas. Originally commissioned by Nureyev for the Paris Opera Ballet, Forsythe's 1987 *In the Middle, Somewhat Elevated* is considered to be one of the most groundbreaking ballets of its time and is usually a hit with audiences today; Boston Ballet added it to its repertoire in 2002. (Recently, Mikko Nissinen, Boston Ballet's current artistic director, entered into a five-year agreement for Forsythe to create new works for the company.) Perhaps the equivalent of "grunge" in the music scene, *In the Middle* is seen by many to be a game changer and is a work that ushered in the kind of hip coolness that many contemporary ballets now impart, the dancers moving with an unsettling mix of nonchalant intensity. Set to a sometimes piercingly loud electronic score by Thom Willems, *In the Middle* thrilled many people, but some were put off by its casual disregard for anything resembling "traditional" balletic lyricism.

Its title notwithstanding, Forsythe's *Love Songs*—set to a series of songs sung by Aretha Franklin and Dionne Warwick—is likewise emotionally jarring, the cast's women dancing with the unabashed anger, frustration, or despair conjured by their relationships with their male partners. In contrast, Kylián's 1976 *Symphony in D* is humorous and brimming with playful invention; set to exuberant music by Franz Josef Haydn, the choreography is indeed rooted in classical vocabulary but often executed at devilish speeds.

Meanwhile, unlike the range of reactions that the original Nijinsky/ Stravinsky production of *Le Sacre du Printemps* garnered in Paris in 1913, when Boston Ballet performed Béjart's erotic 1970 version later that season, it intoxicated some audience members and was met with "polite" interest by others. The famously "puritanical" Boston viewers had certainly come a long way in terms of openness as to what ballet could be; I believe that Virginia's early commitment to an eclectic repertoire laid the groundwork for the audiences Boston Ballet attracts today. In any event, I didn't perform in any of these ballets new to the company; I'd missed the "Iconoclasts" program entirely because I'd torn some cartilage in my knee a couple of months earlier in the *Nutcracker* season, and although I did dance in the company's premiere of Balanchine's witty *Bourrée Fantasque*, I was struggling physically.

––––––––––

DESPITE MY UNFORTUNATE series of injuries at this time, I figured I'd come out of them and continue dancing as usual. Yes, I knew that at this point it wouldn't be for much longer, but I thought I had another couple of years in me. Thankfully, I was able to nurse my knee to a point where it was manageable, and my groin injury (never a dull moment) had healed sufficiently so that by the end of the twenty-fifth-anniversary season I was just able to take on Kitri and *Don Q* again.

And this was just in time, as it turned out, to take my own final bows as a professional dancer. In March 1989, during my annual contract talk with Marks, I learned that he had decided this season ought to be my last, ending with *Don Q*. Oh, there was an offer of *Nutcracker*, but that was no enticement after having performed it for so many seasons. Stunned and not sure what to say, I just sat there in the meeting trying to digest what this would mean for me, both professionally and financially—not to mention my pride. With time, however, I came to understand that Marks saw what I could not at the time. So few dancers, particularly at the principal level, are mentally ready to retire because performing and rehearsing has been part of their daily lives for years, even decades, and they've become attached to their colleagues and local audience. While demoralized because I was not given a warning and therefore didn't see it coming, I'd been in the business long enough to have seen it happen to others; I just didn't foresee it happening to me. I suppose all "veterans" feel the same. Within the company, we referred to ourselves as "MAs," mature artists, knowing full well that the end was nearing. At the moment, however, tired of trying to piece myself back together, from injury after injury, it was easy to acquiesce.

So I did what I'd been doing for nearly three decades: I pulled myself together and dove into rehearsals. And now it was my turn to act as mentor to younger dancers such as Jennifer, who was cast as one of the Kitris for that production. Offering advice to Jennifer reminded me of the company's beginning days, back when I myself was a teenager getting help from dancers such as Sara Leland. I realize, as I think back on it now, that being in that role probably helped to distract me from thinking too much about the unknowns that lay ahead for me. It's said that dancers die twice, the first time being when they retire from the stage. The metaphor is, of course, an exaggeration, but for many of us leaving the stage, it is indeed nothing less than a life-altering experience. How could it not be? Dancers' whole beings—minds, "spirits," and our very instruments, our bodies—are engaged in the daily pursuit of the impossible. The loss of that poetic and physical striving is profound; some experience it immediately, sharply, while others feel it over a longer period of time, like a dull ache. For most of us, thankfully, it doesn't necessarily mean that the "best part" of our lives is over, but it certainly means that a very significant part of our lives has come and gone. Dancing at the level that my peers and I did can be hard to match in terms of whatever's next in one's career. There's an assumption that most dancers will become teachers. Many do, certainly, and fortunate are the students who get to absorb some of the extensive troves of information these former dancers have. But it's not a given that every dancer can transfer his or her performance skills into the craft of teaching. Meanwhile, some dancers simply have no desire to teach, choreograph, or direct a company of their own. Some have a clear idea of what they want to do after retiring from the stage, and sometimes it has nothing to do with dance at all.

But of course, many dancers do stay in the field. After Elaine retired, she continued to teach and became quite an inspirational ballet mistress and coach, both in Boston and later, at Pacific Northwest Ballet (PNB). She and David eventually moved to Seattle, where he had accepted the executive director position at PNB. Dede Myles also became a top-notch teacher and coach, and served as the principal of the Boston campus of the school for several years before moving to Florida where she heads Orlando Ballet's excellent school. Longtime corps de ballet member Arthur Leeth was one of the first to teach in the school's adult program when it was just starting up and continues to do so today, while also serving as Boston Ballet's music administrator, a position he's held for more than twenty years. Some dancers, such as PeeWee (Jerilyn Dana), went into administrative positions within the company, while others such as Sheridan Heynes and Howard Merlin found themselves still involved in the creative process but behind the scenes, finding their new careers in the wardrobe department. Then, of course, there were those who did go on to direct their own ensembles in the region, for instance, David Drummond, Sam Kurkjian, James Reardon, Anthony Williams, and a host of others, and some who were hired to lead bigger groups around the country. After retiring, Fernando became artistic director of Orlando Ballet, although tragically he passed away in 2005, at the untimely age of fifty. Devon Carney is now leading Kansas City Ballet. Many former Boston Ballet dancers went on to teach at other schools, such as the Boston Conservatory, where Anamarie, Elaine, Denise Pons, Leslie Woodies, and I—to name a few from my generation—taught at various times. And many formed their own schools. So many Boston Ballet alums are out there in the world, sharing their gifts and knowledge with the next generations of dancers.

As for me, in addition to directing BBII, I also served for a couple of years as one of the company's ballet mistresses, where I discovered that I enjoyed coaching as much as I enjoyed teaching, and it was an inspiration to work with those young dancers. As the expression goes, by my students, I have been taught. I did, however, pass on one job that Marks offered me: in 1991, he established CityDance, a program that introduced classical ballet to underserved schoolchildren in the area, and he proposed that I be the director. In the same way that I discovered that choreography wasn't in my wheelhouse, so too did I know that teaching very young children was not a strong suit of mine. I am much more comfortable with teenagers and young (and older) adults. I'm convinced that my demurral was better for everyone involved. CityDance, by the way, has grown into an important resource for the community, as well as providing excellent training for students who may not otherwise be able to afford it; it recently celebrated its own twenty-fifth anniversary. Graduates of the program have gone successfully through the school and onto performing careers across the country and Europe. Our own Isaac Akiba is one of those dancers and is now a soloist with BB.

One of my biggest thrills as ballet mistress came when Marks asked me to stage Frederick Ashton's *Monotones I* for the company. Even though I felt I had done a pretty good job with *Monotones I*, and in general with my duties as ballet mistress, I was only kept on in that position for a couple of years. I was disappointed, but I rolled with the punches; I was getting good at it. After more than a decade of directing BBII, I became the principal of the school's Boston campus for ten years and then eventually moved into the same position on the Newton campus for two more years. By now I was no longer directing the summer school intensive in the Boston studio, but I had developed an offshoot of it, a program for 160 serious ballet students aged ten to fourteen. Called DanceLab, each faculty member was responsible for one class, composed of about twenty students, for the entire five weeks— as opposed to the typical practice of summer programs, in which students may have three or even four different teachers in a given day. I thought of us—once again conjuring Virginia—as "mother hens" to the students. We had a wonderful, rich time with our charges. Running both the school-year and the summer programs was rewarding but all consuming, and eventually it was time for me to slow down. It was a joy to finally be able to focus all of my energies solely on teaching, not only at Boston Ballet School, but also at Dean College, where its terrific dance department continues to grow and now offers a major in dance.

———————

AND SO FOR ME, life after performing has brought me many new adventures and pleasures. But there have been great sorrows along the way too: my cherished parents died recently, but at least I was blessed to have them well into their nineties, and many of my dear friends and colleagues have passed away. The AIDS epidemic claimed many of them and cancer took others, and now age is becoming a factor.

Lefty and I are the remaining Gumm Sisters; we lost Rose to cancer in 1999. Not surprisingly, Rose—who'd always been such a physical power-house—put up a strong fight. Her particular cancer wasn't curable, but Rose decided to undergo chemotherapy so that she could have as much time with Al and especially their daughter Jessica, who was then thirteen. Once on a visit, knowing that Rose was now bald, Lefty and I wore schmattes on our heads too, in silly solidarity. Rose laughed, and we all shared fond memories that day, which we knew would be one of the last times we'd be together. After her memorial service Lefty, David, Chris, PeeWee, and I joined Al and Jessica at their house in the Berkshire Hills of western Massachusetts, where we scattered Rose's ashes in her garden.

MY RETIREMENT from the stage didn't quite go off without a hitch. In fact, my opening night turned out to be like the plot of a made-for-TV movie, complete with an over-the-top dramatic twist. The difference, of course, is that this was real life. In the very beginning of the first act of *Don Q*, with Fernando as my Basilio, my left thigh finally gave out completely. The domino effect of my earlier femoral fracture, the torn cartilage in my knee, and my groin pull all finally took a decisive toll right then and there on the stage. The quad was all I had left to do all the work. It gave out, and I simply couldn't straighten my leg anymore. Just as in one of those movies in which the young ingénue gets her big break, Jennifer Gelfand, who was in the audience watching the performance, was hustled into costume during the intermission and finished the rest of the performance with Fernando in my stead.

As you can imagine, I was crushed that my last series of performances began this way; and at first, I assumed that that's how they'd end too, as this was not feeling like something I'd be able to bounce back from. And indeed, Jennifer, who was otherwise cast to dance with Daniel Meja, ended up filling in for my next two scheduled performances, appearing with Fernando again for both. Meanwhile, I quietly worked to get myself back onstage for the final performance. And I did. The strange world of the stage worked its old magic on me, mostly suspending my pain, and on Sunday, May 21, 1989, I danced my own swan song with Boston Ballet with Devon Carney as my Basilio. Of course, nobody wants to just "get through" something as important as their last performance, and I am mystified but eternally grateful that apparently I triumphed. Calling it "the most dazzling performance" she'd seen from the company that season, Christine Temin wrote, "Young set the tone from the instant she tore onstage, launching into a variation filled with voracious backbends and sky-high kicks . . . every once in a while she'd shake her head and let her fingers explode as if she couldn't contain the champagne inside her." Not bad for a forty-two-year-old with a bum leg!

———————

DURING MY FINAL BOW I was so moved by the showers of flowers, the generous ovations from the audience, and once again, by the loving presence of my colleagues, which now included the dancers of BBII, that afterward I only vaguely remember going through the usual postperformance rituals. I scrubbed off my makeup, freed my hair from its ballerina bun, and hung up my costume. Leaving Kitri in the dressing room, I went out the stage door and into the Boston spring. First, I had a party to get to, the one celebrating my career as a Boston Ballerina. After that though, I had the biggest "fourth act" party yet to come—the next chapters of my life.

My Fourth Act

I N 2014 Boston Ballet celebrated its fiftieth anniversary season, which meant that, yes, I observed *fifty-two* years with the organization. As a part of that anniversary celebration, I was asked to assist with the company timeline, which would highlight Boston Ballet's "milestones" from its inception to the current day. Given my long tenure with Boston Ballet, going through that process made me realize the unique position I was in to share my memories of the company's history. This memoir has come about through the bonding and prodding of friends old and new. Thank you all!

I'VE BEEN BLESSED with a very fulfilling life after my symbolic "first death" and am delighted that dancing is still a big part of that life. The new relationships that have developed over the years with my teen, college, and adult students have brought me tremendous joy and personal growth, as they all teach me something new every day. For me, the gratification that comes from teaching supplants the fulfillment of performing and continues to fuel my passion for the art form.

I must confess that I don't miss the chronic aches and pains that accompanied my daily routine as a professional. Naturally, I'm occasionally sore after teaching—and then there are those aches and pains that simply come with getting older—but most of that is nothing in comparison to what used to be commonplace for me. I wasn't completely spared from long-term damage though; like several of my colleagues, I've had replacement surgery on both hips. As scary as the surgery seemed, it was the best thing I could have done for myself as even walking had become agonizing; now, I am no longer hobbled by debilitating pain. But I will be seventy years old in 2017, and though I hope to continue teaching in some capacity as long as I am able, I have reduced my schedule so that I'm no longer carrying a full load of classes day after day.

I have no problem, however, filling my newly freed-up time. Like everyone else, I have my hobbies; I still love cooking, gardening, and reading, and Chris and I enjoy traveling whenever we can. We are partial to tropical beaches but have also loved our trips abroad, especially Italy. We keep going back. Experiencing these destinations purely as a tourist is a rather different experience from earlier visits in which my time was largely consumed by rehearsals and performances. Those tours were, without a doubt, wonderfully enriching, but I appreciate the greater freedom I now have when we travel. We also do a fair amount of trekking within our own vast country, usually planning our routes and itineraries in such a way that we can visit with friends along the way, many of whom are old "ballet" pals. It never ceases to amaze me how we can all just pick up where we left off and howl over the retelling of stories from "back in the day."

Although there has been more turmoil along the way, the company has survived each trial—and then continued forward. After Marks's tenure, Anna-Marie Holmes became the artistic director (AD) for several years. When she left the company, she returned to what I think was her true passion and expertise: staging the classics, something she has done many times both here and abroad. For example, after her successful restaging of the full-length *Le Corsaire* for Boston Ballet, she was immediately asked to stage the production for American Ballet Theatre. After her departure, the search began again for a new leader. When that person decided, after only a few months, that it was not working out, we were in for yet another round of upheaval. In the manner of our old "guerilla ballet" approach, Jonathan McPhee, the company's music director and principal conductor, stepped up to serve as interim AD in order to keep our momentum going. In 2002, Mikko Nissinen became Boston Ballet's new AD and remains in that position today.

Mikko and his artistic staff—along with the board; the executive, administrative, and production staffs; the faculty; the orchestra; and of course, the dancers—have persevered and continued to raise the bar of excellence that was first raised and pressed upward by their predecessors. Boston Ballet has grown up to be an internationally respected company and today ranks among the top ballet companies in the United States. Simply put, the company looks fantastic, which gives me great pleasure and satisfaction that Virginia's dream continues on.

I find what's most satisfying for me as a viewer these days is seeing the promising younger dancers who are just starting to make their mark. Naturally, it's particularly thrilling when a former student makes it into the junior ensemble or even into the main company, as did Lauren Herfindahl. She studied with me at an early age and progressed through those hallowed ranks of the school to the pre-professional class, a trainee, Boston Ballet II, and then the company corps de ballet, and was recently promoted to second soloist. Her special talent was obvious from the start, and what a thrill it is to watch her progress. Oh, the memories of what those early days were like when *I* was that age! It takes so much for a young dancer to make it that far, and there is both potentially so much ahead and so much uncertainty. The pathway of a professional dancer is paved with difficulty: the never-ending work to maintain one's best physical fitness, the occasional disappointments of casting and injuries, and the unpredictability of it all. But it's a journey that, for many of us, is filled with great adventures and deep pleasures. When I think of what Virginia and her staff, faculty, volunteers, board members, and we, her hardworking, earnest disciples—achieved in those early years, I'm proud all over again.

What did it take? Humility, confidence, compassion, passion, and what I like to call "gumption." One must dare to be great, and when you achieve "good," you are halfway there. This daily regimen wasn't a guarantee, but occasionally we did get to hover at the tips of dance's unique odyssey and experience moments of rare beauty and transcendent elation. There is no question of whether or not it was worth it; I would do it all again in a heartbeat.

Raise a toast with me to Boston Ballet's next generation of adventurous dreamers.

Gan bei!

NOTES

3. Return to Forever

17 *Dear Laurie, I think it is time*: E. Virginia Williams, letter to Laura Young, June 7, 1961, in author's possession.

23 *Everything was delightful*: Elinor Hughes, *Boston Herald*, June 1963.

4. Relevé

26 *In Boston, dance has been a stepchild*: Margo Miller, *Boston Globe*, March 15, 1964.

27 *Of the Boston Ballet Company*: Elliot Norton, *Boston Herald*, January 1965.

27 *The opening night of the Boston Ballet*: Elinor Hughes, *Boston Herald*, January 26, 1965.

29 *"Swan Lake" tests the quality*: Kathleen Cannell, *Christian Science Monitor*, February 1965.

29 *the warmest reception*: Elinor Hughes, *Boston Herald*, February 1965.

5. Allegro

36 *its program must have surely constituted*: Clive Barnes, *New York Times*, January 19, 1966.

38 Serenade *stands or falls on its ensemble*: Clive Barnes, *New York Times*, March 21, 1966.

38 *beatnik ballet*: Rolfe Boswell, *Boston Record American*, January 18, 1966.

40 *True, though the government won't help*: Elinor Hughes, *Boston Herald*, n.d.

40 *Disregarding many reasons*: Joan B. Cass, *Boston Herald*, n.d.

6. Onstage, Offstage

45 *It was the first performance*: Alta Maloney, *Boston Traveler*, April 8, 1967.

46 *Boston Ballet's Third Season*: *Boston Globe*, January 22, 1967.

47 *The line is disappearing*: Joan B. Cass, *Boston Herald*, January 22, 1967.

51 *Elaine Bauer taught her*: Christine Temin, *Boston Globe*, May 14, 1989.

7. Pas de Bourrée and Bourrée

52 *The first trouble came*: Joan B. Cass, *Boston Herald*, July 6, 1969.

58 *with a little budget like ours*: Margo Miller, *Boston Globe*, June 16, 1968.

58 *could be very much within*: Elliot Norton, *Boston Herald*, May 1968.

59 *As far as my own career*: Pauline Dubkin, *Patriot Ledger*, May 31, 1969.

8. Arabesque Voyagée

61 *The Boston Ballet WILL*: Margo Miller, *Boston Globe*, February 16, 1969.

62 *is so dominated by mannerisms*: Joan B. Cass, *Boston Herald*, March 1969.

62 *technically faultless*: Elliot Norton, *Boston Herald*, March 1969.

65 *We can be very proud*: Elliot Norton, *Boston Herald*, May 1969.

65 *The high point*: Joan B. Cass, *Boston Herald*, May 1969.

65 *In most of the best*: Elliot Norton, *Boston Herald*, May 1969.

9. Fouetté

73 *Joan Kennedy made a big hit*: Joan B. Cass, *Herald Tribune*, February 1970.

74 *a crown of horns*: Gerald Fitzgerald, *Patriot Ledger*, May 1970.

10. Tour Jeté

79 *All the dancers*: Valerie Restivo, *(Boston) Phoenix*, February 16, 1971.

80 *The young Boston Ballet dancers*: Kathleen Cannell, *Christian Science Monitor*, February 17, 1971.

81 *since then she has researched*: ibid.

11. Ballon

89 *That weakness is one reason*: William A. Henry, *Boston Globe*, August 26, 1973.

91   *Anamarie Sarazin, a vivid dancer*: Walter Terry, *Dance News*, May 1974.

92   *Like many European dancers*: Gerald Fitzgerald, *Patriot Ledger*, November 13, 1973.

92   *two men stars*: Elliot Norton, *Boston Herald-American*, November 9, 1973.

92   *I hope Lowski's arrival*: Laura Shapiro, *Real Paper*, November 28, 1973.

94   *The highlight of the evening*: Jack Zink, *Fort Lauderdale News*, April 22, 1974.

94   *Villella was teamed*: Bob Freund, *Fort Lauderdale News*, April 1974.

95   *Now they're back*: Bonnie Selway, *Boston Herald-American*, March 5, 1974.

96   *One notes that there*: Ella Jackson, *Mass Media*, February 19, 1974.

97   *both on the threshold*: Walter Terry, *Saturday Review*, January 25, 1975.

97   *After watching lovely Laura*: Ella Jackson, *Mass Media*, February 19, 1974.

12. À Terre; en l'Air

99   *satisfaction with the performance*: Carole Mazur, *Patriot Ledger*, October 25, 1974.

105   *idiom has never been*: Christina Robb, *Boston Globe*, April 11, 1975.

105   *far more classical*: Clive Barnes, *New York Times*, April 11, 1975.

106   *The Boston Ballet returned*: Kitty Cunningham, *Berkshire Courier*, August 7, 1975.

107   *The Boston Ballet Company*: Valerie Restivo, (Albany, NY) *Times-Union*, August 6, 1975.

107   *major non-New York*: Walter Terry, *Saturday Review*, January 25, 1975.

109   *new aspects of a familiar work*: Gerald Fitzgerald, *Patriot Ledger*, November 11, 1975.

109   *Miss Young has been*: Elliot Norton, *Boston Herald*, December 13, 1975.

13. La Belle au Bois Dormant

110   *With this production*: Iris Fanger, *Christian Science Monitor*, April 12, 1976.

111   *Chairman of the Board*: Boston Ballet Society, *Newsletter*, March 1976.

112   *Boston Ballet's sumptuous production*: Iris Fanger, *Christian Science Monitor*, April 12, 1976.

113   *Young's dancing has always*: Christine Temin, *Boston Globe*, April 4, 1979.

113   *Edra Toth, who's been on leave*: Elizabeth Varady, *Boston Herald-American*, April 1976.

115   *This scene . . . really has no story*: Clive Barnes, *New York Times*, July 5, 1974.

14. Pas de Chat

118   *I like to nest*: Margo Miller, *Boston Globe*, November 6, 1977.
119   *may not be able*: ibid.
119   *You know each other*: Dorothy Stockbridge, *Sarasota Journal*, January 12, 1977.
119   *We have tremendous rapport*: ibid.
120   *My talents have been mismanaged*: Bonnie Selway, *Boston Herald-American*, March 5, 1974.
121   *Their heavy schedule*: Dorothy Stockbridge, *Sarasota Journal*, January 12, 1977.
126   *a major addition*: Laura Shapiro, *Boston Globe*, March 14, 1977.
126   *Of all the true*: Clive Barnes, *New York Times*, May 15, 1977.

15. Tendu

130   *something has happened*: Elizabeth Varady, *Boston Herald-American*, April 6, 1978.
130   *many of the corps*: Christine Temin, *Boston Globe*, May 21, 1978.
131   *the real substance*: Laura Shapiro, *Real Paper*, March 1978.
135   *whenever the Boston Ballet*: Laura Shapiro, *Real Paper*, March 1978.

16. Tour en l'Air

141   *We all reached a point*: Peter J. Rosenwald, *Wall Street Journal*, February 9, 1979.
146   *been named associate artistic director*: *New York Times*, August 21, 1979.
147   *How do I feel about it?* Gwen Ifill, *Boston Herald-American*, May 24, 1980.
147   *"The Road to China"*: Christine Temin, *Boston Globe*, February 3, 1980.
147   *in the past few weeks*: Elizabeth Varady, *Boston Herald-American*, February 1980.
148   *never seen [the company]*: Clive Barnes, *New York Post*, June 12, 1980.

17. Rudi, Rudi, Rudi

155 *To anyone familiar with Bauer*: Christine Temin, *Boston Globe*, November 10, 1980.

156 *The Boston Ballet made*: Clive Barnes, *New York Post*, November 7, 1980.

157 *unique contribution[s]*: Boston Mayor's Office, letter to Laura Young, August 25, 1980, in author's possession.

159 *made a strong debut*: Christine Temin, *Boston Globe*, February 6, 1981.

159 *a charming rendition*: Elizabeth Varaday, *Boston Herald-American*, May 16, 1980.

159 *Laura Young and Nicolas Pacaña*: Christine Temin, *Boston Globe*, May 16, 1980.

160 *There is no use demanding*: Gerald Fitzgerald, *Patriot Ledger*, March 17, 1981.

160 *pointedly told not to come*: Iris M. Fanger, *Boston Phoenix*, December 29, 1981.

161 *On Thursday, the Boston-born*: Alexander Bland, *Observer*, July 5, 1981.

18. Manèges

164 *I want to dance*: Sharon Basco, *Boston Herald*, August 7, 1983.

165 *Is it really the Boston Ballet?*: Christine Temin, *Boston Globe*, March 16, 1982.

166 *Meanwhile, and here's the true joy*: Gerald Fitzgerald, *Patriot Ledger*, March 16, 1982.

166 *Imagine Laura Young*: Gerald Fitzgerald, *Patriot Ledger*, March 16, 1982.

166 *Last night was also*: Christine Temin, *Boston Globe*, March 13, 1982.

171 *They understand better*: Sharon Basco, *Boston Herald*, August 7, 1983.

174 *Of course, 20 years*: Christine Temin, *Boston Globe*, March 25, 1983.

19. Temps de l'Ange

176 *was given pseudo-serious*: Sharon Basco, *Boston Herald*, April 6, 1984.

179 *She has built The Boston Ballet*: Twentieth-anniversary commemorative booklet (Boston: Boston Ballet, 1984).

180 *The moving performance of Young*: Christine Temin, *Boston Globe*, May 24, 1984.

181   *The Ballet has become*: Christine Temin, *Boston Globe*, September 18, 1984.

183   *Nutcracker Was a Miracle*: Anthony N. Compagnone Jr., *Milford Daily News*, December 4, 1984.

22. Révérence

214   *the most dazzling performance*: Christine Temin, *Boston Globe*, May 22, 1989.

INDEX OF BALLETS

INDEX OF NAMES

Note: *insert1* refers to the image gallery following page 84; *insert2* refers to the image gallery following page 180.